101 Tissue Toppers

in Plastic Canvas

Edited by Laura Scott

HOUSE of
WHITE
BIRCHES

PUBLISHERS
SINCE 1947

Editor: Laura Scott
Associate Editor: Cathy Reef
Design Manager: Vicki Blizzard
Technical Editor: June Sprunger
Copy Editor: Mary Nowak
Publications Coordinator: Tanya Turner

Photography: Andy J. Burnfield, Scott Campbell
Photo Stylists: Martha Coquat, Salway Sabri

Production Coordinator: Brenda Gallmeyer
Graphic Arts Supervisor: Ronda Bechinski
Cover Design: Jessi Butler
Book Design: Erin Augsburger
Graphic Production: Kimberly Wills
Production Assistants: Janet Bowers, Marj Morgan
Technical Artists: Leslie Brandt, Julie Catey, Chad Summers
Traffic Coordinator: Sandra Beres
Publishers: Carl H. Muselman, Arthur K. Muselman

Chief Executive Officer: John Robinson
Marketing Director: Scott Moss
Book Marketing Manager: Craig Scott
Product Development Director: Vivian Rothe
Publishing Services Manager: Brenda Wendling

Printed in the United States of America
First Printing: 2001
Library of Congress Number: 00-109010
ISBN: 1-882138-71-6

Every effort has been made to ensure the accuracy and completeness of the
instructions in this book. However, we cannot be responsible for human
error or for the results when using materials other than those specified in
the instructions, or for variations in individual work.

A Note From The Editor

Tissue box covers are, in my opinion, one of the best projects to stitch and share! Our staff and designers went all out to bring you this collection of toppers with a touch of fun and whimsy, toppers with elegance and beauty, and toppers with seasonal festivity and merriment!

Not only do tissue box covers make attractive and practical accents for every room in your home, but they also make wonderful gifts, whether for birthdays, Mother's Day or Father's Day, to cheer a sick friend or shut-in, for house-warmings, or as a special hostess gift! Nothing touches the heart of a loved one as much as a handstitched gift from you!

Tissue boxes also make festive holiday decorations! Arranged by seasons, this book starts off with a collection of more-than-delightful spring tissue toppers, followed by breezy summer designs, then vibrant autumn tissue box covers and finishes up with magical winter toppers! Each chapter includes a pleasant mix of holiday toppers and all-occasion toppers suited to the season.

As my staff and I selected the projects for this book from the many terrific designs submitted by our freelance designers, we each became more and more excited about this book! In fact, we often wanted to get out our canvas and yarn and start on some of these wonderful projects! I promise, you will not see any "same old, same old" tissue boxes in this collection!

As an added bonus to you, we've filled the pages of this beautiful hardcover book with more than 100 brand-new, never-before-published designs! That means this book is the only place you'll find the projects in this collection.

So get out your needle, yarn and canvas, and pick your favorite project in this book to stitch for yourself, or to share with someone you love!

Warmest regards,

Laura Scott

Contents

Springtime Fresh ❀

Summer Brights 🐝

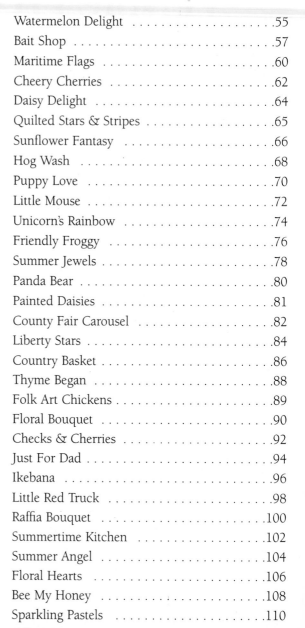

Autumn Glory

Winter Sparkles

General Information

Springtime Fresh!

What's fun, practical, colorful and a great gift idea all in one? Tissue box covers! Following is a collection of 27 terrific springtime tissue box covers in a variety of colors, styles and designs.

Garden Fence Buzz

Design by Vicki Blizzard

Catch up on the latest garden gossip by joining these busy-body flowers having a chat at the garden fence! Stitch it to add a touch of whimsy to your home!

Skill Level: Beginner

Size: Fits regular-size tissue box

Materials

- 2 sheets 7-count plastic canvas
- Uniek Needloft plastic canvas yarn as listed in color key
- DMC #3 pearl cotton as listed in color key
- #16 tapestry needle
- 8 (5mm) round black cabochons from The Beadery
- 18 (4mm) round black cabochons from The Beadery
- Sheet green felt
- Pinking shears
- Jewel glue
- Hot-glue gun

Cutting & Stitching

1. Cut plastic canvas according to graphs (pages 8 and 9).

2. With pinking shears, cut eight elongated almond-shaped leaves from green felt, varying length of leaves from 2½ inches to 3 inches and width from ¾ inch to 1 inch.

3. Following graphs through step 7, work top and sides. Using holly throughout, Overcast inside edges of top and bottom edges of sides. Whipstitch long sides to short sides, then Whipstitch sides to top.

4. For large flowers, stitch one with yellow center and lilac petals as graphed, one with yellow center and watermelon petals, one with yellow center and bright blue petals and one with pink center and yellow petals. Overcast each with petal color.

5. For small flowers, stitch two as graphed, three replacing watermelon with bright blue, one replacing watermelon with lilac, and three replacing watermelon with yellow and yellow French Knot with pink French Knot. Overcast with adjacent colors

6. Stitch leaves and stems with holly. Work Straight Stitches in center of leaves when background stitching is completed. Overcast with holly.

7. Using photo as a guide, for variation in facial expressions of flowers' faces, stitch mouths with very dark rose pearl cotton, changing positions and shapes by working different lengths of stitches. Work French Knots in place of Straight Stitches for some mouths.

Assembly

1. Use photo as a guide throughout assembly. For eyes, using jewel glue, glue 5mm cabochons to large flowers and 4mm cabochons to small flowers. Using graphs only as placement guides, vary positions of cabochons to change expressions of flowers' faces.

2. Using hot glue through step 5, glue one point of two felt leaves to back of each large flower in varying positions.

3. Glue fence to front of box, curving center out slightly from box. Glue one large flower to one end of each stem. Glue stems to back of fence.

4. Glue two flowers and two stitched leaves in a cluster to one short side. Glue remaining flowers and stitched leaves to front of fence as desired.

5. Glue remaining tips of felt leaves in varying positions, placing some close to mouths, some to sides of faces by ears as if listening or some to fence and smaller flowers. ❖

Graphs continued on next page

Garden Fence Buzz

Graphs continued from previous page

COLOR KEY

Plastic Canvas Yarn	Yards
☐ Fern #23	42
■ Holly #27	62
☐ White #41	23
■ Lilac #45	4
▨ Watermelon #55	5
☐ Yellow #57	9
Bright blue #60	6
╱ Holly #27 Straight Stitch	
○ Pink #07 French Knot	1
○ Yellow #57 French Knot	

#3 Pearl Cotton

╱ Very dark rose #326 Straight Stitch	2
● Attach 5mm cabochon	
● Attach 4mm cabochon	

Color numbers given are for Uniek Needloft plastic canvas yarn and DMC #3 pearl cotton.

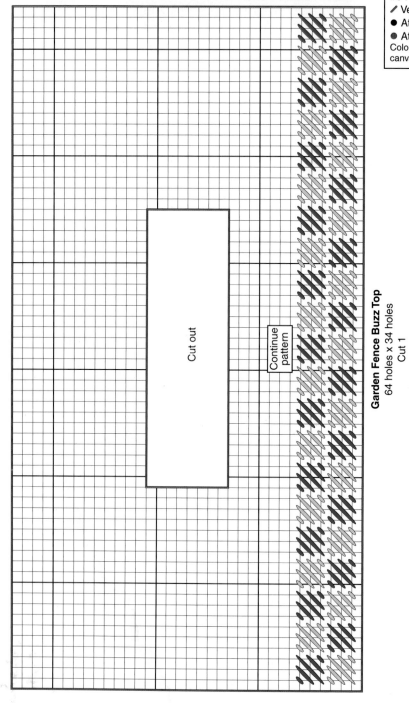

Cut out

Continue pattern

Garden Fence Buzz Top
64 holes x 34 holes
Cut 1

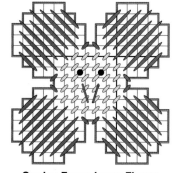

Garden Fence Large Flower
15 holes x 15 holes
Cut 4
Stitch one as graphed,
1 with yellow center and
watermelon petals,
1 with yellow center and
bright blue petals,
1 with pink center and
yellow petals

Garden Fence Small Flower
7 holes x 7 holes
Cut 9
Stitch 2 as graphed
Stitch 3, replacing watermelon
with bright blue
Stitch 1, replacing watermelon
with lilac
Stitch 3, replacing watermelon
with yellow and yellow French Knot
with pink French Knot

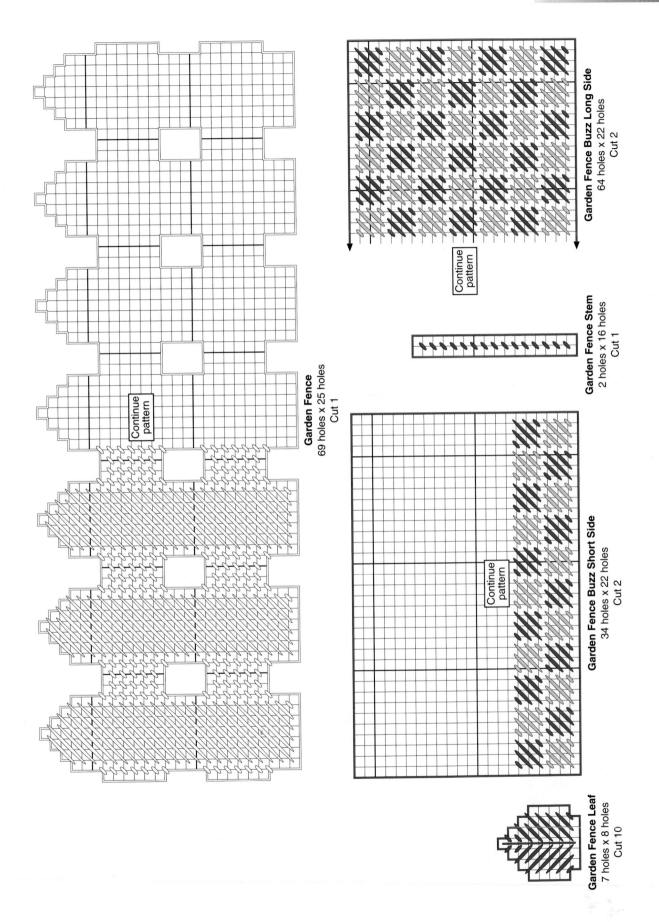

Garden Fence
69 holes x 25 holes
Cut 1

Continue pattern

Garden Fence Buzz Long Side
64 holes x 22 holes
Cut 2

Continue pattern

Garden Fence Stem
2 holes x 16 holes
Cut 1

Garden Fence Buzz Short Side
34 holes x 22 holes
Cut 2

Continue pattern

Garden Fence Leaf
7 holes x 8 holes
Cut 10

- DMC #8 pearl cotton as listed in color key
- DMC 6-strand embroidery floss as listed in color key
- #16 tapestry needle
- Thick white glue

Instructions

1. Cut plastic canvas according to graphs.

2. Following graphs, work borders with Two-Color Herringbone Stitch (Fig. 1), working lily pink stitches first, then eggshell stitches. Work eggshell Slanting Gobelin Stitches on sides and top as indicated.

3. Work all remaining background stitches with Continental Stitches, working uncoded areas in corners, around angel and in center area of sides with eggshell.

4. When background stitching is completed, work Cross Stitches for cheeks with 2-strands salmon floss. Embroider halo and lower portion of wings with Vatican gold medium (#16) braid.

5. Stitch lower portion of wings a second time with black #8 pearl cotton, then work remaining black pearl cotton embroidery, passing over each eye six times.

6. Work remaining embroidery with #3 pearl cotton, wrapping twice for French Knot at center of each bow on sides.

Spring Angel

Design by Janelle Giese

Celebrate the birth of a baby girl by stitching this beautiful tissue box cover for the nursery! It's a keepsake Mother will enjoy now, and Baby will treasure when she's grown up!

Skill Level: Intermediate

Size: Fits boutique-style tissue box

Materials
- 1½ sheets 7-count plastic canvas
- Coats & Clark Red Heart Classic worsted weight yarn Art. E267 as listed in color key
- Kreinik Medium (#16) Braid as listed in color key
- DMC #3 pearl cotton as listed in color key

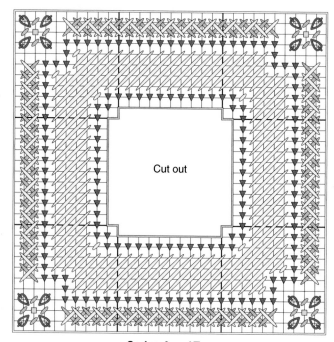

Spring Angel Top
30 holes x 30 holes
Cut 1

7. For hair bows, cut two lengths of medium rose pearl cotton. For each pigtail, thread ends of one length from back to front through holes indicated on graph. Tie each length in a tiny bow, trimming ends as needed. Secure with a dab of glue.

8. Overcast inside edges on top with lily pink. Using eggshell, Whipstitch sides together, then Whipstitch sides to top; Overcast bottom edges. ❖

Fig. 1
Two-Color Herringbone Stitch

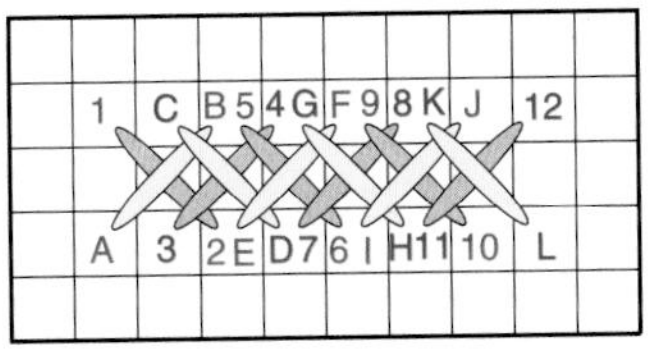

Work a row of lily pink stitches first, then work a row of eggshell stitches on top.

COLOR KEY	
Worsted Weight Yarn	**Yards**
◇ White #1	1
Eggshell #111	48
□ Cornmeal #220	3
◆ Sea coral #246	2
☆ Maize #261	1
▼ Warm brown #336	1
★ Mid brown #339	1
Light lavender #579	1
◆ Honey gold #645	1
Lily pink #719	15
▼ Pale rose #755	14
△ Pale blue #815	2
Uncoded areas are eggshell #111 Continental Stitches	
Medium (#16) Braid	
Vatican gold #102 Backstitch and Straight Stitch	1
#3 Pearl Cotton	
Peach #353 Backstitch, Straight Stitch and Cross Stitch	2
Dark forest green #987 Straight Stitch	2
Medium rose #899 Lazy Daisy Stitch	
Light baby blue #3325 Lazy Daisy Stitch	6
● Peach #353 French Knot	
#8 Pearl Cotton	
Black #310 Backstitch and Straight Stitch	4
6-Strand Embroidery Floss	
✖ Salmon #760 Cross Stitch	1
● Attach hair bow	

Color numbers given are for Coats & Clark Red Heart Classic worsted weight yarn Art. E267, Kreinik Medium (#16) Braid and DMC pearl cotton and 6-strand embroidery floss.

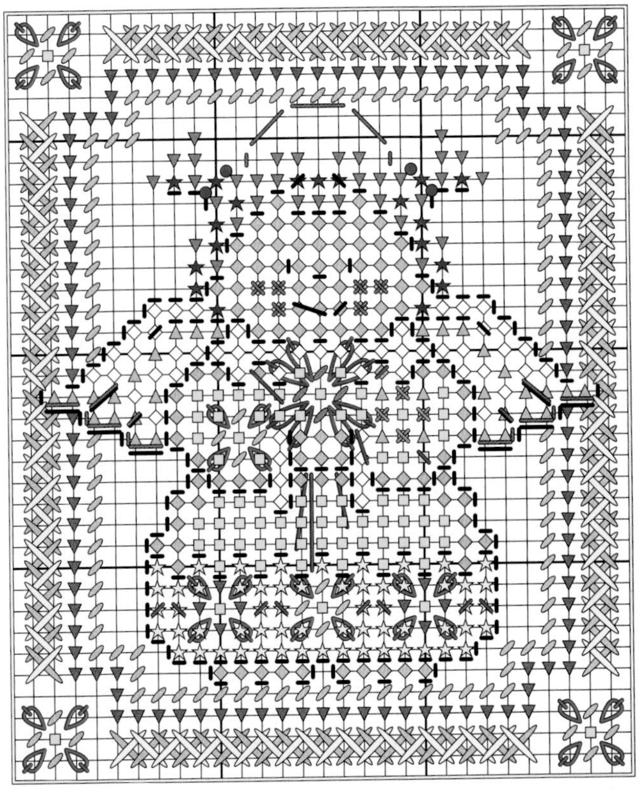

Spring Angel Front
30 holes x 36 holes
Cut 1

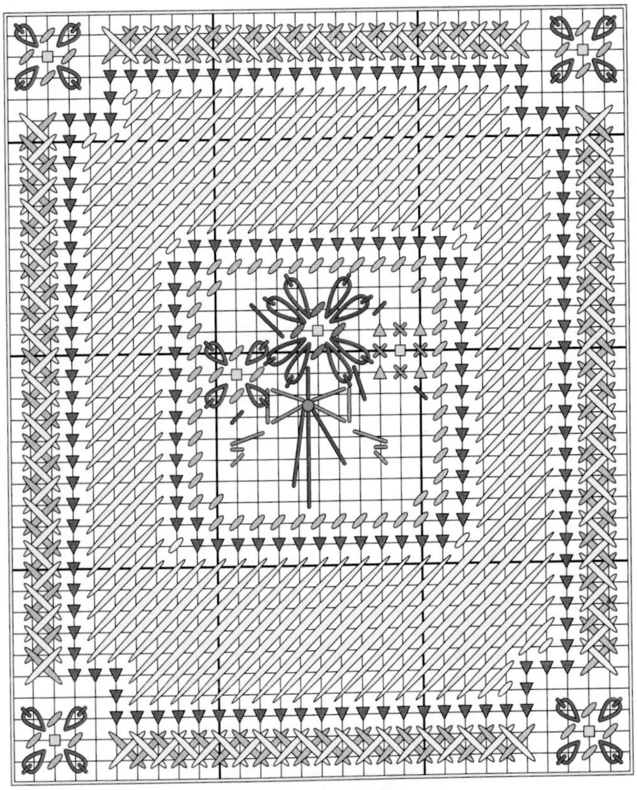

Spring Angel Side
30 holes x 36 holes
Cut 3

Patchwork Tulips

Design by Angie Arickx

Capture a glimpse of the simple life with this colorful Amish-quilt style tissue box cover. Vibrant red and yellow tulips will decorate the inside of your home while your flowering bulbs decorate the outside!

Skill Level: Beginner

Size: Fits boutique-style tissue box

Materials

- 1½ sheets Uniek Quick-Count 7-count plastic canvas
- Uniek Needloft plastic canvas yarn as listed in color key
- #16 tapestry needle

Instructions

1. Cut and stitch plastic canvas according to graphs (page 15).

2. Using fern throughout, Overcast inside edges of top and bottom edges of sides. Whipstitch sides together, then Whipstitch sides to top. ❖

Continued on page 15

Country Cottage

Design by Michele Wilcox

This sweet country cottage is just the right size for holding just enough tissue to get you through a morning at church or an afternoon shopping trip!

Skill Level: Beginner

Size: Fits pocket-size tissue

Materials

- ½ sheet Uniek Quick-Count 7-count plastic canvas
- Uniek Needloft plastic canvas yarn as listed in color key
- DMC #3 pearl cotton as listed in color key
- #16 tapestry needle
- 1 yard 1¼-inch-wide white satin ribbon

Instructions

1. Cut plastic canvas according to graph.

2. Stitch pieces following graph, working uncoded areas with tangerine Continental Stitches.

3. When background stitching is completed, work Backstitches and French Knots with pearl cotton.

4. Overcast inside and outside roof edges with dark royal. Whipstitch wrong sides of cottage pieces together around sides and bottom with tangerine.

5. Cut white satin ribbon in half. Attach one length through each hole at top of roof with a Lark's Head Knot.

6. For easier access, remove tissue from package before placing inside cottage; tie ribbon in a bow. ❖

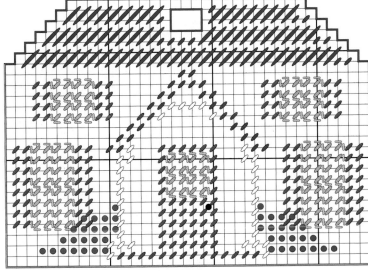

Country Cottage
35 holes x 25 holes
Cut 2

COLOR KEY	
Plastic Canvas Yarn	**Yards**
■ Red #01	8
■ Maple #13	1
■ Sail blue #35	7
□ White #41	2
■ Dark royal #48	8
Uncoded areas are tangerine #11 Continental Stitches	23
╱ Tangerine #11 Whipstitching	
#3 Pearl Cotton	
╱ White Backstitch	3
● Black #310 French Knot	¼
● Bright green #700 French Knot	3
Color numbers given are for Uniek Needloft plastic canvas yarn and DMC #3 pearl cotton.	

Happy Easter

Design by Michele Wilcox

Colorful embroidered Easter eggs and a sweet chick make this delightful tissue box cover a must-have for spring celebrating!

Skill Level: Intermediate

Size: Fits boutique-style tissue box

Materials

- 1¼ sheets Uniek Quick-Count 7-count plastic canvas
- Uniek Needloft plastic canvas yarn as listed in color key
- DMC #5 pearl cotton as listed in color key
- #16 tapestry needle

Instructions

1. Cut plastic canvas according to graphs.

2. Stitch pieces following graphs, working uncoded areas with white Continental Stitches.

3. When background stitching is completed, work embroidery with pearl cotton.

4. Overcast bottom edges of sides with white. With bright blue, Overcast inside edges of top. Whipstitch sides together, then Whipstitch sides to top. ❖

COLOR KEY	
Plastic Canvas Yarn	**Yards**
▢ Pink #07	6
▢ Fern #23	6
▩ Watermelon #55	5
▢ Yellow #57	16
▢ Bright blue #60	16
■ Bright purple #64	2
Uncoded areas are white #41 Continental Stitches	30
#5 Pearl Cotton	
✐ Very light mahogany #402 Backstitch	5
✐ Violet #553 Backstitch	5
✐ Cranberry #603 Backstitch	6
✐ Bright chartreuse #704 Backstitch	3
✐ Dark delft blue #798 Backstitch	10
✐ Medium burnt orange #946 Backstitch and Straight Stitch	1
◐ Violet #553 Lazy Daisy	
● Violet #553 French Knot	
● Cranberry #603 French Knot	
○ Light pale yellow #745 French Knot	2
● Dark delft blue #798 French Knot	
Color numbers given are for Uniek Needloft plastic canvas yarn and DMC #5 pearl cotton.	

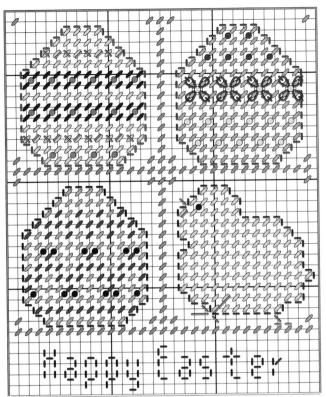

Happy Easter Side
30 holes x 36 holes
Cut 4

COLOR KEY	
Plastic Canvas Yarn	**Yards**
■ Christmas red #02	16
▨ Fern #23	30
■ Holly #27	28
☐ Yellow #57	16
Color numbers given are for Uniek Needloft plastic canvas yarn.	

Patchwork Tulips

Continued from page 12

Patchwork Tulips Side
30 holes x 37 holes
Cut 4

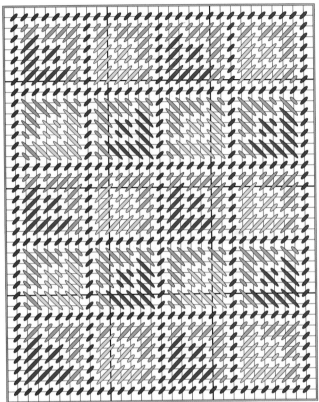

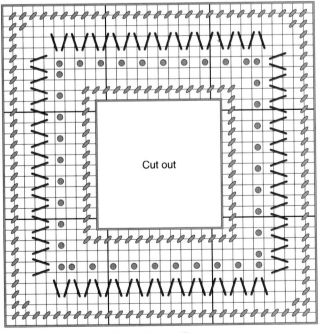

Happy Easter Top
30 holes x 30 holes
Cut 1

Cut out

Patchwork Tulips Top
30 holes x 30 holes
Cut 1

Baby Love

Design by Robin Petrina

Welcome your family's newest arrival with this enchanting tissue box for the nursery.
Sweet satin bows and yarn worked in delicate pastels make this tissue box cover a keepsake!

Skill Level: Beginner

Size: Fits boutique-style tissue box

Materials

- 2 sheets 7-count plastic canvas
- Coats & Clark Red Heart Super Saver worsted weight yarn Art. E301 as listed in color key
- Uniek Needloft iridescent craft cord as listed in color key
- #16 tapestry needle
- 24 inches ¼-inch-wide pink satin ribbon
- Hot-glue gun

Instructions

1. Cut plastic canvas according to graphs.

2. Stitch pieces following graphs, working uncoded background on overlay sides with white Continental Stitches. Work white iridescent craft cord Straight Stitches when background stitching is completed.

3. Using petal pink throughout, Overcast inside edges of top and bottom edges of cover sides, then Whipstitch sides together.

4. With white, Overcast inside and bottom edges of overlay sides. Whipstitch together along side edges, then Whipstitch to top.

5. Place overlay sides; glue in place.

6. Cut ribbon into four 6-inch lengths; tie each in a bow. Glue one bow to center top of each side. ❖

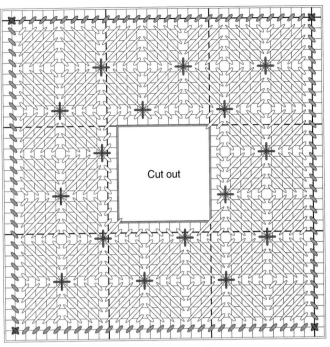

Baby Love Overlay Top
31 holes x 31 holes
Cut 1

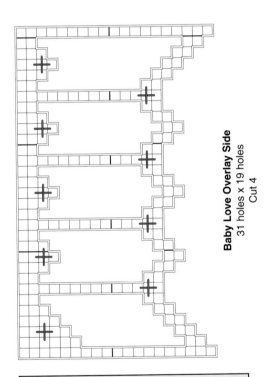

Baby Love Overlay Side
31 holes x 19 holes
Cut 4

COLOR KEY

Worsted Weight Yarn	Yards
☐ White #311	30
▨ Petal pink #373	52

Uncoded background on overlay sides
is white #311 Continental Stitches

Iridescent Craft Cord

■ White #55033	11
✧ White #55033 Straight Stitch	

Color numbers given are for Coats & Clark Red Heart
Super Saver worsted weight yarn Art. E301 and Uniek
Needloft iridescent craft cord.

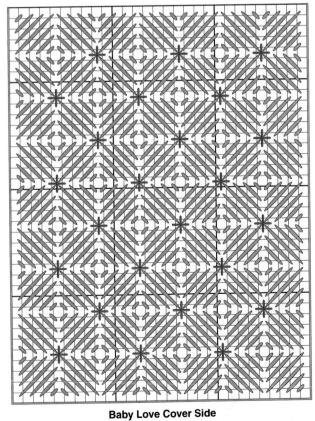

Baby Love Cover Side
29 holes x 37 holes
Cut 4

Bunny Bouquet

Design by Lee Lindeman

You'll want to hug this friendly bunny every time you see him bringing you a pot filled with fresh daisies from his garden! Stitch this topper to add springtime charm to your home!

Skill Level: Beginner

Size: Fits boutique-style tissue box

Materials

- 2 sheets 7-count plastic canvas
- Coats & Clark Red Heart Classic worsted weight yarn Art. E267 as listed in color key
- Coats & Clark Red Heart Super Saver worsted weight yarn Art. E300 as listed in color key
- 6-strand embroidery floss as listed in color key
- #18 tapestry needle
- 2 (6mm) round brown animal eyes
- 12mm triangular black animal nose
- 6 inches ¼-inch-wide yellow satin ribbon
- 4 (1-inch) faux silk daisies
- 1-inch terra-cotta pot
- Tacky craft glue or hot-glue gun

Cutting & Stitching

1. Cut plastic canvas according to graphs (pages 19 and 24).

2. Stitch tissue topper pieces following graphs, working uncoded areas with blue jewel Continental Stitches.

3. When background stitching is completed, work celery Straight Stitches on front, back and sides. Using white yarn, work ⅜-inch-long loops for daisy petals on sides and back where indicated on graph.

4. Overcast inside edges on top with yellow and bottom edges of front, back and sides with celery. Whipstitch front and back to sides with white and blue jewel following graphs, then Whipstitch front, back and sides to top with blue jewel.

5. Stitch bunny pieces following graphs, reversing one arm before stitching and working two ear fronts as graphed and two ear backs entirely with warm brown Continental Stitches.

6. Backstitch and Straight Stitch mouth and whiskers with black 6-strand embroidery floss.

7. Using warm brown through step 8, Overcast ear openings on head front and head back between arrows. Overcast side and bottom edges of head front from dot to dot and bottom edge of head back.

8. For each ear, Whipstitch wrong sides of one ear front to one ear back.

Assembly

1. Using photo as a guide throughout assembly, glue eyes and nose to head front. Glue ears inside openings on head.

2. Glue head to topper front at top of body. Glue top of arms to shoulders of bunny on front.

3. Tie yellow satin ribbon in a bow and glue to neckline.

4. Glue daisies inside terra-cotta pot; glue pot in place between bunny arms so it looks like he is holding the pot. ❖

COLOR KEY

Worsted Weight Yarn	Yards
■ Medium clay #280	8
□ White #311	5
▨ Aran #313	7
▨ Bright yellow #324	2
■ Warm brown #336	15
■ Celery #616	4
▨ Light raspberry #774	1
Uncoded areas on sides and top are	
blue jewel #818 Continental Stitches	40
⁄ Blue jewel #818 Whipstitching	
⁄ Celery #616 Straight Stitch	
● Attach daisy petals	

6-Strand Embroidery Floss

⁄ Black Backstitch and Straight Stitch	1

Color numbers given are for Coats & Clark Red Heart Classic worsted weight yarn Art. E267 and Red Heart Super Saver worsted weight yarn Art. E300.

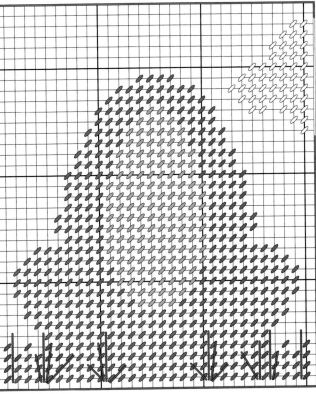

Bunny Bouquet Front
31 holes x 36 holes
Cut 1

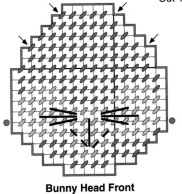

Bunny Head Back
15 holes x 11 holes
Cut 1

Bunny Head Front
15 holes x 16 holes
Cut 1

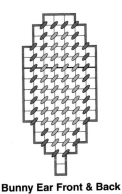

Bunny Ear Front & Back
7 holes x 15 holes
Cut 4
Stitch 2 as graphed for fronts
Stitch 2 entirely with warm brown
Continental Stitches for backs

Bunny Arm
7 holes x 16 holes
Cut 2, reverse 1

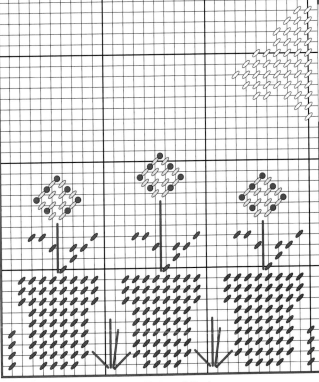

Bunny Bouquet Back
31 holes x 36 holes
Cut 1

Graphs continued on page 24

Pampered Pets

Designs by Christina Laws

Pet lovers will adore this pair of whimsical tissue box covers.
Each design can be easily adapted with color changes to look like your precious pet!

Skill Level: Beginner

Size: Fits boutique-style tissue box

Materials
Each Box Cover

- 2 sheets 7-count plastic canvas
- Worsted weight yarn as listed in color key
- #16 tapestry needle
- Hot-glue gun

Kitty

- 9 inches ⅛-inch-wide green satin ribbon
- ½-inch gold jingle bell

Dalmatian

1. Cut plastic canvas according to graphs.

2. Stitch pieces following graphs, reversing one ear before stitching and working uncoded areas with white Continental Stitches. Do not stitch line highlighted with blue on both front and back.

3. Work white Straight Stitches for eye highlights. Work black Straight Stitches for mouth.

4. Overcast ears with black. Overcast paws with white and black following graph.

5. Using white through step 7, Overcast inside edges of top and bottom edges of sides.

6. With wrong sides together, Whipstitch head back to head on front and tail front to tail on back around sides and top, leaving bottom edges and blue highlighted lines unstitched at this time.

7. Whipstitch front and back to sides; Whipstitch front, back and sides to top, stitching bottom edge of head back to front and bottom edge of tail front to back with Continental Stitches while Whipstitching.

8. Using photo as a guide, glue ears to head and paws to front, making sure bottom edges are even.

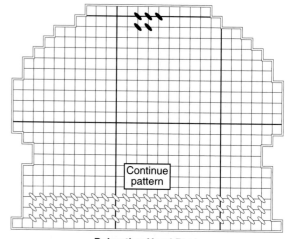

Dalmatian Head Back
26 holes x 21 holes
Cut 1

Dalmatian Ear
14 holes x 13 holes
Cut 2, reverse 1

Pampered Pets Paw
15 holes x 9 holes
Cut 2 for each cover

COLOR KEY	
DALMATIAN	
Worsted Weight Yarn	**Yards**
☐ White	70
■ Black	16
Uncoded areas are white Continental Stitches	
⁄ White Straight Stitch	
⁄ Black Backstitch	

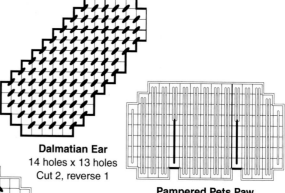

Dalmatian Tail Front
28 holes x 25 holes
Cut 1

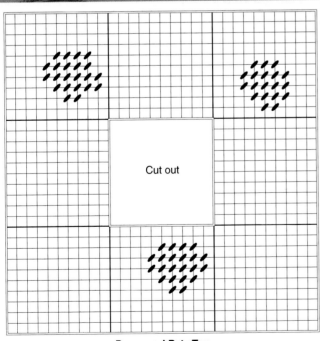

Pampered Pets Top
30 holes x 30 holes
Cut 1 for Dalmatian
Stitch as graphed
Cut 1 for Kitty
Stitch entirely with
gold Continental Stitches

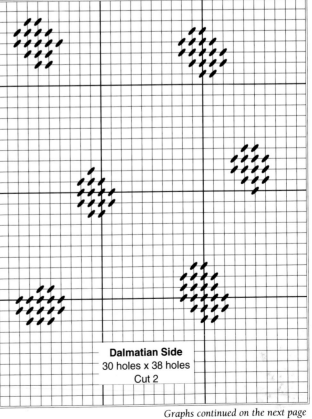

Dalmatian Side
30 holes x 38 holes
Cut 2

Graphs continued on the next page

Dalmation

Continued from the previous page

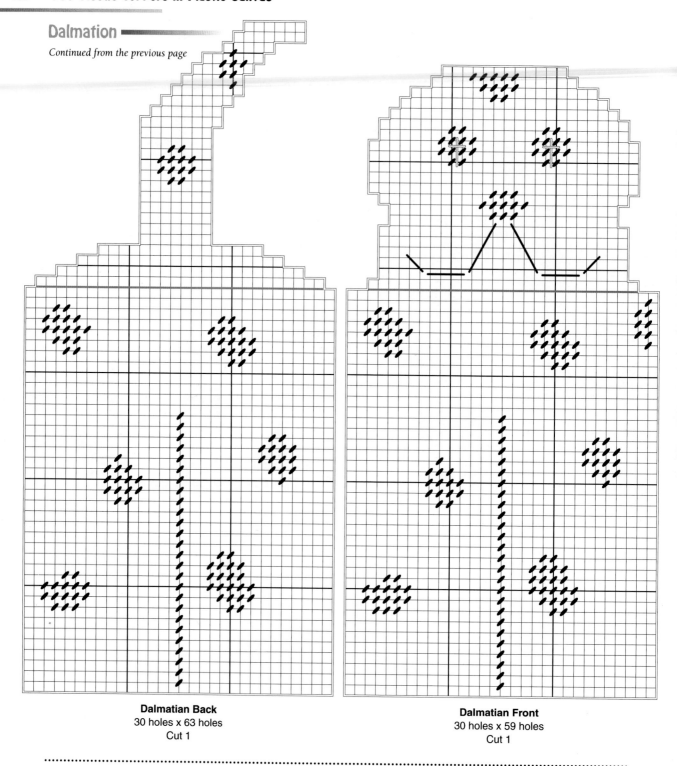

Dalmatian Back
30 holes x 63 holes
Cut 1

Dalmatian Front
30 holes x 59 holes
Cut 1

Kitty

1. Cut plastic canvas according to graphs (pages 21, 23 and 24). Cut two 30-hole x 38-hole pieces for sides.

2. Work kitty sides and top with gold Continental Stitches. Stitch remaining pieces following graphs, working uncoded areas with gold Continental Stitches.

3. Work white Straight Stitches for eye highlights. Work black Straight Stitches for mouth.

4. Overcast paws with white and black following graph. Overcast inside edges of top and bottom edges of sides with gold. Overcast bottom edges of front and back with white.

5. Following graphs, with wrong sides together,

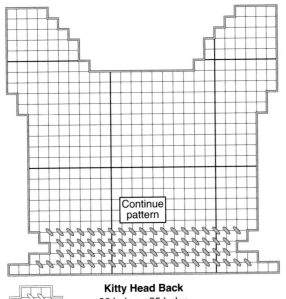

Kitty Head Back
26 holes x 25 holes
Cut 1

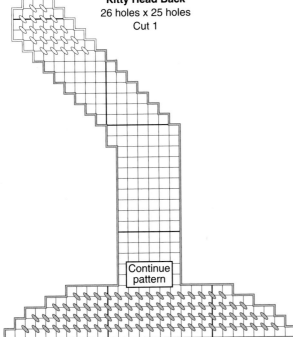

Kitty Tail Front
28 holes x 32 holes
Cut 1

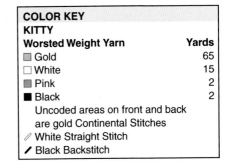

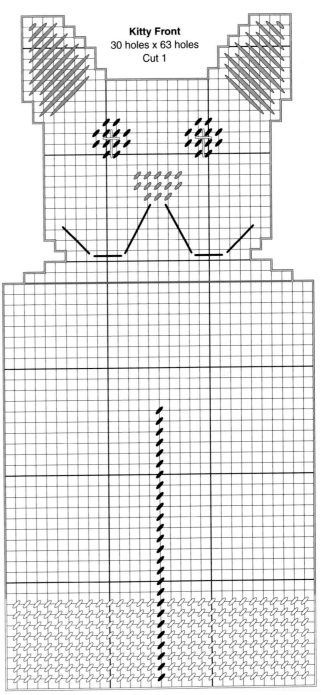

Kitty Front
30 holes x 63 holes
Cut 1

Whipstitch head back to head on front and tail front to tail on back around sides and top, leaving bottom edges and blue highlighted lines unstitched at this time.

6. Using gold and white, Whipstitch front and back to sides following graphs. Using gold, Whipstitch front, back and sides to top, stitching bottom edge of head back to front and bottom edge of tail front to back with Continental Stitches while Whipstitching.

7. Using photo as a guide, glue paws to front, making sure bottom edges are even. Thread gold jingle bell on ribbon and tie around neck. ❖

Graphs continued on the next page

Kitty

Continued from the previous page

Bunny Bouquet

Continued from page 19

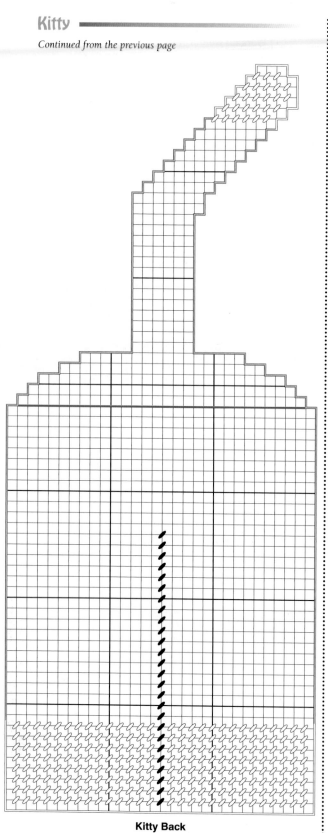

Kitty Back
30 holes x 70 holes
Cut 1

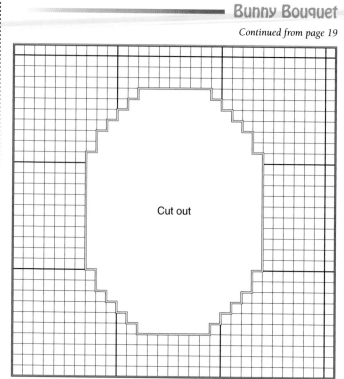

Bunny Bouquet Top
31 holes x 31 holes
Cut 1

Cut out

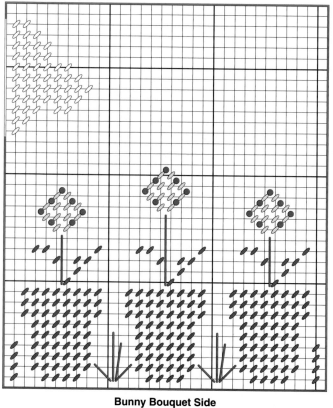

Bunny Bouquet Side
31 holes x 36 holes
Cut 2

Bees & Blooms

Design by Michele Wilcox

Combine two favorite sights of spring, bumblebees and flowers, into one charming and practical tissue holder!

Skill Level: Beginner

Size: Fits pocket-size tissue package

Materials

- ½ sheet Uniek Quick-Count 7-count plastic canvas
- Uniek Needloft plastic canvas yarn as listed in color key
- DMC #5 pearl cotton as listed in color key
- #16 tapestry needle

Instructions

1. Cut plastic canvas according to graphs.

2. Stitch pieces following graphs, working uncoded areas with white Continental Stitches.

3. When background stitching is completed, work black pearl cotton Backstitches.

4. Using white throughout, Overcast top edge of one top piece and bottom edge of remaining top piece. Place top pieces on bottom with Overcast edges in the center, then Whipstitch together along outside edges. ❖

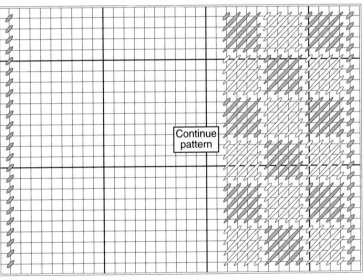

Continue pattern

Bees & Blooms Bottom
35 holes x 25 holes
Cut 1

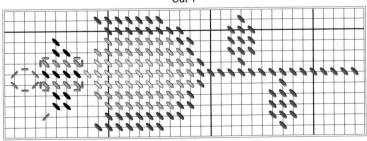

Bees & Blooms Top
35 holes x 12 holes
Cut 2

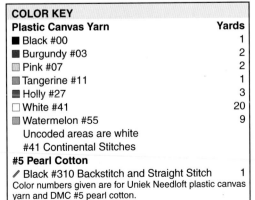

COLOR KEY	
Plastic Canvas Yarn	**Yards**
■ Black #00	1
■ Burgundy #03	2
▨ Pink #07	2
▨ Tangerine #11	1
■ Holly #27	3
☐ White #41	20
▨ Watermelon #55	9
Uncoded areas are white #41 Continental Stitches	
#5 Pearl Cotton	
✎ Black #310 Backstitch and Straight Stitch	1
Color numbers given are for Uniek Needloft plastic canvas yarn and DMC #5 pearl cotton.	

Strawberry Patch

Design by Vicki Blizzard

Savor one of the season's favorite fruits with this charming tissue topper!
Juicy berries and a friendly bluebird will add a warm touch to your home!

Skill Level: Beginner

Size: Fits regular-size tissue box

Materials

- 2 sheets 7-count plastic canvas
- Uniek Needloft plastic canvas yarn as listed in color key
- #16 tapestry needle
- 2 (5mm) round black cabochons from The Beadery
- 1 (4.54 gram) package Mill Hill Products yellow glass seed beads #00128 from Gay Bowles Sales Inc.
- Jewel glue
- Hot-glue gun

Cutting & Stitching

1. Cut plastic canvas according to graphs (this page and pages 27 and 29).

2. Stitch cover pieces following graphs (this page and pages 27 and 29). Using baby yellow throughout, Overcast inside edges of top and bottom edges of sides. Whipstitch long sides to short sides; Whipstitch sides to top.

3. Stitch and Overcast bluebird, blossoms, leaves, strawberries and strawberry caps following graphs, reversing four large strawberries and three strawberry caps before stitching.

4. Using jewel glue through step 5,

glue cabochons to bird's face for eyes where indicated on graph.

5. Using photo as a guide through step 9, glue seed beads to strawberries as desired and to blossoms where indicated on graph.

6. Using hot glue throughout assembly, glue strawberry caps to tops of large strawberries.

7. Set aside three large strawberries, two small strawberries, four blossoms, four small leaves and four large leaves.

8. For cover front, glue bluebird and remaining strawberries, leaves and blossoms to one long side, placing tops of small strawberries under large strawberries, blossoms and leaves.

9. Glue one large strawberry, one small strawberry, two blossoms, two small leaves and one large leaf in a cluster to each of the two corners on top piece adjacent to cover front. Glue one large strawberry and two large leaves in a cluster to one short side. ❖

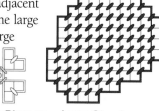

Strawberry Blossom
5 holes x 5 holes
Cut 8

Large Strawberry
11 holes x 10 holes
Cut 8, reverse 4

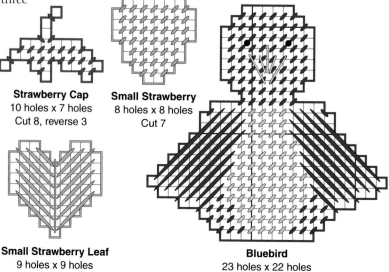

Strawberry Cap
10 holes x 7 holes
Cut 8, reverse 3

Small Strawberry
8 holes x 8 holes
Cut 7

Small Strawberry Leaf
9 holes x 9 holes
Cut 6

Bluebird
23 holes x 22 holes
Cut 1

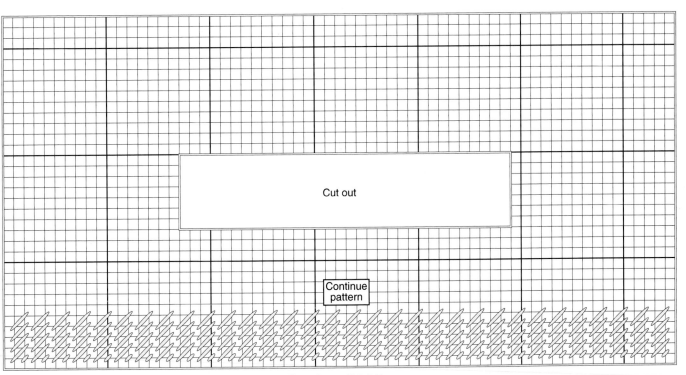

Strawberry Patch Top
65 holes x 33 holes
Cut 1

Graphs continued on page 29

Cottage Garden

Design by Angie Arickx

Each window box on this lovely cottage has its own enchanting garden filled with pretty dimensional flowers!

Skill Level: Beginner

Size: Fits boutique-style tissue box

Materials

- 1½ sheets Uniek Quick-Count 7-count plastic canvas
- Uniek Needloft plastic canvas yarn as listed in color key
- #16 tapestry needle

Instructions

1. Cut plastic canvas according to graphs (pages 28 and 29).

2. Stitch pieces following graphs, working uncoded areas with sail blue Continental Stitches.

3. When background stitching is completed, work Straight Stitches and French Knots.

4. Using white throughout, Overcast top edges of chimney pieces. Whipstitch chimney pieces together, then Whipstitch bottom edges of chimney to inside edges of box top.

5. Whipstitch front and sides together with beige, sail blue and white following graphs; Whipstitch front and sides to top with beige.

6. Overcast bottom edges of front with fern and white following graph; Overcast bottom edges of sides with white. ❖

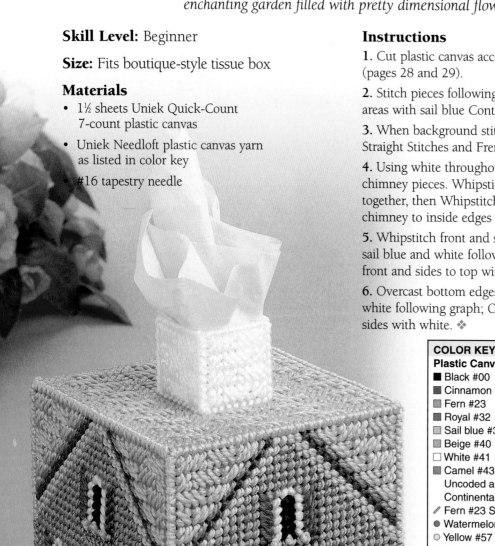

COLOR KEY	
Plastic Canvas Yarn	**Yards**
■ Black #00	7
■ Cinnamon #14	4
▨ Fern #23	6
■ Royal #32	8
□ Sail blue #35	30
▨ Beige #40	30
□ White #41	22
▨ Camel #43	12
Uncoded areas are sail blue #35 Continental Stitches	
╱ Fern #23 Straight Stitch	
● Watermelon #55 French Knot	2
○ Yellow #57 French Knot	3
● Bright purple #64 French Knot	2
Color numbers given are for Uniek Needloft plastic canvas yarn.	

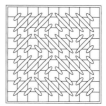

Cottage Garden Chimney
9 holes x 9 holes
Cut 4

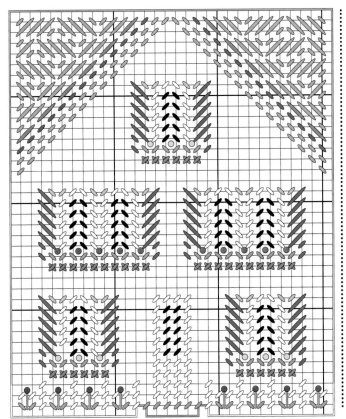

Cottage Garden Front
31 holes x 38 holes
Cut 1

Strawberry Patch

Continued from page 27

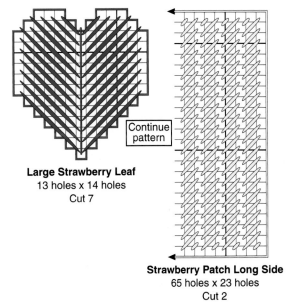

Large Strawberry Leaf
13 holes x 14 holes
Cut 7

Continue pattern

Strawberry Patch Long Side
65 holes x 23 holes
Cut 2

Strawberry Patch Short Side
33 holes x 23 holes
Cut 2

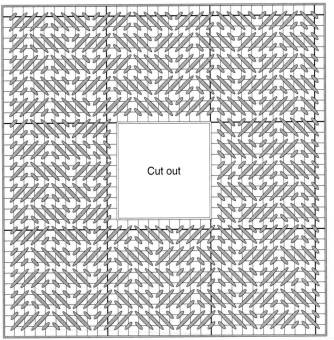

Cut out

Cottage Garden Top
31 holes x 31 holes
Cut 1

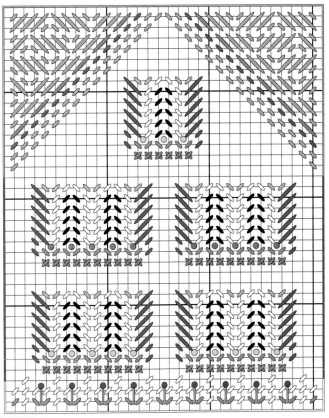

Cottage Garden Side
31 holes x 38 holes
Cut 3

Rose Lattice

Design by Nancy Marshall

A quick-to-learn pattern with a lattice look creates a lovely background for vibrant, ready-made ribbon rose accents on this pretty boutique tissue topper!

Skill Level: Intermediate

Size: Fits boutique-style tissue box

Materials

- 1¼ sheets Uniek Quick-Count pastel blue 7-count plastic canvas
- Uniek Needloft plastic canvas yarn as listed in color key
- #16 tapestry needle
- 6 light pink #117 swirl Ribbon Boutique roses with willow leaves by Offray
- Mini swirl Ribbon Boutique roses with willow leaves by Offray: 10 hot pink #156 and 8 daffodil #645
- 18 purple #465 small Ribbon Boutique roses with leaves by Offray
- Tacky craft glue or hot-glue gun

Instructions

1. Cut plastic canvas according to graphs (page 32).

2. Following graphs, work sail blue Cross Stitches of Rice Stitch pattern (Fig. 1) first; top with white stitches. Work white borders when Rice Stitches are completed.

3. Using white throughout, Overcast inside edges of top and bottom edges of sides. Whipstitch sides together; Whipstitch sides to top.

4. Using photo as a guide throughout, glue one light pink rose, two hot pink roses, two daffodil roses and four purple roses to each side.

5. Glue one light pink rose, one hot pink rose and one purple rose to two opposite corners on top. ❖

Fig. 1: Rice Stitch

Step 1
Using sail blue yarn, bring needle up at 1, down at 2, up at 3, down at 4.

Step 2
Using white yarn, bring needle up at 5, down at 6, up at 7, down at 8.

Step 3
Continuing with white yarn, bring needle up at 9, down at 10, up at 11, down at 12.

Graphs continued on page 32

Springtime Plaid

Design by Celia Lange Designs

Combine all the prettiest colors of spring into one unique project! Or, easily adapt the colors to coordinate with a room in your home.

Skill Level: Beginner

Size: Fits boutique-style tissue box

Materials

- 2 sheets Darice Ultra Stiff 7-count plastic canvas
- Coats & Clark Red Heart Classic worsted weight yarn Art. E267 as listed in color key
- Coats & Clark Red Heart Super Saver worsted weight yarn Art. E301 as listed in color key
- #16 tapestry needle

Instructions

1. Cut plastic canvas according to graphs (this page and page 32).

2. Stitch pieces following graphs, working uncoded areas with white Continental Stitches.

3. Overcast inside edges on top with blue jewel. Whipstitch sides together with lavender; Whipstitch sides to top with mint. Overcast bottom edges with pink. ❖

Graphs continued on next page

COLOR KEY	
Worsted Weight Yarn	**Yards**
☐ White #1	35
☐ Yellow #230	11
▨ Sea coral #246	11
■ Mint #366	14
▨ Kiwi #651	6
▨ Blue jewel #818	18
■ Lavender #584	10
▨ Pink #737	12
Uncoded areas are white #1 Continental Stitches	
Color numbers given are for Coats & Clark Red Heart Classic worsted weight yarn Art. E267 and Red Heart Super Saver worsted weight yarn Art. E301.	

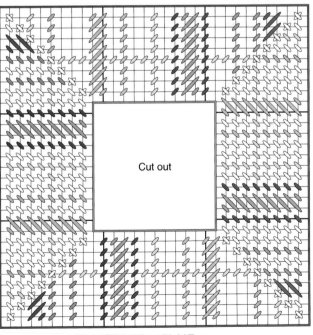

Springtime Plaid Top
30 holes x 30 holes
Cut 1

Springtime Plaid

Continued from page 30

Rose Lattice

Continued from page

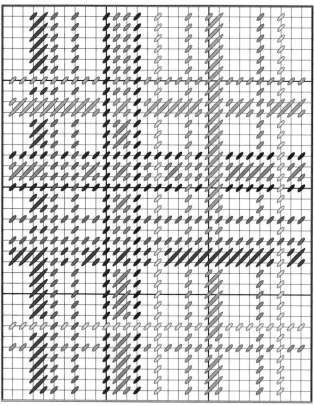

Springtime Plaid Side
30 holes x 37 holes
Cut 4

COLOR KEY

Worsted Weight Yarn	Yards
☐ White #1	35
☐ Yellow #230	11
☐ Sea coral #246	11
■ Mint #366	14
☐ Kiwi #651	6
■ Blue jewel #818	18
■ Lavender #584	10
☐ Pink #737	12
Uncoded areas are white #1 Continental Stitches	

Color numbers given are for Coats & Clark Red Heart Classic worsted weight yarn Art. E267 and Red Heart Super Saver worsted weight yarn Art. E301.

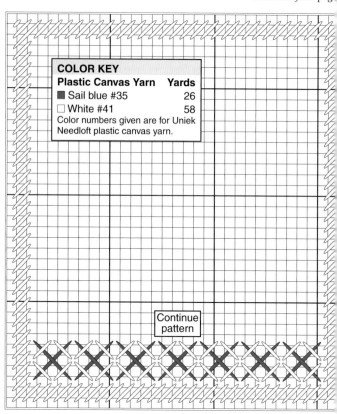

COLOR KEY

Plastic Canvas Yarn	Yards
■ Sail blue #35	26
☐ White #41	58

Color numbers given are for Uniek Needloft plastic canvas yarn.

Continue pattern

Rose Lattice Side
33 holes x 37 holes
Cut 4

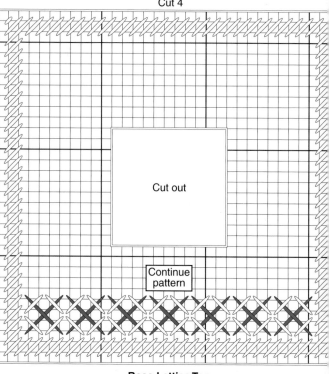

Cut out

Continue pattern

Rose Lattice Top
33 holes x 33 holes
Cut 1

Wishing Well

Design by Ruby Thacker

Whether your wish is for good luck, or simply good health, this decorative topper is sure to help you get over a case of the sniffles!

Continued on next page

Wishing Well

Continued from previous

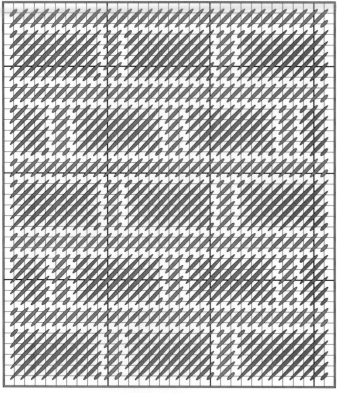

Wishing Well Front & Back
32 holes x 36 holes
Cut 2

Wishing Well Roof Support
20 holes x 30 holes
Cut 2

Skill Level: Intermediate

Size: Fits boutique-style tissue box

Materials

- 2 sheets 7-count plastic canvas
- Uniek Needloft plastic canvas yarn as listed in color key
- Nylon plastic canvas yarn as listed in color key
- #16 tapestry needle
- 2 (1-inch) floral napkin rings with attached floral spray in coordinating color
- Hot-glue gun

Instructions

1. Cut plastic canvas according to graphs.

2. Stitch pieces following graphs, working uncoded areas with camel Continental Stitches. Do not stitch bars highlighted with blue on roof pieces at this time.

3. Using gray throughout, Overcast inside edges on top. With right sides facing, Whipstitch bottom edge of one support to one side of top between arrows. Whipstitch remaining support to opposite side of top between arrows.

4. Using camel through step 5, Whipstitch wrong sides of roof pieces together along top edges; Overcast remaining edges.

5. With wrong sides together and matching edges, place one support next to support on one side; Whipstitch together along side edges and inside the "Y"; do not Whipstitch top edges together between blue dots. Repeat with remaining supports.

6. With gray, Whipstitch top to front, back and sides, then Whipstitch sides together.

7. Place roof on supports. Using camel yarn and a Continental Stitch, Whipstitch unworked top edges of supports to bars on roof indicated with blue lines.

8. Using photo as a guide, glue floral napkin rings with sprays to sides and to supports. ❖

COLOR KEY	
Plastic Canvas Yarn	**Yards**
■ Gray #38	40
■ Antique rose	35
Uncoded areas are camel #43 Continental Stitches	51
⁄ Camel #43 Overcasting and Whipstitching	
Color numbers given are for Uniek Needloft plastic canvas yarn.	

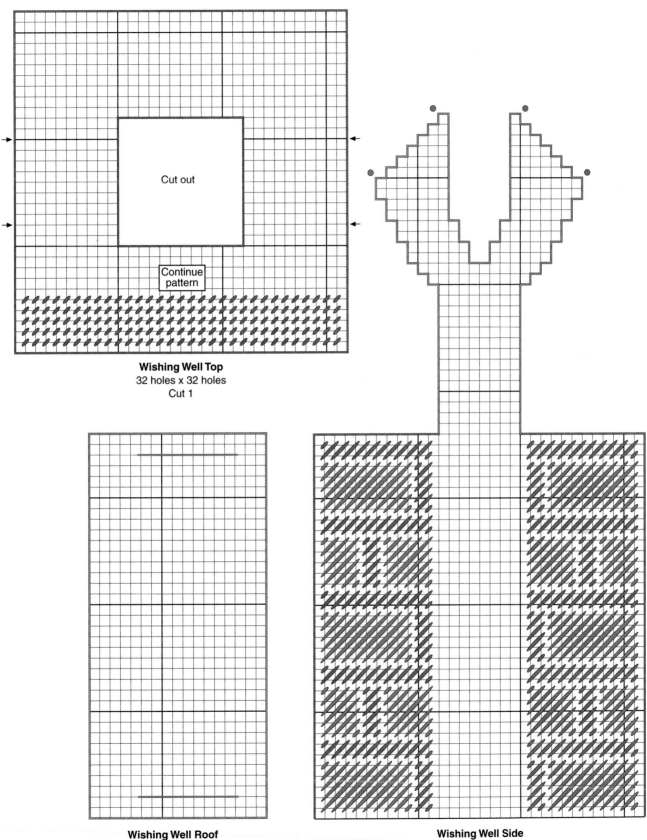

Wishing Well Top
32 holes x 32 holes
Cut 1

Wishing Well Roof
36 holes x 17 holes
Cut 2

Wishing Well Side
32 holes x 66 holes
Cut 2

Cut out

Continue
pattern

Forget-Me-Not

Design by Susan Leinberger

Just as springtime forget-me-nots delight us with their cheerful blue color and dainty petals, so this charming tissue topper will please you with its pearl-centered flowers and dimensional design!

Skill Level: Beginner

Size: Fits boutique-style tissue box

Materials

- 1½ sheets Uniek Quick-Count 7-count plastic canvas
- Uniek Needloft plastic canvas yarn as listed in color key
- Uniek Needloft iridescent craft cord as listed in color key
- #16 tapestry needle
- 1 yard ³⁄₁₆-inch-wide white picot satin ribbon
- 10 inches 4mm transparent round crystal beads on a string
- 28 (4mm) transparent round crystal beads
- 72 (2.5mm) round white pearl beads
- Tacky craft glue
- Hot-glue gun

Cutting & Stitching

1. Cut plastic canvas according to graphs.

2. Following graphs through step 5, stitch top and sides, working uncoded areas on sides with white Continental Stitches.

3. When background stitching is completed, work Backstitches, Straight Stitches and Lazy Daisy Stitches with one ply yarn.

4. Using turquoise throughout, Overcast inside edges on top. Whipstitch sides together; Whipstitch sides to top. Overcast bottom edges.

5. Using one-ply yarn throughout, stitch and Overcast leaves and large flower. Overcast 23 small flowers with bright blue and 15 with turquoise.

Assembly

1. Using tacky craft glue, attach one 2.5mm white pearl bead to center of each forget-me-knot on upper sides. Glue one 4mm transparent round crystal bead to center of each small flower. Glue one small bright blue flower to top of large flower. Allow to dry.

2. Cut three 12-inch lengths of white satin ribbon. Place three lengths together as one; tie in a bow.

3. Cut beads on a string into one 6-inch length and one 4-inch length.

4. Using photo as a guide and hot-glue gun through step 6, glue satin ribbon bow and both lengths of beads on a string to one corner on top; glue two single leaves and large flower on top of bow and beads on a string.

5. On sides, glue one small turquoise flower at top of each vertical bright blue Slanting Gobelin Stitch row and one small bright blue flower at top of each turquoise Slanting Gobelin Stitch row.

6. Glue three double leaves, two small bright blue flowers and one small turquoise flower to each remaining corner on top. ❖

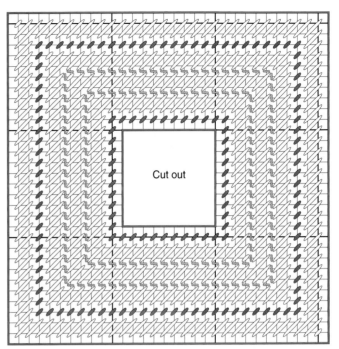

Forget-Me-Not Top
31 holes x 31 holes
Cut 1

COLOR KEY

Plastic Canvas Yarn	Yards
☐ White #41	56
▨ Mermaid #53	5
■ Turquoise #54	20
▨ Bright blue #60	15

Uncoded areas on sides are white #41 Continental Stitches
╱ Turquoise #54 Backstitch
╱ Mermaid #53 Backstitch
╱ Bright blue #60 Backstitch and Straight Stitch
𝒪 Mermaid #53 Lazy Daisy Stitch

Iridescent Craft Cord

	Yards
■ Blue #55049	6

Color numbers given are for Uniek Needloft plastic canvas yarn and iridescent craft cord.

Large Flower
5 holes x 5 holes
Cut 1

Small Flower
3 holes x 3 holes
Cut 38
Overcast 23 as graphed
Overcast 15 with turquoise

Single Leaf
3 holes x 3 holes
Cut 2

Double Leaf
4 holes x 4 holes
Cut 9

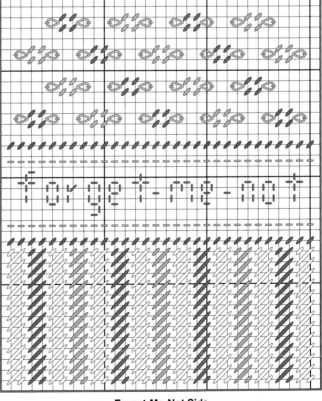

Forget-Me-Not Side
31 holes x 37 holes
Cut 4

Seeds of the Spirit

Design by Vicki Blizzard

*Plant the seeds today that will bear the fruit of the Spirit tomorrow
by extending love and spreading joy wherever you go.*

Skill Level: Beginner

Size: Fits boutique-style tissue box

Materials

- 2 sheets 7-count plastic canvas
- Uniek Needloft plastic canvas yarn as listed in color key
- DMC #3 pearl cotton as listed in color key
- DMC 6-strand metallic embroidery floss as listed in color key
- #16 tapestry needle
- 26 (16ss/5mm) round light rose AB Austrian crystal heat-set rhinestones from Creative Crystals Co.
- BeJeweler heat-set tool from Creative Crystals Co.
- Hot-glue gun

Cutting & Stitching

1. Cut plastic canvas according to graphs (this page and pages 39 and 53).

2. Following graphs through step 5, stitch signs, top and sides, working uncoded areas with white Continental Stitches.

3. When background stitching is completed, work lettering with medium dark antique mauve pearl cotton and Backstitches on sides with silver metallic embroidery floss.

4. Using lavender throughout, Overcast inside edges of top and bottom edges of sides. Whipstitch sides together; then Whipstitch sides to top. Overcast signs with silver floss.

5. Stitch and Overcast individual letters, flowers and leaves. When background stitching and overcasting are completed, work moss Straight Stitches on leaves and silver floss Straight Stitches on letters.

Assembly

1. Using heat-set tool, attach one rhinestone to each flower center and two to each sign.

2. Using hot glue through step 6, center and glue one sign over silver Backstitches on each side.

3. Glue letters to spell "LOVE" along bottom edge of one side; glue love flowers and leaves as desired to this side.

4. Glue letters to spell "JOY" along bottom edge of second side; glue joy flowers and leaves to this side.

5. Glue letters to spell "HOPE" along bottom edge of third side; glue hope flowers and leaves to this side.

6. Glue letters to spell "PEACE" along bottom edge of last side, gluing letters in a slight curve if necessary to fit. Glue peace flowers and leaves as desired to this side. ❖

Graphs continued on page 53

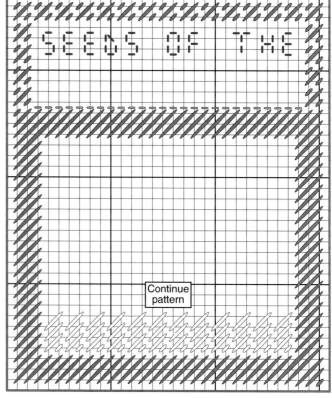

Seeds of the Spirit Side
31 holes x 37 holes
Cut 4

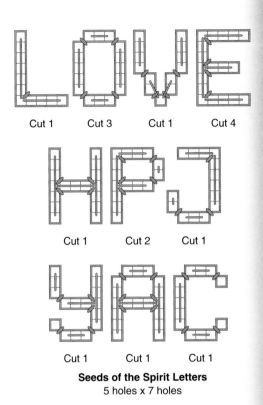

Cut 1 Cut 3 Cut 1 Cut 4

Cut 1 Cut 2 Cut 1

Cut 1 Cut 1 Cut 1

Seeds of the Spirit Letters
5 holes x 7 holes

Seeds of the Spirit Sign
15 holes x 5 holes
Cut 4

Peace Flower
5 holes x 5 holes
Cut 5

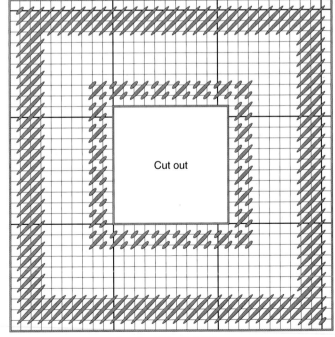

Cut out

Seeds of the Spirit Top
31 holes x 31 holes
Cut 1

COLOR KEY

Plastic Canvas Yarn	Yards
■ Lavender #05	34
□ Pink #07	3
□ Lemon #20	5
■ Moss #25	24
■ Sail blue #35	3
□ White #41	70
■ Lilac #45	5

Uncoded areas are white #41
Continental Stitches
╱ Moss #25 Straight Stitch

#3 Pearl Cotton
╱ Medium dark antique mauve #315
Backstitch and Straight Stitch | 6

6-Strand Metallic Embroidery Floss
╱ Silver #5283 Backstitch, Straight Stitch
and Overcasting | 8
● Attach rhinestone

Color numbers given are for Uniek Needloft plastic canvas yarn and DMC #3 pearl cotton and 6-strand metallic floss.

April Showers

Design by Robin Howard-Will

April showers bring fun afternoons of splashing and stomping in puddles. May brings a bounty of lovely flowers. Remember both with this easy-to-stitch tissue box cover!

Skill Level: Beginner

Size: Fits boutique-style tissue box

Materials

- 1½ sheets 7-count plastic canvas
- Coats & Clark Red Heart Classic worsted weight yarn Art. E267 as listed in color key
- Coats & Clark Red Heart Super Saver worsted weight yarn Art. E300 as listed in color key
- DMC 6-strand embroidery floss as listed in color key
- #16 tapestry needle

Instructions

1. Cut plastic canvas according to graphs.

2. Stitch pieces following graphs, working uncoded areas on top and May sides with light blue Continental Stitches and uncoded areas on April sides with light blue Reverse Continental Stitches.

3. When background stitching is completed, work sun's rays with bright yellow Straight Stitches and letters with black embroidery floss.

4. Overcast inside edges on top with light blue and bottom edges on sides with grass green.

5. Whipstitch April sides to May sides with light blue and grass green following graphs. *Note: Same months will be on opposite sides.* Whipstitch sides to top with light blue. ❖

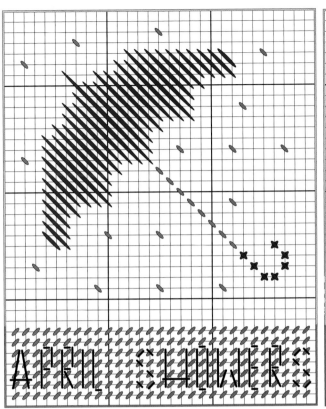

April Side
30 holes x 37 holes
Cut 2

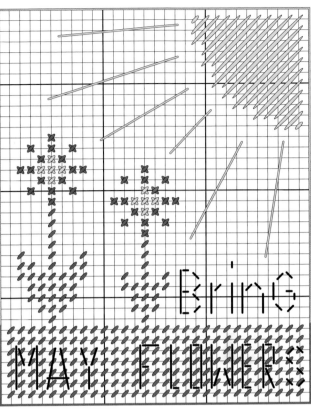

May Side
30 holes x 37 holes
Cut 2

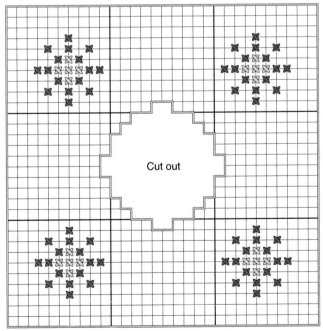

April Showers Top
30 holes x 30 holes
Cut 1

COLOR KEY

Plastic Canvas Yarn	Yards
☐ Bright yellow #324	9
■ Raspberry #375	5
■ Skipper blue #380	2
■ Nickel #401	1
■ Amethyst #588	5
■ Grass green #687	14
Uncoded areas on May sides and top are light blue #381 Continental Stitches	44
Uncoded areas on April sides are light blue #381 Reverse Continental Stitches	
╱ Light blue #381 Overcasting and Whipstitching	
╱ Bright yellow #324 Straight Stitch	

6-Strand Embroidery Floss

╱ Black #310 Backstitch and Straight Stitch

Color numbers given are for Coats & Clark Red Heart Classic worsted weight yarn Art. E267 and Red Heart Super Saver worsted weight yarn Art. E300 and DMC 6-strand embroidery floss.

Mini Critters Tissue Pockets

Designs by Christina Laws

Tuck a pocket-sized packet of tissue in one of these whimsical holders for kids or yourself!

Skill Level: Intermediate

Size:

Cat: 2⅝ inches W x 4⅞ inches L x 3¼ H

Dog: 3½ inches W x 4⅞ inches L x 3 H

Pig: 2½ inches W x 4⅞ inches L x 2⅞ H

Elephant: 3¾ inches W x 4⅞ inches L x 3½ H

Materials

- 2 sheets 7-count plastic canvas
- Worsted weight yarn as listed in color key
- #16 tapestry needle
- Hot-glue gun

Cutting & Stitching

1. Following graphs through step 9, cut and stitch cat pieces (page 42), working uncoded areas with white Continental Stitches. Do not stitch blue Whipstitch lines at this time.

2. Overcast cat muzzle, working pink Straight Stitches while Overcasting. Work white French Knot for center of each eye.

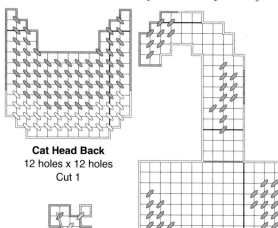

Cat Head Back
12 holes x 12 holes
Cut 1

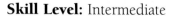

Cat Muzzle
4 holes x 4 holes
Cut 1

Cat Pocket Back
16 holes x 21 holes
Cut 1

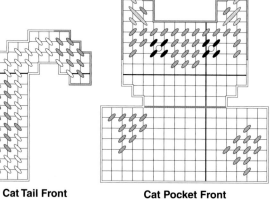

Cat Tail Front
10 holes x 14 holes
Cut 1

Cat Pocket Front
16 holes x 19 holes
Cut 1

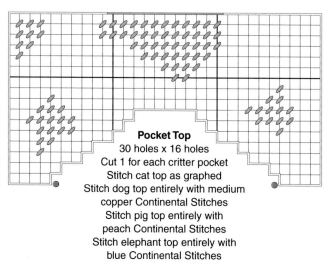

Pocket Top
30 holes x 16 holes
Cut 1 for each critter pocket
Stitch cat top as graphed
Stitch dog top entirely with medium
copper Continental Stitches
Stitch pig top entirely with
peach Continental Stitches
Stitch elephant top entirely with
blue Continental Stitches

COLOR KEY	
CAT	
Worsted Weight Yarn	**Yards**
☐ White	14
▨ Pumpkin	7
☐ Pink	1
■ Black	1
Uncoded areas are white Continental Stitches	
⁄ Pink Straight Stitch	
○ White French Knot	

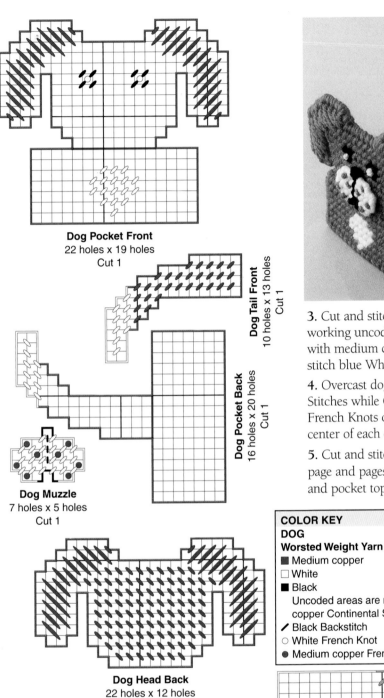

Dog Pocket Front
22 holes x 19 holes
Cut 1

Dog Tail Front
10 holes x 13 holes
Cut 1

Dog Pocket Back
16 holes x 20 holes
Cut 1

Dog Muzzle
7 holes x 5 holes
Cut 1

Dog Head Back
22 holes x 12 holes
Cut 1

Pocket Side A
30 holes x 7 holes
Cut 1 for each critter pocket
Stitch cat side A as graphed
Stitch dog side A entirely
with medium copper Continental Stitches
Stitch pig side A entirely with
peach Continental Stitches
Stitch elephant side A entirely with
blue Continental Stitches

3. Cut and stitch dog pieces (this page and page 42), working uncoded areas and pocket top and sides with medium copper Continental Stitches. Do not stitch blue Whipstitch lines at this time.

4. Overcast dog muzzle, working black Straight Stitches while Overcasting. Work medium copper French Knots on muzzle and white French Knot for center of each eye.

5. Cut and stitch pig pieces following graphs (this page and pages 42 and 47), working uncoded areas and pocket top and sides with peach Continental Stitches; Overcast tail while stitching back piece. Do not stitch blue Whipstitch line at this time.

6. Overcast snout, then work black French Knots. Work white French Knot for center of each eye.

COLOR KEY	
DOG	
Worsted Weight Yarn	**Yards**
■ Medium copper	19
□ White	2
■ Black	1
Uncoded areas are medium copper Continental Stitches	
╱ Black Backstitch	
○ White French Knot	
● Medium copper French Knot	

Pocket Side B
30 holes x 7 holes
Cut 1 for each critter pocket
Stitch cat side B as graphed
Stitch dog side B entirely
with medium copper Continental Stitches
Stitch pig side B entirely with
peach Continental Stitches
Stitch elephant side B entirely with
blue Continental Stitches

Continued on next page

Mini Critter Tissue Pockets

Continued from page 44

7. Cut and stitch elephant pieces following graphs (this page and pages 42 and 43), working uncoded areas and pocket top and sides with blue Continental Stitches. Do not stitch blue Whipstitch lines at this time.

8. Overcast trunk. Work white French Knot for center of each eye.

9. Using white for cat pieces and adjacent colors for dog, pig and elephant pieces, Overcast uneven edges on pocket tops and on sides A from dot to dot.

Assembly

1. Following graphs and working with corresponding pieces through step 4, with wrong sides together, Whipstitch head backs to heads on pocket fronts around side and top edges only. Repeat for cat, dog and elephant tail fronts.

2. Using white and pumpkin for cat pieces, medium copper for dog pieces, peach for pig pieces and blue for elephant pieces through step 3, Whipstitch side edges of pocket tops to fronts and backs, working Continental Stitches along Whipstitch lines and catching bottom edges of tail fronts and head backs while stitching.

3. Whipstitch sides A and B to tops, fronts and backs. Overcast bottom edges of cat pocket with white and bottom edges of remaining pockets with adjacent colors.

4. Using photo as a guide, glue muzzles, snout and elephant trunk to heads. ❖

Continued on page 47

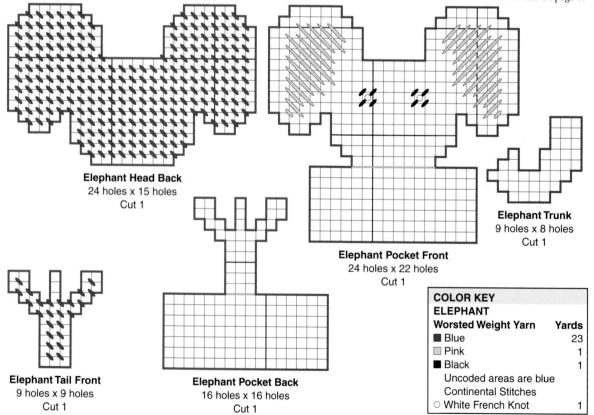

Elephant Head Back
24 holes x 15 holes
Cut 1

Elephant Trunk
9 holes x 8 holes
Cut 1

Elephant Pocket Front
24 holes x 22 holes
Cut 1

Elephant Tail Front
9 holes x 9 holes
Cut 1

Elephant Pocket Back
16 holes x 16 holes
Cut 1

COLOR KEY	
ELEPHANT	
Worsted Weight Yarn	**Yards**
■ Blue	23
▨ Pink	1
■ Black	1
Uncoded areas are blue Continental Stitches	
○ White French Knot	1

Bless You!

Design by Cynthia Roberts

Tuck a few tissues inside this slim tissue holder. It's just the right size for tucking in your purse!

Skill Level: Beginner

Size: Fits purse-size tissue package

Materials

- ½ sheet 7-count plastic canvas
- Worsted weight yarn as listed in color key
- #16 tapestry needle

Instructions

1. Cut plastic canvas according to graphs.

2. Stitch pieces following graphs, working uncoded areas with blue Continental Stitches. When background stitching is completed, work burgundy French Knots.

3. Using blue throughout, Overcast bottom edge of Front A and top edge of Front B.

4. With wrong sides together and matching outside edges, Whipstitch remaining edges of top pieces to back, Overcasting the two center holes on each side of back while Whipstitching. ❖

COLOR KEY	
Worsted Weight Yarn	**Yards**
■ Blue	22
□ White	3
▨ Pink	1
■ Green	½
Uncoded areas are blue Continental Stitches	
● Burgundy French Knot	½

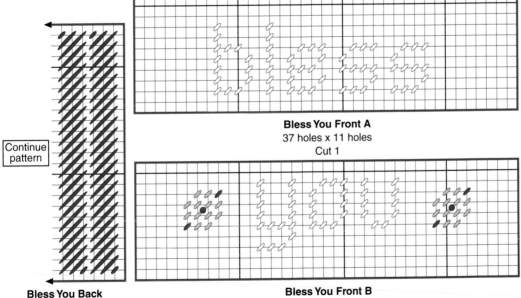

Bless You Front A
37 holes x 11 holes
Cut 1

Continue pattern

Bless You Back
37 holes x 24 holes
Cut 1

Bless You Front B
37 holes x 11 holes
Cut 1

You're the Star!

Design by Joan Green

Celebrate your child's achievements with this photo frame tissue cover! Metallic gold and silver yarn adds just the right amount of sparkle!

Skill Level: Beginner

Size: Fits boutique-style tissue box

Materials

- 1¼ sheets 7-count plastic canvas
- 5-inch plastic canvas star shape by Uniek
- Coats & Clark Red Heart Classic worsted weight yarn Art. E267 as listed in color key
- ⅛ inch-wide Plastic Canvas 7 Metallic Needlepoint Yarn by Rainbow Gallery as listed in color key
- #16 tapestry needle
- Fabric glue

Instructions

1. Cut plastic canvas according to graphs, cutting away gray area in center of large star.

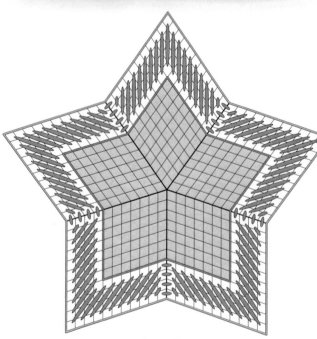

Large Star
Cut 1,
cutting away gray area

You're the Star Side
30 holes x 37 holes
Cut 4

2. Following graphs through step 3, stitch top and sides, working pale blue Continental Stitches first. Fill in squares with Scotch Stitches, working in diagonal rows.

3. Stitch and Overcast large star. Stitch small stars, working three stars in gold and three in silver; Overcast edges while stitching.

4. Center and glue photo behind opening on large star.

5. Using pale blue, Overcast inside opening on top. Whipstitch sides to top, making sure skipper blue square is in the upper left-hand corner on each side.

6. Tack large star to one side with gold metallic yarn. Tack one gold and one silver star to each remaining side with matching metallic yarn.

7. Using pale blue, Whipstitch sides together; Overcast bottom edges. ❖

Small Star
11 holes x 10 holes
Cut 6
Stitch 3 as graphed
Stitch 3 with silver

COLOR KEY

Worsted Weight Yarn	Yards
☐ Pale blue #815	40
▨ Blue jewel #818	18
■ True blue #822	18
■ Skipper blue #848	20
⅛-Inch-Wide Metallic Needlepoint Yarn	
▨ Gold #PC1	11
▨ Silver #PC2	14

Color numbers given are for Coats & Clark Red Heart Classic worsted weight yarn Art. E267 and Rainbow Gallery Plastic Canvas 7 Metallic Needlepoint Yarn.

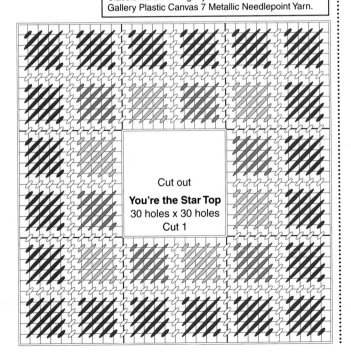

Cut out
You're the Star Top
30 holes x 30 holes
Cut 1

Mini Critter Tissue Pockets

Continued from page 44

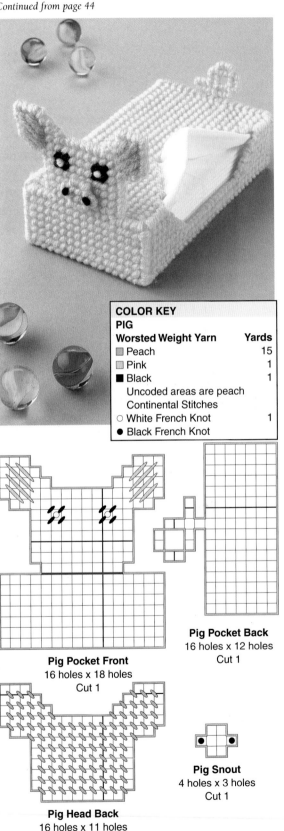

COLOR KEY
PIG

Worsted Weight Yarn	Yards
☐ Peach	15
▨ Pink	1
■ Black	1
Uncoded areas are peach Continental Stitches	
○ White French Knot	1
● Black French Knot	

Pig Pocket Back
16 holes x 12 holes
Cut 1

Pig Pocket Front
16 holes x 18 holes
Cut 1

Pig Snout
4 holes x 3 holes
Cut 1

Pig Head Back
16 holes x 11 holes
Cut 1

Spring Garden

Design by Michele Wilcox

Capture the beauty of an aromatic perennial garden with this artistic tissue box cover!

Skill Level: Beginner

Size: Fits regular-size tissue box

Materials

- 1½ sheets Uniek Quick-Count 7-count plastic canvas
- Uniek Needloft plastic canvas yarn as listed in color key
- DMC #5 pearl cotton as listed in color key
- #16 tapestry needle

Instructions

1. Cut plastic canvas according to graphs.

2. Stitch pieces following graph, working uncoded areas with white Continental Stitches.

3. When background stitching is completed, work medium delft blue Lazy Daisy Stitches and cranberry and light pale yellow Straight

Stitches. Work light pale yellow and medium delft blue French Knots last.

4. Using white throughout, Whipstitch front and back to sides; Whipstitch front, back and sides to top, aligning edges on top and front pieces to create opening for tissues. Overcast all remaining edges. ❖

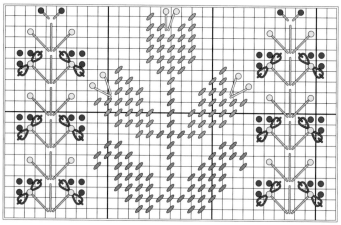

Spring Garden Side
32 holes x 20 holes
Cut 2

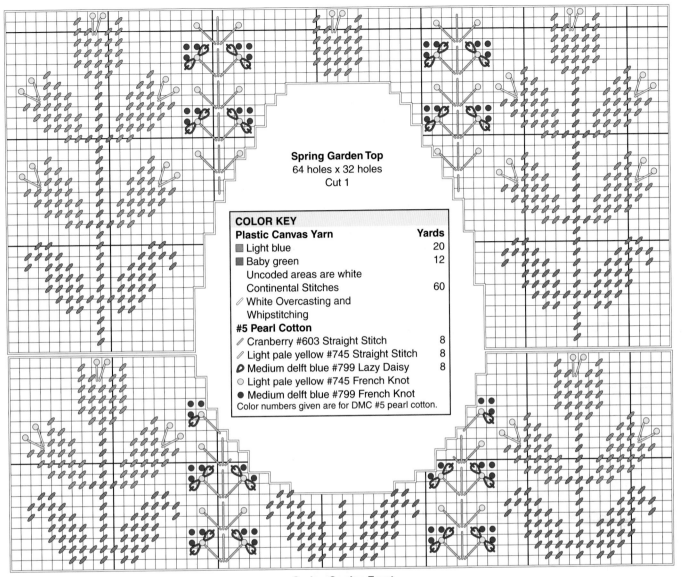

Spring Garden Top
64 holes x 32 holes
Cut 1

COLOR KEY

Plastic Canvas Yarn	Yards
■ Light blue	20
■ Baby green	12
Uncoded areas are white Continental Stitches	60
╱ White Overcasting and Whipstitching	

#5 Pearl Cotton

	Yards
╱ Cranberry #603 Straight Stitch	8
╱ Light pale yellow #745 Straight Stitch	8
⫸ Medium delft blue #799 Lazy Daisy	8
○ Light pale yellow #745 French Knot	
● Medium delft blue #799 French Knot	

Color numbers given are for DMC #5 pearl cotton.

Spring Garden Front
64 holes x 20 holes
Cut 1

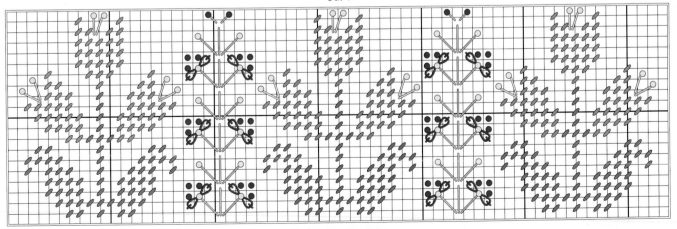

Spring Garden Back
64 holes x 20 holes
Cut 1

Count Your Bless-You's!

Design by Vicki Blizzard

Anytime you are sick or just feeling blue, the darling angel on this tissue topper will remind you to count your bless-you's!

Skill Level: Beginner

Size: Fits boutique-style tissue box

Materials

- 2 sheets 7-count plastic canvas
- Uniek Needloft plastic canvas yarn as listed in color key
- Kreinik ⅛-inch Metallic Ribbon as listed in color key
- DMC #3 pearl cotton as listed in color key
- #16 tapestry needle
- 2 (4mm) round black cabochons from The Beadery
- 8 inches ⅛-inch-wide red satin ribbon
- Brown mini-curl doll hair
- Jewel glue
- Hot-glue gun

Cutting & Stitching

1. Cut plastic canvas according to graphs.

2. Following graphs through step 7, work top and sides. When background stitching is completed, work Backstitches with 1 ply watermelon.

3. Using red yarn throughout, Overcast inside edges of top and bottom edges of sides. Whipstitch sides together; Whipstitch sides to top.

4. Stitch and Overcast halo with Aztec gold.

5. Stitch remaining pieces, working uncoded area on sign with white Continental Stitches and uncoded areas on head and hands with flesh tone Continental Stitches. Stitch and Overcast 22 hearts with watermelon and 22 with Christmas red.

6. Overcast sign with watermelon, wings with white, hands with flesh tone and head with flesh tone and cinnamon.

7. Using 1 ply yarn, work flesh tone Straight Stitches on hands and pink French Knot for nose. Using bright red pearl cotton, work mouth on head and words on sign.

Assembly

1. Use photo as a guide throughout assembly. Using jewel glue, glue cabochons to head for eyes.

2. Use hot glue through step 5. Following manufacturer's instructions, glue hair in bunches to head around face where Overcast with cinnamon.

3. Tie ribbon in a bow and glue to hair on one side of head.

4. Glue five hearts along each top and bottom edge of sides, alternating colors. Glue one watermelon and one Christmas red heart each to opposite corners on top.

5. Glue face and hands to top upper left corner of sign. Glue wings to back of sign behind head and hands. Glue halo to upper back edge of head. Glue completed unit to one side. ❖

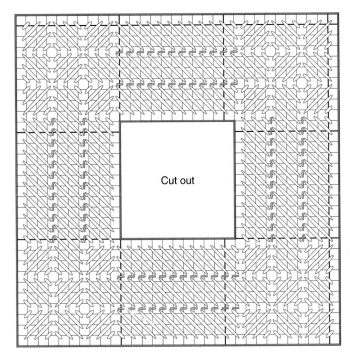

Count Your Bless-You's Top
31 holes x 31 holes
Cut 1

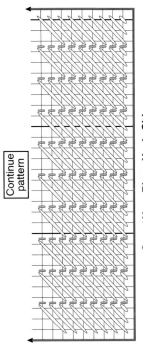

Count Your Bless-You's Side
31 holes x 37 holes
Cut 4

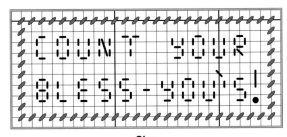

Sign
26 holes x 11 holes
Cut 1

Angel Wing
11 holes x 7 holes
Cut 2

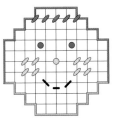

Angel Head
10 holes x 10 holes
Cut 1

COLOR KEY	
Plastic Canvas Yarn	**Yards**
■ Christmas red #02	13
☐ Pink #07	1
■ Cinnamon #14	1
☐ White #41	70
■ Watermelon #55	13
Uncoded background on sign is white #41 Continental Stitches	7
Uncoded areas on head and hands are flesh tone #56 Continental Stitches	3
╱ Red #01 Overcasting and Whipstitching	
╱ Watermelon #55 Backstitch	
╱ Flesh tone #56 Straight Stitch and Overcasting	
◯ Pink #07 French Knot	
⅛-Inch Metallic Ribbon	1
■ Aztec gold #202	
#3 Pearl Cotton	
╱ Bright red #666 Backstitch and Straight Stitch	3
● Bright red #666 French Knot	
● Attach 4mm cabochon	

Color numbers given are for Uniek Needloft plastic canvas yarn, Kreinik ⅛-inch Metallic Ribbon and DMC #3 pearl cotton.

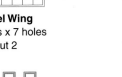

Count Your Bless-You's Heart
5 holes x 5 holes
Cut 44
Stitch 22 as graphed
Stitch 22 with Christmas red

Angel Hand
5 holes x 4 holes
Cut 2

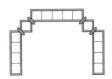

Angel Halo
9 holes x 6 holes
Cut 1

Hearts & Daisies

Design by Judy Collishaw
Perfect for keeping in the car or at the office,
this small tissue box cover holds a purse-size package of tissues!

Skill Level: Beginner

Size: Fits purse-size tissue package

Materials

- ⅔ sheet 7-count plastic canvas
- Worsted weight yarn as listed in color key
- #16 tapestry needle

Instructions

1. Cut plastic canvas according to graphs. Cut one 30-hole x 16-hole piece for bottom and one 28-hole x 6-hole piece for flap.

2. Stitch pieces following graphs, working bottom, flap and uncoded areas on all remaining pieces with navy blue Continental Stitches.

3. When background stitching is completed, work daisies petals with white Straight Stitches.

4. Using navy blue through step 6, Overcast inside edges of top. Whipstitch ends to front, forming one long strip, then Whipstitch ends and front to top and bottom. *Note: There will be one open end.*

5. Whipstitch top edge of back piece to remaining edge on top piece. Center and Whipstitch one long edge of flap to bottom edge of back piece.

6. Overcast all remaining edges. ❖

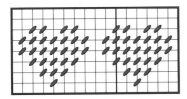

Hearts & Daisies End
16 holes x 8 holes
Cut 2

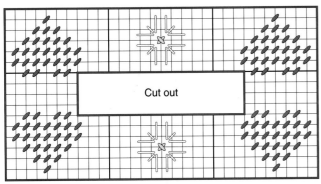

Hearts & Daisies Top
30 holes x 16 holes
Cut 1

Cut out

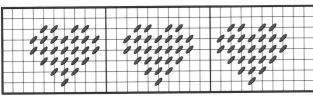

Hearts & Daisies Front & Back
30 holes x 8 holes
Cut 2

COLOR KEY	
Worsted Weight Yarn	**Yards**
■ Bright red	6
☐ Yellow	1
Uncoded areas are navy blue Continental Stitches	20
⁄ Navy blue Overcasting and Whipstitching	
⁄ White Straight Stitch	1

Seeds of the Spirit

Continued from page 39

COLOR KEY	
Plastic Canvas Yarn	**Yards**
■ Lavender #05	34
☐ Pink #07	3
☐ Lemon #20	5
■ Moss #25	24
■ Sail blue #35	3
☐ White #41	70
■ Lilac #45	5
Uncoded areas are white #41 Continental Stitches	
⁄ Moss #25 Straight Stitch	
#3 Pearl Cotton	
⁄ Medium dark antique mauve #315 Backstitch and Straight Stitch	6
6-Strand Metallic Embroidery Floss	
⁄ Silver #5283 Backstitch, Straight Stitch and Overcasting	8
● Attach rhinestone	
Color numbers given are for Uniek Needloft plastic canvas yarn and DMC #3 pearl cotton and 6-strand metallic floss.	

Joy Flower
7 holes x 7 holes
Cut 3

Love Flower
7 holes x 7 holes
Cut 3

Joy Leaf
5 holes x 11 holes
Cut 2

Love/Peace Leaf
5 holes x 6 holes
Cut 4 for love leaf
Cut 4 for peace leaf

Hope Leaf
3 holes x 4 holes
Cut 5

Hope Flower
3 holes x 3 holes
Cut 9

Summer Brights!

Add vivid colors and lively summer designs to every room in your home with this collection of breezy and beautiful tissue box covers!

Watermelon Delight

Design by Angie Arickx

Nothing says summertime quite like a big, juicy slice of watermelon! Stitch it today for a unique tissue topper!

Skill Level: Beginner

Size: Fits regular-size tissue box

Materials
- 1 sheet Uniek Quick-Count artist-size 7-count plastic canvas
- Uniek Needloft plastic canvas yarn as listed in color key
- #16 tapestry needle

Instructions

1. Cut two sides from plastic canvas according to graph (page 56). Cut one 121-hole x 33-hole piece for top according to graph, cutting left half first, then turning graph and cutting right half.

2. Stitch sides following graph, working uncoded area with watermelon Continental Stitches.

3. Stitch one half of top following graph, working uncoded areas with holly Continental Stitches; turn graph and stitch remaining half.

4. Overcast bottom edges of sides with adjacent colors. Using holly, Overcast inside edges and short edges of top, then Whipstitch long edges on top to curved edges on sides. ❖

Graphs continued on next page

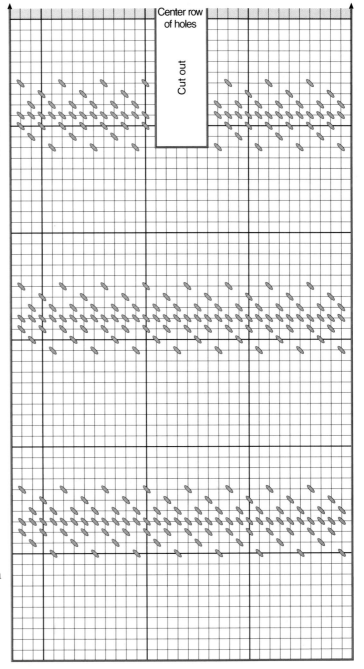

Watermelon Delight Top
121 holes x 33 holes
Cut 1
Cut left half first
Turn graph and cut right half
Stitch left half as shown
Turn graph and stitch right half

Watermelon Delight

Continued from previous page

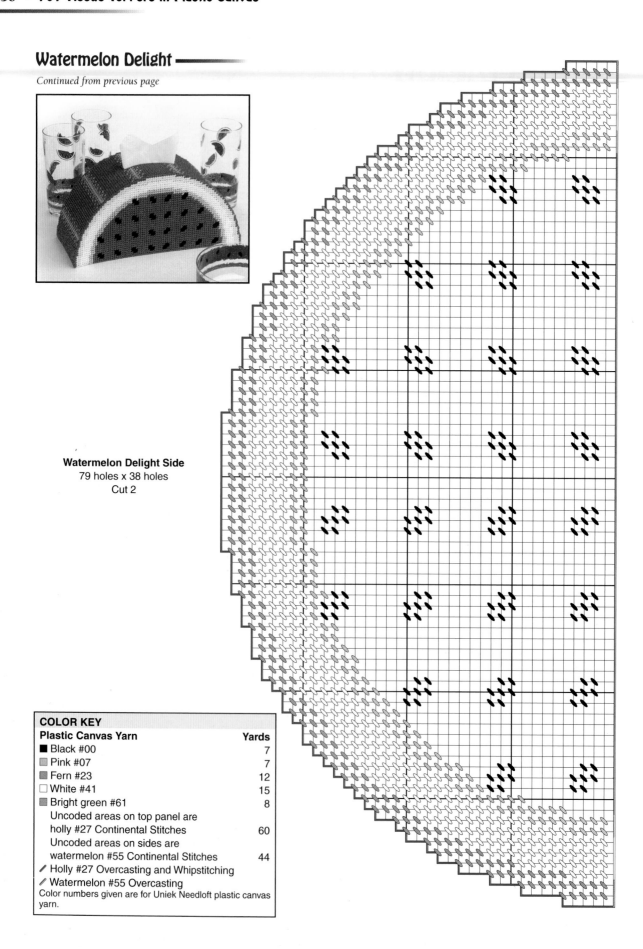

Watermelon Delight Side
79 holes x 38 holes
Cut 2

COLOR KEY

Plastic Canvas Yarn	Yards
■ Black #00	7
▨ Pink #07	7
▨ Fern #23	12
☐ White #41	15
▨ Bright green #61	8
Uncoded areas on top panel are holly #27 Continental Stitches	60
Uncoded areas on sides are watermelon #55 Continental Stitches	44
╱ Holly #27 Overcasting and Whipstitching	
╱ Watermelon #55 Overcasting	

Color numbers given are for Uniek Needloft plastic canvas yarn.

Bait Shop

Design by Robin Petrina

Please the fisherman in your family with this whimsical tissue box cover! At last— a Father's Day gift Dad will truly enjoy!

Skill Level: Beginner

Size: Fits boutique-style tissue box

Materials

- 2 sheets clear 7-count plastic canvas
- Small amount peach 7-count plastic canvas from Darice
- Small amount clear 10-count plastic canvas
- Coats & Clark Red Heart Super Saver worsted weight yarn Art. E300 as listed in color key
- DMC 6-strand embroidery floss: ¼ yard white and as listed in color key
- #16 tapestry needle
- Hot-glue gun

Cutting and Stitching

1. Cut large and small fish from clear 10-count plastic canvas and fishing rod from peach 7-count plastic canvas according to graphs (pages 58 and 59), cutting away blue lines on fishing rod.

2. Cut all remaining pieces from clear 7-count plastic canvas according to graphs (pages 58 and 59).

3. Place medium forest green and pearl gray 6-strand embroidery floss together; stitch and Overcast fish following graphs. Work eye on large fish with 2 plies hunter green.

4. Overcast windows with hunter green. Stitch remaining pieces with yarn following graphs, reversing one side before stitching and working uncoded background on sign with hunter green Continental Stitches.

5. Overcast plaque with warm brown, outside edges of base with grass green and top edges of front back and sides with light gray. Overcast door, sign and inside and outside edges of roof with hunter green.

6. Embroider words on sign with white and door knob on door with light gray.

Assembly

1. Use photo as a guide throughout assembly. Using light gray, Whipstitch long side edges of sides to front; Whipstitch short side edges to back. Whipstitch front back and sides to inside edges of base with grass green.

2. Center and glue roof to top edges of bait shop. Glue one set of windows to each side. Center and glue door front at base.

3. Center and glue large fish to plaque; glue plaque to front above door. Glue sign to front above plaque.

4. For fishing rod, following Fig. 1 and using 2 strands white floss, wrap floss around reel and secure; do not cut off. Tie floss in a knot around rod halfway to end, then again at end of rod. Allow a 1¼-inch-length floss to hang from end of rod.

5. Glue end of floss to back of small fish. Prop fishing rod against bait shop front; then glue in place to front and base. ❖

Graphs continued on next page

Bait Shop

Continued from previous page

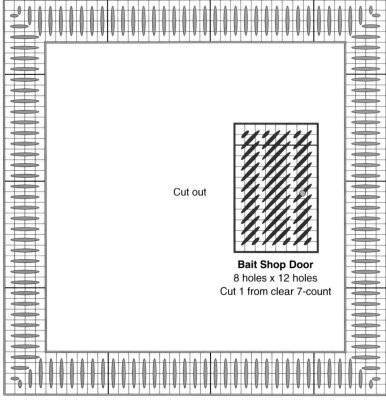

Cut out

Bait Shop Door
8 holes x 12 holes
Cut 1 from clear 7-count

Bait Shop Base
37 holes x 37 holes
Cut 1 from clear 7-count

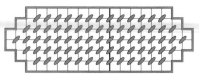

Bait Shop Plaque
18 holes x 6 holes
Cut 1 from clear 7-count

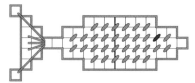

Large Fish
17 holes x 7 holes
Cut 1 from clear 10-count

Fishing Rod
16 holes x 1 holes
Cut 1 from peach 7-count
Cut away blue lines
Do not stitch

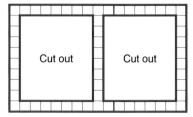

Cut out   Cut out

Bait Shop Windows
17 holes x 10 holes
Cut 2 from clear 7-count
Do not stitch

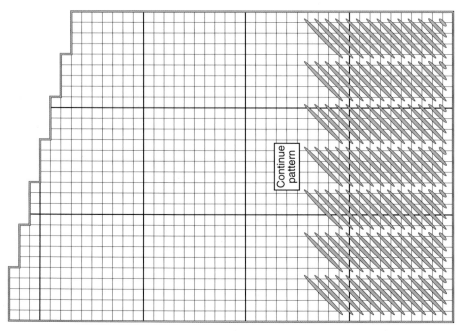

Continue pattern

Bait Shop Side
29 holes x 43 holes
Cut 2, reverse 1,
from clear 7-count

COLOR KEY

Worsted Weight Yarn	Yards
■ Warm brown #336	2
▨ Light gray #341	55
■ Hunter green #389	26
▨ Grass green #687	26
Uncoded background on sign is hunter green #389 Continental Stitches	
⁄ White #311 Backstitch and Straight Stitch	1
● Light gray #341 French Knot	
6-Strand Embroidery Floss	
■ Medium forest green #988 and	2
pearl gray #415 combined	2
⁄ Medium forest green #988 and pearl gray #415 Straight Stitch	

Color numbers given are for Coats & Clark Red Heart Super Saver worsted weight yarn Art. E300 and DMC 6-strand embroidery floss.

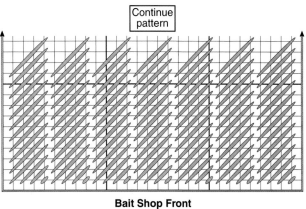

Bait Shop Front
29 holes x 43 holes
Cut 1 from clear 7-count

Bait Shop Back
29 holes x 37 holes
Cut 1 from clear 7-count

Fig. 1

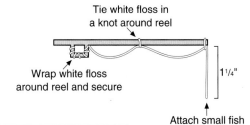

Tie white floss in a knot around reel

Wrap white floss around reel and secure

1¼"

Attach small fish

Bait Shop Sign
26 holes x 9 holes
Cut 1 from clear 7-count

Small Fish
6 holes x 3 holes
Cut 1 from clear 10-count

Continue pattern

Cut out

Continue pattern

Continue pattern

Bait Shop Roof
41 holes x 41 holes
Cut 1 from clear 7-count

Maritime Flags

Design by Joan Green

Ahoy, stitchers! Boat lovers will love stitching this maritime flag and rope-decorated topper for the summer cottage on the lake!

Skill Level: Beginner

Size: Fits regular-size tissue box

Materials

- 1¼ sheets 7-count plastic canvas
- Coats & Clark Red Heart Classic worsted weight yarn Art. E267 as listed in color key
- ⅛-inch-wide Plastic Canvas 7 Metallic Needlepoint Yarn by Rainbow Gallery as listed in color key
- #16 tapestry needle

Instructions

1. Cut plastic canvas according to graphs (this page and pages 61 and 63).

2. Stitch long and short sides A and top following graphs, working uncoded areas with blue jewel Continental Stitches. Work remaining long and short sides, replacing flags with side B flags as

graphed and working uncoded areas with blue jewel Continental Stitches.

3. When background stitching is completed, work dark gold metallic yarn Straight Stitches on top and short sides.

4. Overcast inside edges of top with dark gold metallic yarn. Overcast bottom edges with blue jewel. Whipstitch long sides to short sides with tan and blue jewel, following graphs; Whipstitch sides to top with blue jewel. ❖

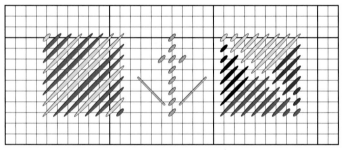

Short Side B Flags

COLOR KEY

Plastic Canvas Yarn	Yards
□ White #1	8
■ Black #12	2
□ Yellow #230	6
□ Tan #334	22
■ Warm brown #336	7
■ Skipper blue #848	10
■ Jockey red #902	8
Uncoded areas are blue jewel #818	
Continental Stitches	46
╱ Blue jewel #818 Overcasting and Whipstitching	
⅛-Inch-Wide Metallic Needlepoint Yarn	
□ Dark gold #PC18	5
╱ Dark gold #PC18 Straight Stitch	

Color numbers given are for Coats & Clark Red Heart Classic worsted weight yarn Art. E267 and Rainbow Gallery Plastic Canvas 7 Metallic Needlepoint yarn.

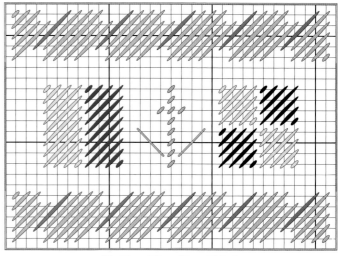

Maritime Flags Short Side A
32 holes x 23 holes
Cut 2
Stitch 1 as graphed
Stitch 1, replacing flags with
short side B flags

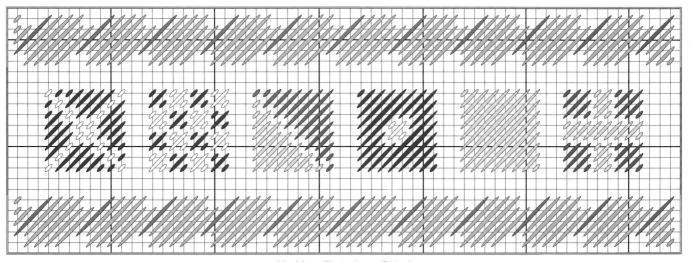

Maritime Flags Long Side A
65 holes x 23 holes
Cut 2
Stitch 1 as graphed
Stitch 1, replacing flags with
long side B flags

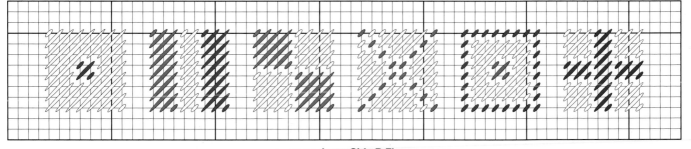

Long Side B Flags

Graphs continued on page 63

Cheery Cherries

Design by Vicki Blizzard

Brighten a corner of your kitchen with this bright and cheery tissue topper! Juicy cherries decorate the sides, accented by an easy-to-stitch background pattern.

Skill Level: Beginner

Size: Fits boutique-style tissue box

Materials

- 2 sheets 7-count plastic canvas
- Uniek Needloft plastic canvas yarn as listed in color key
- #16 tapestry needle
- Hot-glue gun

Instructions

1. Cut plastic canvas according to graphs.

2. Stitch top and sides following graphs. Overcast inside edges of top with holly. Using Christmas red, Overcast bottom edges of sides; Whipstitch sides together; Whipstitch sides to top.

3. Stitch and Overcast cherries and leaves following graphs, working uncoded area on cherries with Christmas red. Work holly Straight Stitches on leaves.

4. Using photo as a guide, glue three cherries and two leaves to each side, placing leaves at top of cherry stems. ❖

COLOR KEY	
Plastic Canvas Yarn	**Yards**
■ Black #00	18
■ Red #01	4
■ Maple #13	12
■ Holly #27	17
□ White #41	49
□ Yellow #57	5
Uncoded areas are Christmas red #02 Continental Stitches	9
╱ Christmas red #02 Overcasting and Whipstitching	
╱ Holly #27 Straight Stitch	
Color numbers given are for Uniek Needloft plastic canvas yarn.	

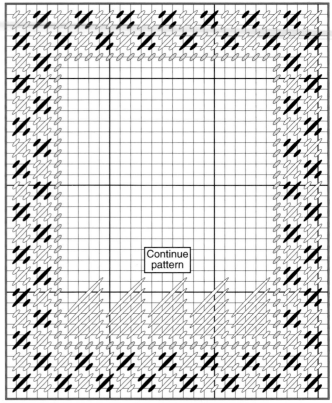

Cheery Cherries Side
31 holes x 37 holes
Cut 4

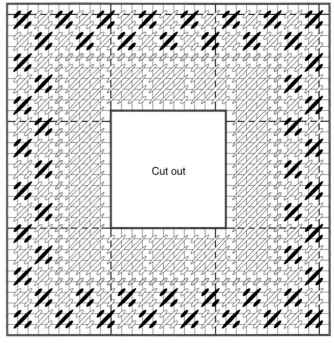

Cheery Cherries Top
31 holes x 31 holes
Cut 1

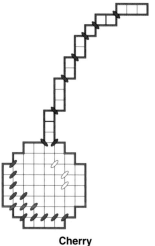

Cherry
14 holes x 21 holes
Cut 12

Cheery Cherries Leaf
9 holes x 14 holes
Cut 8

Maritime Flags

Continued from page 61

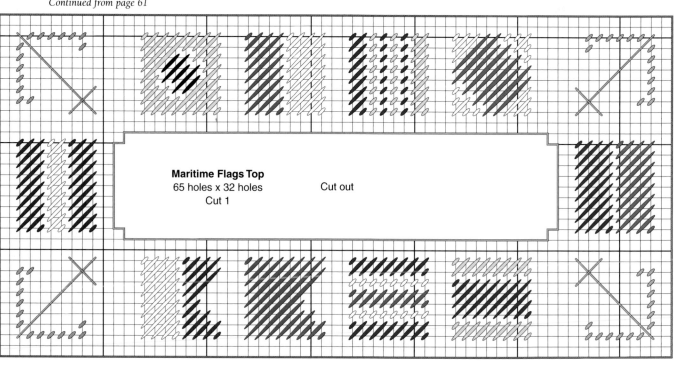

Maritime Flags Top
65 holes x 32 holes   Cut out
Cut 1

Daisy Delight

Design by Celia Lange Designs

Even teenage girls will like this project! Backed with a magnetic strip, this pocket-sized tissue topper can be stuck to a school locker, filing cabinet or any metallic surface.

Skill Level: Beginner

Size: Fits pocket-size tissue package

Materials

- 1 sheet 7-count plastic canvas
- Coats & Clark Red Heart Classic worsted weight yarn Art. E267 as listed in color key
- #16 tapestry needle
- Small amount DMC #5 pearl cotton: light straw #3822
- 2 (⅜-inch) light yellow shirt buttons
- 3 (¾-inch) Dress It Up yellow-and-white daisy shank buttons #100211 by Jesse James Button & Co.
- 3 tiny silk daisy-style leaves
- Sewing needle and pale yellow sewing thread
- 1½-inch x 3½-inch sheet magnet
- Hot-glue gun

Instructions

1. Cut and stitch plastic canvas according to graphs (this page and page 67).

2. Using maize through step 3, Whipstitch front and back to sides; then Whipstitch front, back and sides to top. Overcast opening.

3. Whipstitch bottom to remaining edge on front piece. Overcast all remaining edges.

4. With sewing needle and pale yellow thread, sew shirt buttons to back piece where indicated on graph near open end.

5. Secure two lengths of light straw pearl cotton on wrong side of bottom piece, thread through holes indicated and tie in a knot around edge, securing knot on backside. Tie a knot in each length 2 inches from edge; trim excess.

6. Cut shanks off daisy buttons; glue leaves and buttons to front, using photo as a guide. Glue magnet to back ¼ inch above buttons.

7. Insert tissue pack in cover; close bottom by wrapping pearl cotton around buttons on back. ❖

Graphs continued on page 67

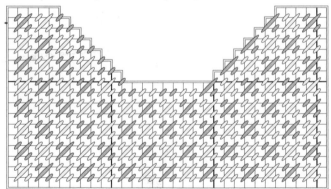

Daisy Delight Front
31 holes x 17 holes
Cut 1

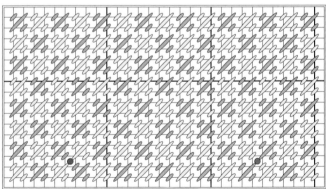

Daisy Delight Back
31 holes x 17 holes
Cut 1

Quilted Stars & Stripes

Design by Angie Arickx

*Stitched with hints of gold metallic yarn, this patriotic topper will add
the perfect accent to your home this Independence Day!*

Skill Level: Beginner

Size: Fits boutique-style tissue box

Materials

- 1½ sheets Uniek Quick-Count 7-count plastic canvas
- Uniek Needloft plastic canvas yarn as listed in color key
- Uniek Needloft metallic craft cord as listed in color key
- #16 tapestry needle

Instructions

1. Cut and stitch plastic canvas according to graphs (this page and 67).

2. Overcast inside edges of top with dark royal and bottom edges of sides with burgundy.

3. Whipstitch sides together with dark royal and burgundy; Whipstitch sides to top with dark royal. ❖

Quilted Stars & Stripes Top
31 holes x 31 holes
Cut 1

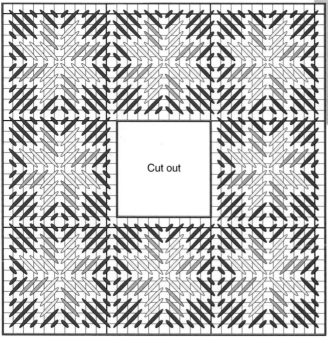

Cut out

COLOR KEY	
Plastic Canvas Yarn	**Yards**
■ Burgundy #03	26
□ Eggshell #39	32
■ Dark royal #48	25
Metallic Craft Cord	
▨ White/gold #55007	6
Color numbers given are for Uniek Needloft plastic canvas yarn and metallic craft cord.	

Graphs continued on page 67

Sunflower Fantasy

Design by Angie Arickx

Sunflower lovers will adore this cheerful tissue topper covered with pretty sunflowers "growing" along a picket fence!

Skill Level: Beginner

Size: Fits boutique-style tissue box

Materials

- 2 sheets Uniek Quick-Count 7-count plastic canvas
- Uniek Needloft plastic canvas yarn as listed in color key
- #16 tapestry needle
- Hot-glue gun

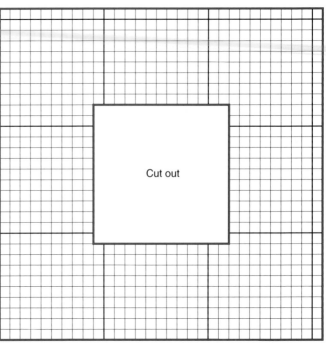

Sunflower Fantasy Top
31 holes x 31 holes
Cut 1

Instructions

1. Cut plastic canvas according to graphs.

2. Stitch top and sides following graphs. Overcast inside edges of top and bottom edges of sides with holly. Whipstitch sides together with white; Whipstitch sides to top with holly.

3. Stitch and Overcast sunflowers and leaves following graphs.

4. Using photo as a guide, glue five sunflowers and six leaves to each side; glue four sunflowers and eight leaves to top. ❖

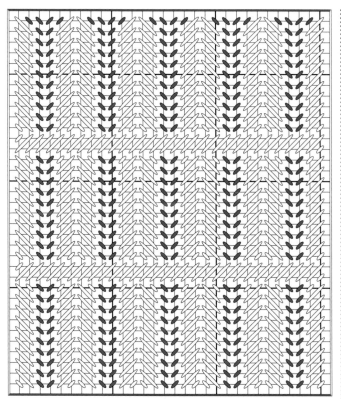

Sunflower Fantasy Side
31 holes x 36 holes
Cut 4

Quilted Stars & Stripes

Continued from page 65

Quilted Stars & Stripes Side
31 holes x 36 holes
Cut 4

COLOR KEY	
Plastic Canvas Yarn	**Yards**
■ Brown #15	10
■ Fern #23	14
■ Holly #27	40
□ White #41	50
□ Yellow #57	20

Uncoded area on top is holly
#27 Continental Stitches
Color numbers given are for Uniek Needloft
plastic canvas yarn.

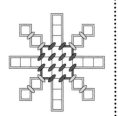

Sunflower
9 holes x 9 holes
Cut 24

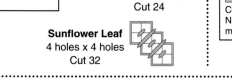

Sunflower Leaf
4 holes x 4 holes
Cut 32

COLOR KEY	
Plastic Canvas Yarn	**Yards**
■ Burgundy #03	26
□ Eggshell #39	32
■ Dark royal #48	25
Metallic Craft Cord	
□ White/gold #55007	6

Color numbers given are for Uniek
Needloft plastic canvas yarn and
metallic craft cord.

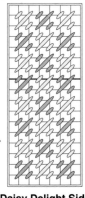

Daisy Delight Side
7 holes x 17 holes
Cut 2

Daisy Delight

Continued from page 65

COLOR KEY	
Worsted Weight Yarn	**Yards**
■ Cornmeal #220	16
□ Maize #261	20
● Attach shirt button	
● Attach pearl cotton	

Color numbers given are for Coats & Clark
Red Heart Classic worsted weight yarn
Art. E267.

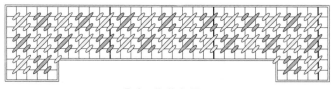

Daisy Delight Top
31 holes x 7 holes
Cut 1

Daisy Delight Bottom
31 holes x 7 holes
Cut 1

Hog Wash

Design by Vicki Blizzard

You don't have to love pigs to laugh every time you see this hilarious tissue box cover! Stitch it to add a whimsical touch to your bathroom!

Skill Level: Beginner

Size: Fits boutique-style tissue box

Materials

- 2 sheets 7-count plastic canvas
- Uniek Needloft plastic canvas yarn as listed in color key
- DMC #3 pearl cotton as listed in color key
- #16 tapestry needle
- 10 (5mm) round black cabochons from The Beadery
- Approximately 100 (3mm and 5mm) clear iridescent pearl beads
- 1 inch 18-gauge magenta Wild Wire copper wire from Natural Science Industries
- Jewel glue
- Hot-glue gun

Instructions

1. Cut plastic canvas according to graphs.

2. Stitch top and sides following graphs, working one side as graphed. Work remaining three sides eliminating white Continental Stitches and filling in with Christmas red and white checkered pattern.

3. Using Christmas red throughout, Overcast inside edges of top and bottom edges of sides. Whipstitch sides together; Whipstitch sides to top.

4. Stitch and Overcast remaining pieces following graphs, working uncoded area on wash tub with silver Continental Stitches and reversing five ears before stitching.

5. When background stitching is completed, work black pearl cotton Straight Stitches on snouts.

6. Use photo as a guide through step 9. Glue snouts to faces with hot glue. For eyes glue cabochons to faces above snouts with jewel glue. Hot glue ears to top corners of heads.

7. Using hot glue through step 8, glue side edges of washtub to side with white Continental Stitches, keeping bottom edges even and curving tub so there is a gap at center between tub and side.

8. Glue faces, front legs and rear legs as desired, both inside and outside of washtub. Twist and bend magenta wire into a small coil. Glue coil to rear legs for tail.

9. For soap suds, apply jewel glue to washtub, pigs and side as desired. Cover glue with clear iridescent pearl beads. When dry, apply a second layer of pearl beads over first layer for extra dimension. ❖

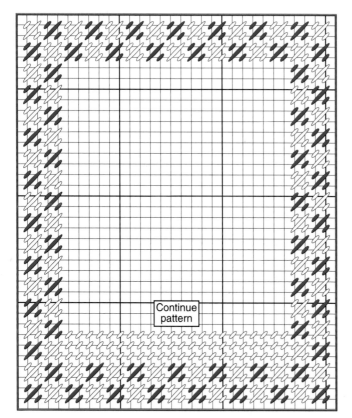

COLOR KEY

Plastic Canvas Yarn	Yards
■ Black #00	2
■ Christmas red #02	41
▨ Pink #07	15
□ White #41	54
Uncoded areas are silver #37 Continental Stitches	6
╱ Silver #37 Overcasting	
#3 Pearl Cotton	
╱ Black #310 Straight Stitch	2

Color numbers given are for Uniek Needloft plastic canvas yarn and DMC #3 pearl cotton.

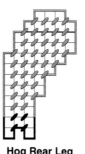

Hog Rear Leg
7 holes x 12 holes
Cut 2

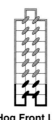

Hog Front Leg
3 holes x 9 holes
Cut 4

Hog Wash Side
31 holes x 37 holes
Cut 4
Stitch 1 as graphed

Stitch 3, replacing white
Continental Stitches with
Christmas red and white
checkered pattern

Hog Snout
4 holes x 4 holes
Cut 5

Hog Face
9 holes x 8 holes
Cut 5

Hog Ear
3 holes x 3 holes
Cut 10, reverse 5

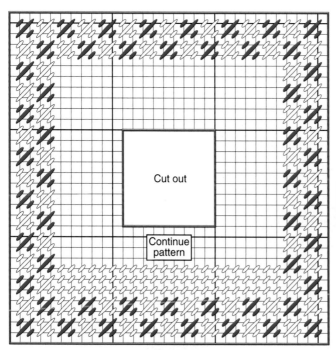

Hog Wash Top
31 holes x 31 holes
Cut 1

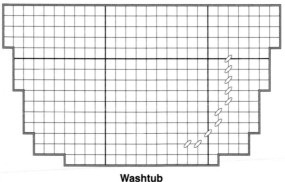

Washtub
27 holes x 15 holes
Cut 1

Puppy Love

Design by Janna Britton

Kids will love showing off this decorative, yet practical puppy tissue topper to all their friends!

Skill Level: Intermediate

Size: Fits boutique-style tissue box

Materials

- 1 sheet Uniek Quick-Count clear 7-count plastic canvas
- 1 sheet Uniek Quick-Count almond 7-count plastic canvas
- Uniek Needloft plastic canvas yarn as listed in color key
- #16 tapestry needle
- 2 (18mm) movable eyes
- 2 inch, adhesive-backed hook-and-loop tape
- Low-temperature glue gun

Instructions

1. Cut one face, one body, one tongue, one nose and two ears from clear plastic canvas according to graphs (pages 71 and 73).

2. Cut one rear from almond plastic canvas according to graph (page 71). Also cut one 29-hole x 37-hole piece for base and one 28-hole x 9-hole piece for flap from almond plastic canvas. Base and flap will remain unstitched.

3. Stitch remaining pieces following graphs, reversing one ear before stitching. Work white, cinnamon and black Continental Stitches on head first and white and cinnamon Continental Stitches on body first, filling in with sandstone pattern last.

4. Overcast ears, nose and tongue and inside edges of rear with adjacent colors.

5. Using sandstone through step 6, Whipstitch face to one long edge of body, easing around curves. Whipstitch rear piece to remaining long edge of body.

6. Whipstitch one short edge of base to bottom edge of face. Center and Whipstitch flap to remaining short edge of base. Overcast bottom edges of body and rear.

7. Using photo as a guide throughout, tack ears to face with cinnamon. Tack nose above smile with black; tack tongue to right side of face with red.

8. Glue eyes in place. Adhere hook-and-loop tape to inner flap and to inside of rear piece so pieces are aligned. ❖

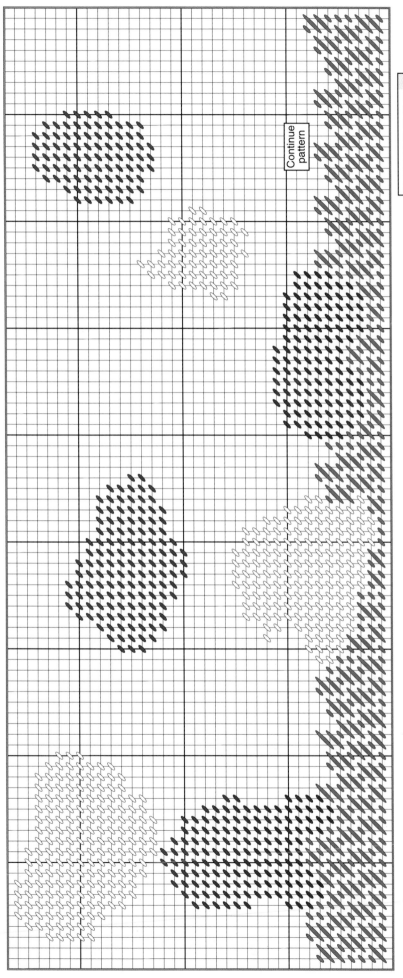

Continue pattern

Puppy Body
90 holes x 37 holes
Cut 1 from clear

COLOR KEY

Plastic Canvas Yarn	Yards
■ Black #00	2
▨ Red #01	2
■ Cinnamon #14	15
▨ Sandstone #16	70
□ White #41	17

Color numbers given are for Uniek Needloft plastic canvas yarn.

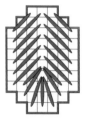

Puppy Tongue
7 holes x 10 holes
Cut 1 from clear

Puppy Nose
6 holes x 6 holes
Cut 1 from clear

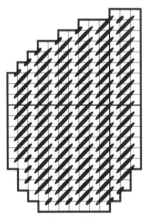

Puppy Ear
13 holes x 19 holes
Cut 2, reverse 1, from clear

Graphs continued on page 73

Little Mouse

Design by Michele Wilcox

Quick and easy to stitch, this sweet pocket-sized tissue holder is closed with a simple rainbow-striped bow!

Skill Level: Beginner

Size: Fits pocket-size tissue package

Materials

- ¾ sheet Uniek Quick-Count 7-count plastic canvas
- Uniek Needloft plastic canvas yarn as listed in color key
- Nylon plastic canvas yarn as listed in color key
- DMC #5 pearl cotton as listed in color key
- #16 tapestry needle
- ½ yard ¼-inch-wide rainbow ribbon
- Hot-glue gun

Instructions

1. Cut plastic canvas according to graphs.

2. Stitch pieces following graphs. Overcasting inside edges on holder pieces with white while stitching.

3. Using a double strand black pearl cotton, work French Knot for eye and Overcast body edge indicated for nose, stitching as often as necessary to cover well. Overcast all remaining edges on mouse pieces with gray.

4. Using lemon, Overcast top edges of holder pieces; Whipstitch wrong sides together along side and bottom edges.

5. Using photo as a guide, glue mouse body, ear and legs to one holder piece.

6. For easier access, remove tissue from package before placing inside holder. Thread rainbow ribbon through holes at top of holder; tie in a bow. ❖

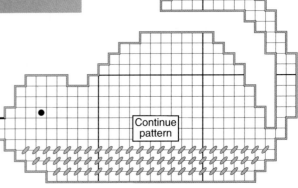

Mouse Body
29 holes x 18 holes
Cut 1

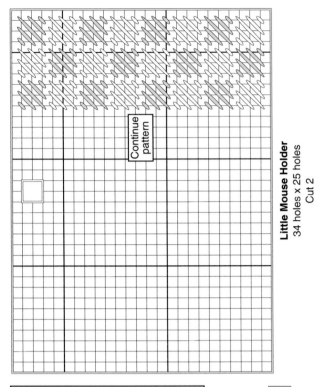

Little Mouse Holder
34 holes x 25 holes
Cut 2

PUPPY LOVE

Continued from page 71

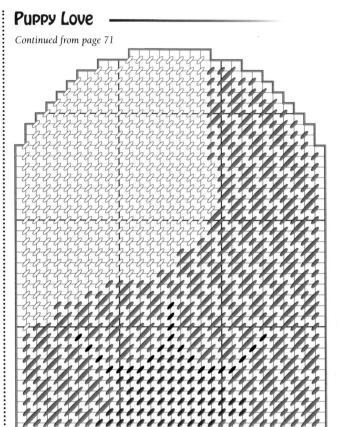

Puppy Face
30 holes x 36 holes
Cut 1 from clear

COLOR KEY

Plastic Canvas Yarn	Yards
☐ Lemon #20	16
▨ Gray #38	12
☐ White #41	12
☐ Baby pink	1
#5 Pearl Cotton	
╱ Black #310 Overcasting	1
● Black #310 French Knot	

Color numbers given are for Uniek Needloft plastic canvas yarn and DMC #5 pearl cotton.

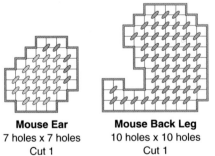

Mouse Front Leg
8 holes x 8 holes
Cut 1

Mouse Ear
7 holes x 7 holes
Cut 1

Mouse Back Leg
10 holes x 10 holes
Cut 1

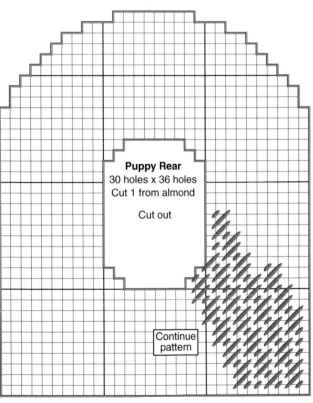

Puppy Rear
30 holes x 36 holes
Cut 1 from almond

Cut out

Continue pattern

COLOR KEY

Plastic Canvas Yarn	Yards
■ Black #00	2
▨ Red #01	2
■ Cinnamon #14	15
▨ Sandstone #16	70
☐ White #41	17

Color numbers given are for Uniek Needloft plastic canvas yarn.

Unicorn's Rainbow

Design by Christina Laws

Capture a glimpse of a magical world of unicorns and vibrant rainbows with this colorful topper!

Skill Level: Beginner

Size: Fits boutique-style tissue box

Materials

- 1½ sheets 7-count plastic canvas
- Worsted weight yarn as listed in color key
- Metallic craft cord as listed in color key
- #16 tapestry needle

Instructions

1. Cut plastic canvas according to graphs (this page and page 75).

2. Stitch pieces following graphs, working uncoded areas on sides with light blue Continental Stitches and uncoded area on unicorns with white Continental Stitches.

3. Overcast inside edges of top with light blue and bottom edges of sides with dark green. Matching edges so rainbows form an arc,

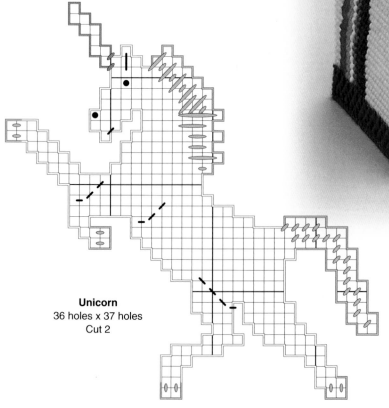

Unicorn
36 holes x 37 holes
Cut 2

Whipstitch sides A to sides B with adjacent colors; then Whipstitch top to sides with light blue.

4. Overcast unicorns with adjacent colors following graph; then work embroidery with black yarn.

5. Using photo as a guide, glue unicorns to sides B. ❖

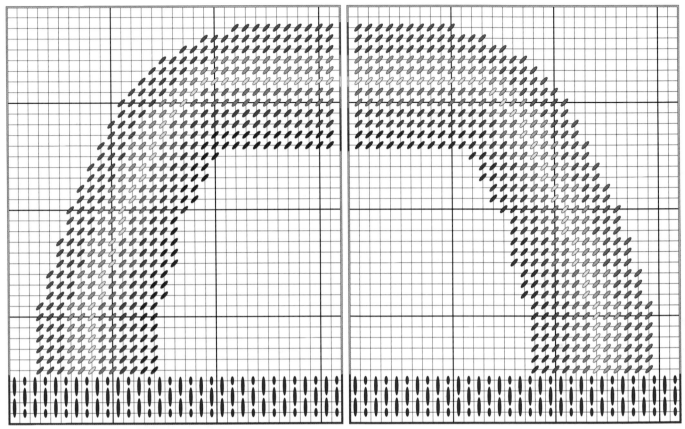

Unicorn's Rainbow Side A
32 holes x 39 holes
Cut 2

Unicorn's Rainbow Side B
32 holes x 39 holes
Cut 2

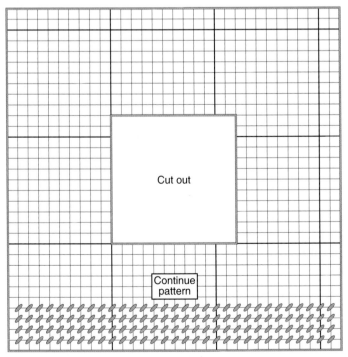

Cut out

Continue
pattern

Unicorn's Rainbow Top
32 holes x 32 holes
Cut 1

COLOR KEY	
Worsted Weight Yarn	**Yards**
▨ Light blue	34
▧ Red	6
▨ Dark green	5
▨ Green	4
▨ Purple	4
▨ Royal blue	4
▨ Orange	4
▨ Yellow	3
Uncoded areas on sides are light blue Continental Stitches	
Uncoded area on unicorn is white Continental Stitches	12
╱ White Overcasting	
╱ Black Backstitch and Straight Stitch	1
● Black French Knot	
Metallic Craft Cord	
▨ White/gold	4
▨ Solid gold	1

Friendly Froggy

Design by Judy Collishaw

Who can resist this delightfully friendly frog? She's sure to bring smiles to everyone, even those with the worst of colds!

Skill Level: Intermediate

Size: Fits boutique-style tissue box

Materials

- 2 sheets 7-count plastic canvas
- Coats & Clark Red Heart Classic worsted weight yarn Art. E267 as listed in color key
- #5 pearl cotton as listed in color key
- #16 tapestry needle
- 4-inch length black wire
- 2 (15mm) movable eyes
- 4-inch-diameter woven straw hat
- Small amount polyester fiberfill
- 2-inch silk daisy with 2-inch stem
- Low-temperature glue gun
- Fast-drying craft glue

Instructions

1. Cut plastic canvas according to graphs (this page and page 77).

2. Stitch pieces following graphs; reversing two legs and one arm before stitching.

3. Overcast hands with kiwi, then work black pearl cotton Backstitches on hands and legs.

4. Using kiwi through step 6, Overcast inside edges of top and bottom edges of body front, back and sides.

Fig. 1

COLOR KEY

Worsted Weight Yarn	Yards
■ Kiwi #651	95
#5 Pearl Cotton	
✎ Black Backstitch	2

Color numbers given are for Coats & Clark Red Heart Classic worsted weight yarn Art. E267.

Bottom Edge →

Frog Eyelid
5 holes x 5 holes
Cut 2

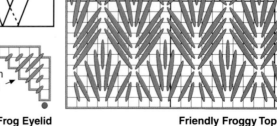

Cut out

Friendly Froggy Top
31 holes x 31 holes
Cut 1

Whipstitch front and back to sides; Whipstitch front, back and sides to top.

5. Overcast bottom edges of eyelids from dot to dot; Whipstitch remaining edges of one eyelid from arrow on side of head to middle arrow. Repeat with remaining eyelid, Whipstitching to other side of head. Overcast remaining edges of head.

6. Overcast straight edges of legs from dot to dot. For each leg, Whipstitch wrong sides of two leg pieces together along remaining edges. Stuff legs with fiberfill.

7. Using photo as a guide through step 9, hot-glue open part of legs to body sides near body back, making sure bottom edges are even.

8. Following Fig. 1 (page 77), glue arms to body front, keeping bottom edges even. Glue flower behind hands; then glue hands to bottom of arms.

9. Bend wire into mouth shape and carefully glue to head with fast-drying craft glue. With glue gun, glue eyes slightly under eyelids. Glue hat to back of head; glue head to top edge of body front between arms. ❖

COLOR KEY

Worsted Weight Yarn	Yards
■ Kiwi #651	95
#5 Pearl Cotton	
╱ Black Backstitch	2

Color numbers given are for Coats & Clark Red Heart Classic worsted weight yarn Art. E267.

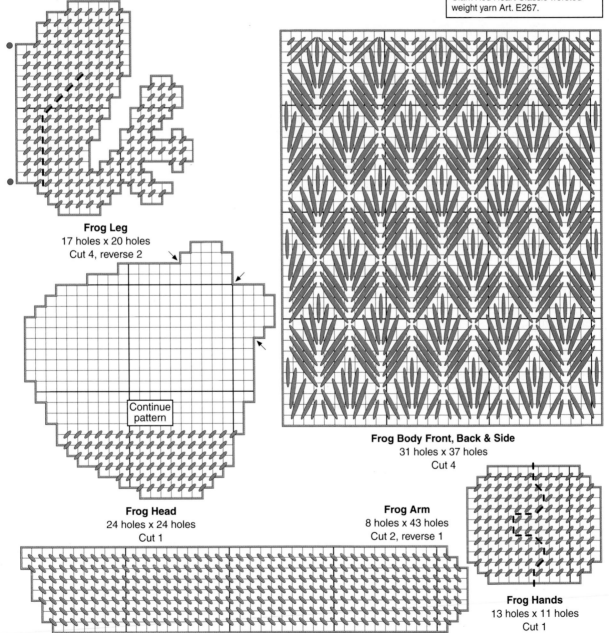

Frog Leg
17 holes x 20 holes
Cut 4, reverse 2

Continue pattern

Frog Head
24 holes x 24 holes
Cut 1

Frog Body Front, Back & Side
31 holes x 37 holes
Cut 4

Frog Arm
8 holes x 43 holes
Cut 2, reverse 1

Frog Hands
13 holes x 11 holes
Cut 1

Summer Jewels

Design by Janna Britton

*Variegated yarn, metallic silver floss and frosted cabochons create
a kaleidoscope effect on this unique tissue topper!*

Skill Level: Intermediate

Size: Fits regular-size tissue box

Materials

- 2 sheets Uniek Quick-Count 7-count plastic canvas
- Coats & Clark Red Heart Classic worsted weight yarn Art. E267 as listed in color key
- DMC 6-strand metallic embroidery floss as listed in color key
- #16 tapestry needle
- 48 (15mm x 7mm) navette dark amethyst frosted acrylic cabochons from The Beadery
- 74 (9mm) round emerald frosted acrylic cabochons from The Beadery
- 40 (7mm) round emerald frosted acrylic cabochons from The Beadery
- Amethyst art paper
- Low-temperature glue gun

Instructions

1. Cut plastic canvas according to graphs (page 79).

2. For each piece, cut amethyst art paper slightly smaller all around, cutting out center hole for top.

3. Stitch pieces following graphs. When background stitching is completed, work silver metallic floss Backstitches and Straight Stitches.

4. Using gemstone yarn, Overcast inside edge of top and bottom edges of sides.

5. Whipstitch long sides to short sides from top to bottom, then from bottom to top, forming a Cross Stitch. Repeat, Whipstitching sides to top with Cross Stitch pattern.

6. Glue amethyst art paper inside cover for lining. Glue cabochons in place following graphs. ❖

COLOR KEY

Worsted Weight Yarn	**Yards**
■ Peacock green #508	25
■ Soft navy #835	25
■ Gemstone #959	65

6-Strand Metallic Embroidery Floss

✎ Silver #5283 Backstitch and Straight Stitch	3
✎ Attach navette cabochon	
○ Attach 9mm round cabochon	
○ Attach 7mm round cabochon	

Color numbers given are for Coats & Clark Red Heart Classic worsted weight yarn Art. E267 and DMC 6-strand metallic embroidery floss.

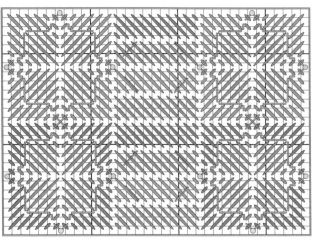

Summer Jewels Short Side
35 holes x 25 holes
Cut 2

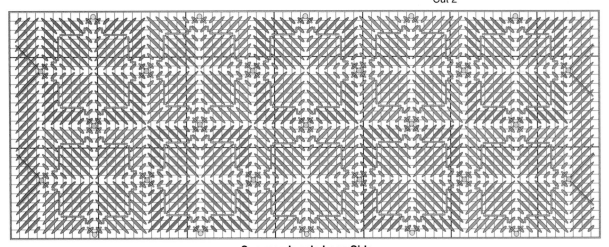

Summer Jewels Long Side
67 holes x 25 holes
Cut 2

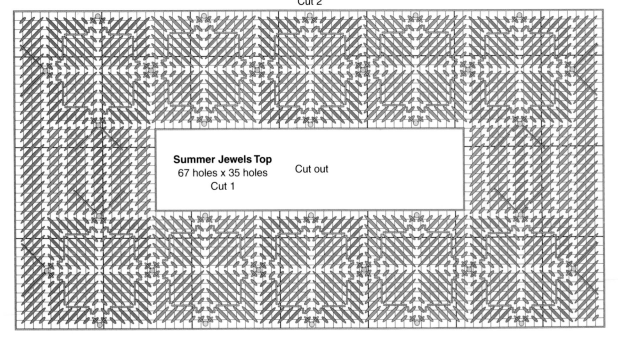

Summer Jewels Top
67 holes x 35 holes
Cut 1

Cut out

Panda Bear

Design by Nancy Dorman

Celebrate the lives of the few remaining panda bears with this keepsake tissue topper!

Skill Level: Beginner

Size: Fits boutique-style tissue box

Materials

- 1½ sheets 7-count plastic canvas
- Worsted weight yarn as listed in color key
- #16 tapestry needle

Instructions

1. Cut plastic canvas according to graphs.

2. Stitch sides and top following graphs, working uncoded areas with country blue Continental Stitches.

3. When background stitching is completed, work medium green and tan Straight Stitches on sides.

4. Using white and a regular Whipstitch or Braided Cross Stitch (see stitching diagram on page 90), Whipstitch sides together. Using same stitch throughout, Overcast inside edges of top; Whipstitch top to sides. Overcast bottom edges. ❖

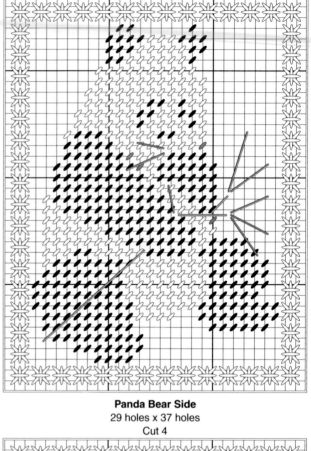

Panda Bear Side
29 holes x 37 holes
Cut 4

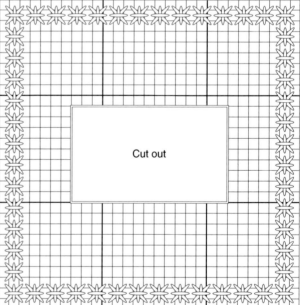

Cut out

Panda Bear Top
29 holes x 29 holes
Cut 1

COLOR KEY	
Worsted Weight Yarn	**Yards**
☐ White	60
■ Black	25
■ Dark gray	2
Uncoded areas are country blue Continental Stitches	50
╱ Tan Straight Stitch	5
╱ Medium green Straight Stitch	3

Painted Daisies

Design by Terry Ricioli

Just as pretty as their flower-garden name-sake, these pretty painted daisies are perfect for quick and easy summer stitching!

Skill Level: Beginner

Size: Fits boutique-style tissue box

Materials

- 1¼ sheets yellow 7-count plastic canvas
- ½ sheet clear 7-count plastic canvas
- Uniek Needloft plastic canvas yarn as listed in color key
- #16 tapestry needle
- 2 yards ⅜-inch-wide yellow satin ribbon
- Hot-glue gun

Instructions

1. Cut sides and top from yellow plastic canvas; cut flowers and bent stems from clear plastic canvas according to graphs (this page and page 82). Cut four 1-hole x 21-hole pieces from clear plastic canvas for straight stems.

2. Stitch sides and top following graphs. Using white throughout, Overcast inside edges of top and bottom edges of sides. Whipstitch sides together; then Whipstitch sides to top.

3. Overcast stems with moss, reversing four bent stems before Overcasting.

4. Stitch daisies and leaves following graphs, working four daisies with pink petals, four with sail blue petals and four with lilac petals. Overcast with adjacent colors.

5. Using photo as a guide, place three stems, two leaves and one daisy of each color on each side so that straight stem is in the middle and stems with opposite bends are on the sides. Glue in place, leaving centers of stems unglued so that ribbon can be slipped underneath.

6. Cut ribbon in four equal lengths. Slide one ribbon under center of stems on each side and tie in a bow, trimming ends as desired. ❖

Graphs continued on page 83

COLOR KEY	
Plastic Canvas Yarn	**Yards**
☐ Pink #07	8
▨ Moss #25	20
Sail blue #35	8
☐ White #41	100
Lilac #45	8
☐ Bright yellow #57	4
Color numbers given are for Uniek Needloft plastic canvas yarn.	

Painted Daisies Side
33 holes x 37 holes
Cut 4 from yellow

County Fair Carousel

Design by Christina Laws

Delight a young girl who loves horses with this colorful carousel tissue topper reminiscent of that favorite ride at the fair!

Skill Level: Beginner

Size: Fits boutique-style tissue box

Materials

- 2 sheets 7-count plastic canvas
- Worsted weight yarn as listed in color key
- #16 tapestry needle

Instructions

1. Cut plastic canvas according to graphs.

2. Stitch sides and tops following graphs, working uncoded areas on sides with light blue Continental Stitches and uncoded area on horses with pale yellow Continental Stitches.

3. Using two stitches per hole where indicated throughout, work two sides as graphed; work remaining two replacing medium blue on awning with red. Work two tops with red and two with medium blue.

4. When background stitching is completed, work gold Backstitches on sides and black French Knots on horses.

5. Overcast top edges of top pieces with adjacent colors. Overcast bottom edges of sides with medium blue. Overcast horses with adjacent colors following graph.

6. With medium blue, light blue and gold, Whipstitch sides together, alternating red and medium blue awnings.

7. Using red, Whipstitch medium blue tops to sides with red awnings. Using medium blue, Whipstitch red tops to sides with medium blue awnings. Whipstitch top pieces together with gold. ❖

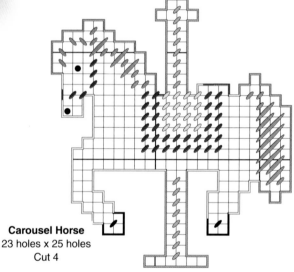

Carousel Horse
23 holes x 25 holes
Cut 4

COLOR KEY	
Worsted Weight Yarn	**Yards**
▨ Medium blue	24
▨ Red	19
☐ White	10
▨ Rust	6
▨ Light raspberry	4
▨ Gray	4
▨ Purple	2
☐ Yellow	2
▨ Dark blue	1
Uncoded areas on sides are light blue Continental Stitches	19
Uncoded areas on horses are pale yellow Continental Stitches	7
╱ Light blue Whipstitching	
╱ Pale yellow Overcasting	
╱ Gold Backstitch and Whipstitching	5
● Black French Knot	1

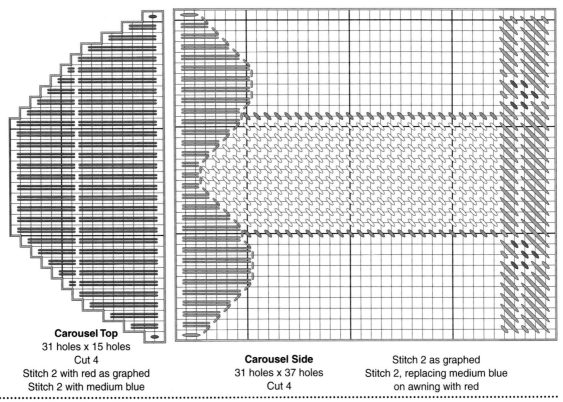

Carousel Top
31 holes x 15 holes
Cut 4
Stitch 2 with red as graphed
Stitch 2 with medium blue

Carousel Side
31 holes x 37 holes
Cut 4

Stitch 2 as graphed
Stitch 2, replacing medium blue
on awning with red

Painted Daisies

Continued from page 81

COLOR KEY	
Plastic Canvas Yarn	**Yards**
▨ Pink #07	8
▨ Moss #25	20
Sail blue #35	8
☐ White #41	100
Lilac #45	8
▨ Bright yellow #57	4
Color numbers given are for Uniek Needloft plastic canvas yarn.	

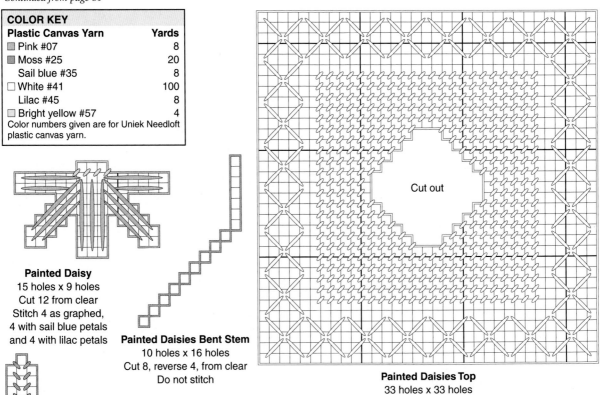

Painted Daisy
15 holes x 9 holes
Cut 12 from clear
Stitch 4 as graphed,
4 with sail blue petals
and 4 with lilac petals

Painted Daisies Bent Stem
10 holes x 16 holes
Cut 8, reverse 4, from clear
Do not stitch

Painted Daisies Leaf
3 holes x 8 holes
Cut 8 from clear

Painted Daisies Top
33 holes x 33 holes
Cut 1 from yellow

Cut out

Liberty Stars

Design by Judy Collishaw

Show your pride in America year-round by stitching and displaying this patriotic project!

Skill Level: Beginner

Size: Fits regular-size tissue box

Materials

- 1 sheet 7-count plastic canvas
- Worsted weight yarn as listed in color key
- Kreinik Heavy (#32) Braid as listed in color key
- #16 tapestry needle

Instructions

1. Cut plastic canvas according to graphs.

2. Stitch pieces following graphs, working uncoded areas with royal blue Continental Stitches.

3. When background stitching is completed, Straight Stitch stars with gold heavy (#32) braid.

4. Using royal blue, Overcast inside edges of top and bottom edges of sides. Whipstitch long sides to short sides with white, then Whipstitch sides to top with royal blue. ❖

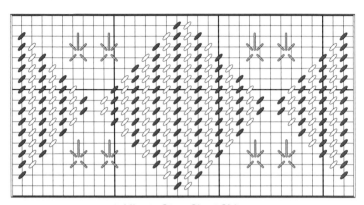

Liberty Stars Short Side
33 holes x 17 holes
Cut 2

COLOR KEY

Worsted Weight Yarn	Yards
☐ White	20
■ Red	20
Uncoded areas are royal blue Continental Stitches	50

Heavy (#32) Braid

╱ Gold #002HL Straight Stitch	10

Color numbers given are for Kreinik Heavy (#32) Braid.

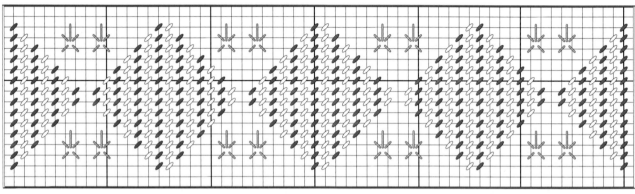

Liberty Stars Long Side
61 holes x 17 holes
Cut 2

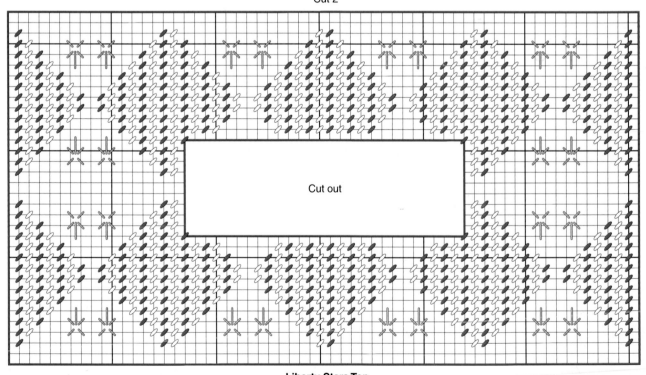

Cut out

Liberty Stars Top
61 holes x 33 holes
Cut 1

Country Basket

Design by Ronda Bryce

Dress up a corner in your country home with this charming picnic-basket tissue box cover decorated with handles, napkins, and slices of apple and watermelon!

Skill Level: Intermediate

Size: Fits boutique-style tissue box

Materials

- 1 sheet Uniek Quick-Count clear 7-count plastic canvas
- 1 sheet Uniek Quick-Count almond 7-count plastic canvas
- 2 (4-inch) plastic canvas radial circles by Uniek
- Uniek Needloft plastic canvas yarn as listed in color key
- Coats & Clark Red Heart Super Saver worsted weight yarn Art. E301 as listed in color key
- #16 tapestry needle
- 1¼ yards 1⅜-inch-wide red gingham ribbon
- Pinking shears
- 20 small black bugle beads
- Sewing needle
- Red and white sewing thread
- Hot-glue gun

Cutting & Stitching

1. Cut one top, three napkins and two apples from clear plastic canvas; cut four sides from almond plastic canvas according to graphs.

2. Cutting away gray areas and following graph, cut one handle and one watermelon slice from one radial circle; cut one handle from remaining radial circle.

3. Stitch pieces following graphs. When background stitching is completed, work brown Cross Stitches on sides.

4. Using brown, Overcast curved edges of handles, leaving bottom edges unworked at this time; Overcast bottom edges of sides.

5. Using burgundy, Overcast napkins, apples and

inside edges of top. Overcast watermelon with forest, fern and red following graph.

Assembly

1. Using warm brown, Whipstitch top to bar on sides indicated with blue line.

2. Using brown throughout, Whipstitch sides together. Overcast top edges of sides, Whipstitching bottom edges of handles to opposite sides while Overcasting.

3. Following graph, attach four black bugle beads to each apple with sewing needle and white thread.

4. Using photo as a guide through step 6, attach remaining 12 bugle beads to watermelon slice with sewing needle and red thread.

5. Using sewing needle and red thread, attach one apple and one napkin to opposite sides; attach watermelon slice and remaining napkin to front.

6 Wrap ribbon around sides just under cross-stitch border, making a bow in front; cut ends with pinking shears. Tack top edge of ribbon to topper with sewing thread. ❖

Country Basket Side
30 holes x 40 holes
Cut 4 from almond

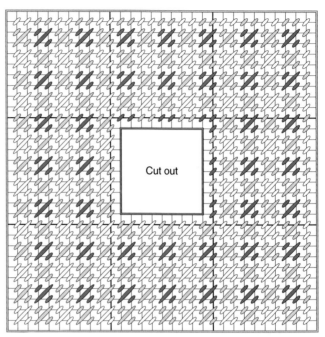

Country Basket Top
30 holes x 30 holes
Cut 1 from clear

COLOR KEY

Worsted Weight Yarn	Yards
■ Brown #328	48
■ Warm brown #336	29
✖ Brown #328 Cross Stitch	
Plastic Canvas Yarn	
◻ Red #01	14
■ Burgundy #03	11
◻ Fern #23	1
◻ White #41	14
⁄ Forest #29 Overcasting	1
⁄ Attach black bugle bead	

Color numbers given are for Coats & Clark Red Heart Super Saver worsted weight yarn Art. E301 and Uniek Needloft plastic canvas yarn.

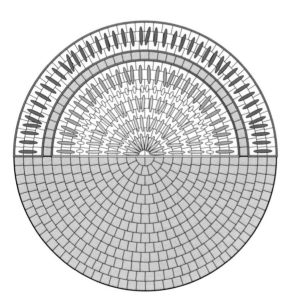

**Country Basket Handle &
Watermelon Slice**
Cut 1 handle and 1 watermelon
slice from one circle
Cut 1 handle from remaining circle
Cut away gray areas

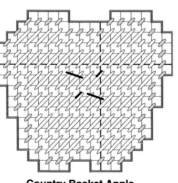

Country Basket Apple
17 holes x 15 holes
Cut 2 from clear

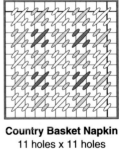

Country Basket Napkin
11 holes x 11 holes
Cut 3 from clear

Thyme Began

Design by Michele Wilcox

Buzzing bees and blooming flowers surround a timeless expression,
"Thyme began in a garden," on this pretty project.

Skill Level: Beginner

Size: Fits boutique-style tissue box

Materials

- 1¼ sheets Uniek Quick-Count 7-count plastic canvas
- Uniek Needloft plastic canvas yarn as listed in color key
- DMC #5 pearl cotton as listed in color key
- #16 tapestry needle

Instructions

1. Cut plastic canvas according to graphs.

2. Using Continental Stitches throughout, stitch pieces following graphs, working uncoded areas with eggshell.

3. When background stitching is completed, using pearl cotton, embroider words with dark pistachio green, stems with ultra dark pistachio green and stitches around bees with black.

4. Work French Knots for flowers with a double strand of pearl cotton.

5. Overcast inside edges of top with eggshell. Using moss, Whipstitch sides together, then Whipstitch sides to top; Overcast bottom edges. ❖

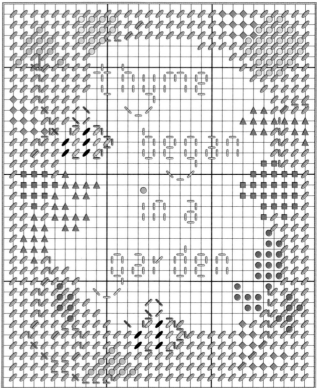

Thyme Began Side
30 holes x 36 holes
Cut 4

COLOR KEY	
Plastic Canvas Yarn	**Yards**
✏ Black #00	2
■ Red #01	6
✏ Tangerine #11	2
✏ Moss #25	55
◆ Holly #27	6
▲ Forest #29	8
Uncoded areas are eggshell #39	
Continental Stitches	50
✏ Eggshell #39 Overcasting	
#5 Pearl Cotton	
✏ Black #310 Backstitch and Straight Stitch	1
✏ Dark pistachio green #367 Backstitch	10
✏ Ultra dark pistachio green #890 Backstitch	
● Dark dark violet #327 French Knot	15
● Medium baby blue #334 French Knot	15
● Dark pistachio green #367 French Knot	
○ Very light topaz #727 French Knot	1
○ Medium carnation #892 French Knot	15
Color numbers given are for Uniek Needloft plastic canvas yarn and DMC #5 pearl cotton.	

Graphs continued on page 91

Folk Art Chickens

Design by Joan Green

If you decorate your kitchen with chickens, then you'll want to add this colorful topper to your decor!

Skill Level: Beginner

Size: Fits boutique-style tissue box

Materials

- 1¼ sheets 7-count plastic canvas
- Coats & Clark Red Heart Classic worsted weight yarn Art. E267 as listed in color key
- #16 tapestry needle

Instructions

1. Cut plastic canvas according to graphs (pages 89 and 93).

2. Stitch pieces following graphs. Overcast wings and inside edges of top with jockey red. Overcast bottom edges of sides with skipper blue.

3. Using 4 plies black, work French Knot eye on hens and Straight Stitches for legs and feet on hens. Using 4 plies orange, work Straight Stitches for beaks on hens and chicks and polka dots on hens and cover top.

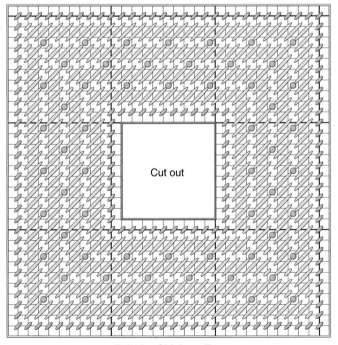

Folk Art Chickens Top
31 holes x 31 holes
Cut 1

4. Using 2 plies black, Backstitch around hens, chicks and eggs and work French Knots for eyes on chicks.

5. Using photo as a guide for placement and using jockey red, tack one wing to each hen from dot to dot around left side of wing, leaving wing tip edges free.

6. Using light periwinkle, Whipstitch sides together, then Whipstitch sides to top. ❖

Graphs continued on page 93

Floral Bouquet

Design by Nancy Dorman

Delicate pink and rose flowers, accented with French Knot centers, make this tissue box cover perfect for those who decorate with a feminine touch!

Skill Level: Beginner

Size: Fits boutique-style tissue box

Materials

- 1½ sheets 7-count plastic canvas
- ¼ sheet 10-count plastic canvas
- 4-ply worsted weight yarn as listed in color key
- 3-ply sport weight yarn as listed in color key
- #16 tapestry needle

Instructions

1. Cut top and sides from 7-count plastic canvas, cut flowers from 10-count plastic canvas according to graphs (pages 89 and 90).

2. Stitch sides and top with ivory and medium green 4-ply yarn following graphs, working uncoded areas with ivory Continental Stitches.

3. When background stitching is completed, work medium green Straight Stitches with 3-ply yarn.

4. Using 3-ply yarn through step 5, Overcast four large flowers and 20 small flowers with pink, tacking to sides where indicated on graph. Overcast 16 medium flowers with rose, tacking to sides where indicated on graph.

5. Work pink and rose French Knots where indicated on graph. Work rose French Knot in center of each large and small pink flower. Work white French Knot in center of rose flowers.

6. With ivory 4-ply yarn and using a regular Whipstitch or Braided Cross Stitch (Fig. 1), Whipstitch sides together. Using same stitch throughout, Overcast inside edges of top and then Whipstitch top to sides. Overcast bottom edges. ❖

Floral Bouquet Top
29 holes x 29 holes
Cut 1 from 7-count

Floral Bouquet Medium Flower
3 holes x 3 holes
Cut 16 from 10-count

Floral Bouquet Small Flower
3 holes x 3 holes
Cut 20 from 10-count

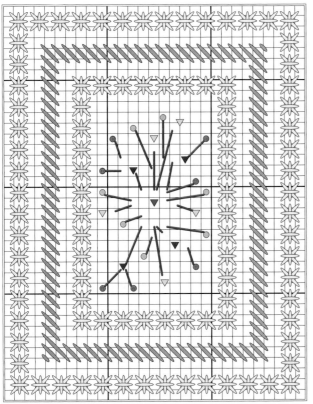

Floral Bouquet Side
29 holes x 37 holes
Cut 4 from 7-count

Thyme Began

Continued from page 88

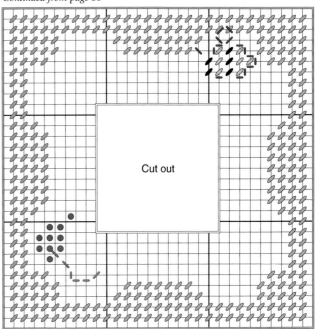

Thyme Began Top
30 holes x 30 holes
Cut 1

COLOR KEY	
4-Ply Worsted Weight Yarn	**Yards**
☐ Ivory	120
▨ Medium green	15
Uncoded areas are ivory	
Continental Stitches	
3-Ply Sport Weight Yarn	
╱ Rose Overcasting	10
╱ Pink Overcasting	10
╱ Medium green Straight Stitch	6
○ White French Knot	2
● Rose French Knot	
● Pink French Knot	
▼ Attach large pink flower	
▽ Attach small pink flower	
▼ Attach medium rose flower	

Fig. 1
Braided Cross Stitch

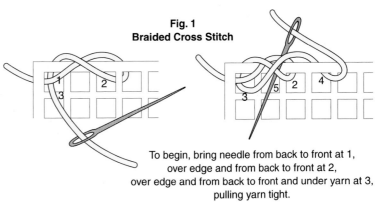

To begin, bring needle from back to front at 1,
over edge and from back to front at 2,
over edge and from back to front and under yarn at 3,
pulling yarn tight.

Pulling yarn tight with each stitch,
continue by bringing needle over edge
and from back to front at 4,
over edge and from back to front at 5, etc.

Floral Bouquet Large Flower
5 holes x 5 holes
Cut 4 from 10-count

Checks & Cherries

Design by Susan Leinberger

*Add a bright and cheery touch
to your kitchen with this
delightful topper designed
with vibrant colors
and sweet cherries!*

Skill Level: Beginner

Size: Fits boutique-style
tissue box

Materials

- 1½ sheets Uniek Quick-Count
  7-count plastic canvas
- Coats & Clark Red Heart
  Super Saver worsted weight
  yarn Art. E301 as listed in
  color key
- #16 tapestry needle

Instructions

1. Cut plastic canvas according
to graphs.

2. Stitch pieces following graphs.
Work uncoded area with top
cherries in white Continental Stitches and
uncoded area with bottom cherries in
Reverse Continental Stitches.

3. Work brown Straight Stitches when
background stitching is completed.

4. Using cherry red and white and alternating colors, Overcast inside edges of top and
bottom edges of sides. Whipstitch sides
together; then Whipstitch sides to top. ❖

Checks & Cherries Top
32 holes x 32 holes
Cut 1

Checks & Cherries

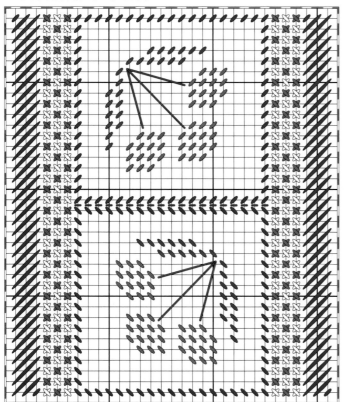

COLOR KEY

Worsted Weight Yarn	Yards
☐ White #311	42
◼ Cherry red #319	20
◼ Paddy green #368	4
◼ Royal #385	24
Uncoded area with top cherries is white #311 Continental Stitches	
Uncoded area with bottom cherries is white #311 Reverse Continental Stitches	
✎ Brown #328 Straight Stitch	2
✎ Royal #385 Backstitch	

Color numbers given are for Coats & Clark Red Heart Super Saver worsted weight yarn Art. E301.

Checks & Cherries Side
32 holes x 37 holes
Cut 4

Folk Art Chickens

Continued from page 89

COLOR KEY

Worsted Weight Yarn	Yards
☐ White #1	12
☐ Yellow #230	22
◼ Orange #245	14
◼ Tan #334	3
◼ Light periwinkle #827	25
◼ Skipper blue #848	22
◼ Jockey red #902	8
✎ Black #12 Backstitch and Straight Stitch	8
✎ Orange #245 Straight Stitch	
● Black #12 French Knot	
● Orange #245 French Knot	

Color numbers given are for Coats & Clark Red Heart Classic worsted weight yarn Art. E267.

Chicken Wing
8 holes x 6 holes
Cut 4

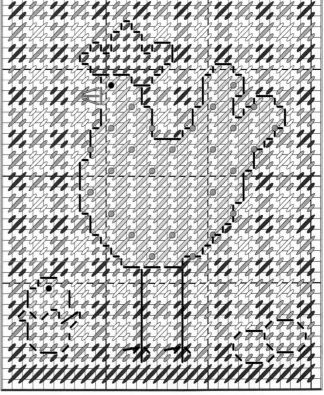

Folk Art Chickens Side
31 holes x 37 holes
Cut 4

Just for Dad

Design by Kimberly A. Suber

*Give Dad a gift he'll cherish this Father's Day—
a handsome tissue box with mallard ducks and cattails.*

Skill Level: Beginner

Size: Fits boutique-style tissue box

Materials
- 2 sheets Uniek Quick-Count 7-count plastic canvas
- Worsted weight yarn as listed in color key
- #16 tapestry needle
- Hot-glue gun

Instructions

1. Cut plastic canvas according to graphs .

2. Using tan throughout, stitch sides and top following graphs. Overcast inside edges of top and bottom edges of sides. Whipstitch sides together; Whipstitch sides to top.

Following graphs through step 7, stitch and Overcast cattails with brown and beige.

4. Stitch four tall leaves with medium green; reverse three and stitch with forest. Stitch one medium leaf with medium green and two with forest. Stitch one short leaf with medium green and one with forest. Overcast with adjacent colors.

5. Stitch mallard, sign and sign ends, working uncoded areas on sign pieces with off-white Continental Stitches.

6. When background stitching is completed, work rust French Knot for eye on mallard and Backstitches and Straight Stitches for words on sign with forest.

7. Overcast mallard with adjacent colors. Overcast sign pieces with off white and forest.

8. Using photo as a guide through step 9, glue sign pieces, two cattails, mallard, one tall leaf, one medium leaf and two short leaves to topper front, making sure bottom edges of front, mallard and leaves are even.

9. Glue three tall leaves, one medium leaf and two cattails to each side, making sure bottom edges of sides and leaves are even. ❖

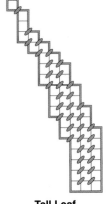

Tall Leaf
9 holes x 18 holes
Cut 7
Stitch 4 as graphed
Reverse 3 and stitch with forest

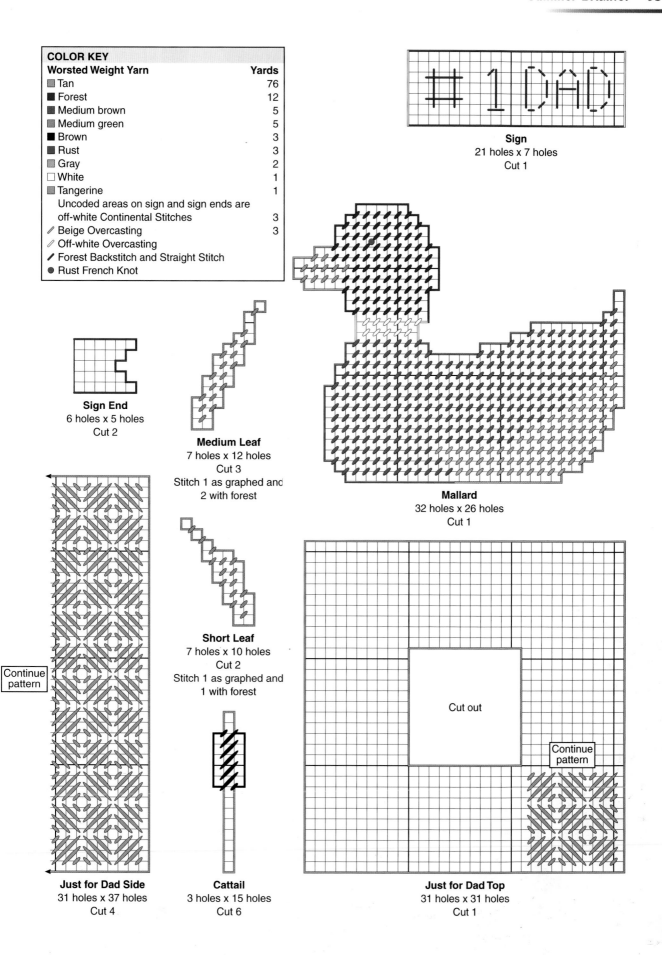

COLOR KEY

Worsted Weight Yarn	Yards
☐ Tan	76
■ Forest	12
■ Medium brown	5
■ Medium green	5
■ Brown	3
■ Rust	3
☐ Gray	2
☐ White	1
☐ Tangerine	1
Uncoded areas on sign and sign ends are off-white Continental Stitches	3
✎ Beige Overcasting	3
✎ Off-white Overcasting	
✎ Forest Backstitch and Straight Stitch	
● Rust French Knot	

Sign
21 holes x 7 holes
Cut 1

Sign End
6 holes x 5 holes
Cut 2

Medium Leaf
7 holes x 12 holes
Cut 3
Stitch 1 as graphed and
2 with forest

Mallard
32 holes x 26 holes
Cut 1

Short Leaf
7 holes x 10 holes
Cut 2
Stitch 1 as graphed and
1 with forest

Continue
pattern

Just for Dad Side
31 holes x 37 holes
Cut 4

Cattail
3 holes x 15 holes
Cut 6

Cut out

Continue
pattern

Just for Dad Top
31 holes x 31 holes
Cut 1

Ikebana

Design by Celia Lange Designs

Designed after the Japanese art of flower arranging, ikebana, this oriental tissue box cover will grace your home with timeless elegance.

Skill Level: Beginner

Size: Fits boutique-style tissue box

Materials

- 2 sheets Darice Ultra Stiff 7-count plastic canvas
- Coats & Clark Red Heart Classic worsted weight yarn Art. E267 as listed in color key
- Coats & Clark Red Heart Super Saver worsted weight yarn Art. E300 as listed in color key
- #16 tapestry needle
- Hot-glue gun

Instructions

1. Cut plastic canvas according to graphs.

2. Stitch pieces following graphs, working uncoded areas on sides and top with pale blue Continental Stitches and uncoded areas on pots with seafoam Continental Stitches. Work shoji screens with eggshell and off-white Alternating Continental Stitches.

3. When background stitching is completed, work embroidery on side A and top with mid brown, grenadine and pink. Work Straight Stitches on screens with black.

4. Using pale blue throughout, Overcast inside edges on top and bottom edges of sides. Whipstitch sides A to sides B; then Whipstitch sides to top.

5. Overcast pots with light seafoam and stands with brown. Using black, Whipstitch two screens together along one long side. Overcast remaining edges. Repeat with remaining two screens.

6. Using photo as a guide through step 7, and making sure bottom edges are even, glue screens to opposite corners of tissue topper so they wrap around corners with pale blue Continental Stitches.

7. Center and glue one pot and one pot stand under floral arrangements on sides A, making sure bottom edges of stand and cover are even. ❖

COLOR KEY	
Worsted Weight Yarn	**Yards**
☐ Off-white #3	12
■ Black #12	24
☐ Eggshell #111	12
☐ Yellow #230	3
☐ Maize #261	1
☐ Gold #321	1
■ Brown #328	2
☐ Amethyst #588	3
☐ Light seafoam #683	2
■ Paddy green #686	3
☐ Grass green #687	2
Uncoded areas on pot are seafoam #684 Continental Stitches	1
Uncoded areas on sides and top are pale blue #815 Continental Stitches	20
✎ Pale blue #815 Overcasting and Whipstitching	
✎ Black #12 Straight Stitch	
✎ Mid brown #339 Backstitch and Straight Stitch	3
● Grenadine #730 French Knot	3
● Pink #737 French Knot	1
Color numbers given are for Coats & Clark Red Heart Classic worsted weight yarn Art. E267 and Red Heart Super Saver worsted weight yarn Art. E300.	

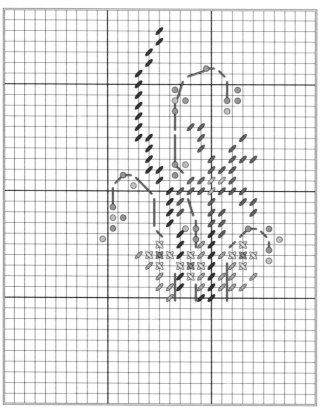

Ikebana Side A
30 holes x 37 holes
Cut 2

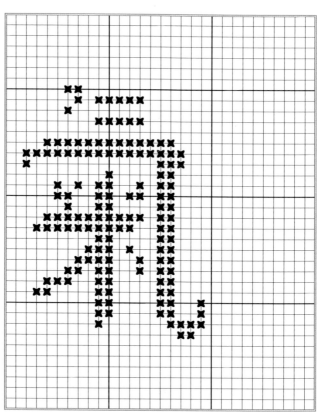

Ikebana Side B
30 holes x 37 holes
Cut 2

Ikebana Pot Stand
16 holes x 5 holes
Cut 2

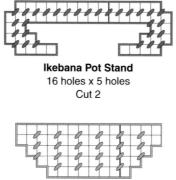

Ikebana Pot
14 holes x 5 holes
Cut 2

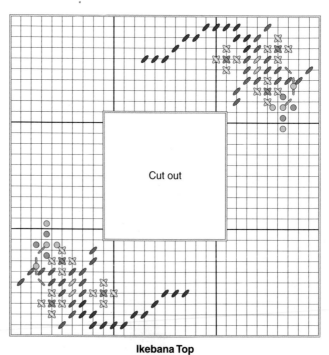

Shoji Screen
9 holes x 38 holes
Cut 4

Ikebana Top
30 holes x 30 holes
Cut 1

Little Red Truck

Design by Lee Lindeman

Here's a perfect pick-me-up for a sick little boy—a bright red, tissue-topper truck with shiny bumpers and lights!

Skill Level: Intermediate

Size: Fits travel-size tissue box

Materials

- 2½ sheets 7-count plastic canvas
- Coats & Clark Red Heart Super Saver worsted weight yarn Art. E301 as listed in color key
- ⅛-inch-wide Plastic Canvas 7 Metallic Needlepoint Yarn by Rainbow Gallery as listed in color key
- #16 tapestry needle
- Small amount taupe ultra suede or felt
- 6 inches ¼-inch-wide yellow satin ribbon
- 2 (16mm) red faceted stones
- 2 (20mm) crystal faceted stones
- 4 (1½-inches in diameter x ½-inch) wooden toy wheels with ¼-inch opening
- 4 (⅜-inch-wide) wooden axle pegs
- 12mm round red bead
- ½-inch wooden furniture button
- 1-inch wooden furniture button
- Small amount mini-curl doll hair in desired color
- Acrylic craft paint: black, yellow, flesh tone and pink
- Black fine-point permanent marker
- ½-inch flat paintbrush
- Small detail paintbrush
- Glossy acrylic spray
- Small amount polyester fiberfill
- Small hand saw
- Sandpaper
- Wood glue
- Tacky glue
- Hot-glue gun

Cutting & Stitching

1. Cut plastic canvas according to graphs. Cut one 33-hole x 46-hole piece for truck bottom, two 46-hole x 10-hole pieces for truck sides and one 33-hole x 10-hole piece for truck front. Truck bottom will remain unstitched.

2. Using pattern given, cut dog ears from taupe ultra suede or felt. Cut one ⅜-inch x ⅛-inch piece of ultra suede for dog's collar. Set aside.

3. Continental Stitch sides and front with cherry red. Stitch remaining pieces following graphs.

4. Overcast cab roof edges, grill, bumpers and inside edges of truck top/bed with adjacent colors.

5. Using cherry red through step 7, Whipstitch cab front and back to cab sides; Overcast top and bottom edges.

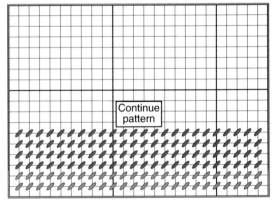

Truck Cab Roof
25 holes x 18 holes
Cut 1

6. Whipstitch truck sides to truck front, forming one long strip. Whipstitch strip to top/bed and to unstitched bottom, placing front edge of top/bed next to truck front.

Continued on page 101

Truck Cab Front & Back
21 holes x 12 holes
Cut 2

Back Edge

Cut out

Continue pattern

Front Edge

Truck Top/Bed
33 holes x 46 holes
Cut 1

Truck Tailgate
43 holes x 10 holes
Cut 1

Truck Front & Back Bumper
38 holes x 3 holes
Cut 2

Dog Ears
Cut 1 from taupe
ultra suede or felt

Driver's Face

Dog's Face

COLOR KEY	
Worsted Weight Yarn	**Yards**
■ Black #312	18
■ Cherry red #319	44
⅛-Inch Metallic Needlepoint Yarn	
■ Silver #PC2	26

Color numbers given are for Coats & Clark Red Heart Super Saver worsted weight yarn Art. E301.

Truck Cab Side
15 holes x 12 holes
Cut 2

Truck Grill
13 holes x 11 holes
Cut 1

Raffia Bouquet

Design by Robin Petrina

Raffia ribbon adds a delicate, almost transparent look to the pastel flowers decorating this creative tissue topper.

Skill Level: Beginner

Size: Fits boutique-style tissue box

Materials

- 1½ sheets 7-count plastic canvas
- Darice straw satin raffia cord as listed in color key
- #16 tapestry needle
- Hot-glue gun

Instructions

1. Cut plastic canvas according to graphs.

2. Stitch sides and top following graphs. Using white, Overcast inside edges of top and bottom edges of sides; Whipstitch sides together, and then Whipstitch sides to top.

3. Overcast leaves and flowers; then work Straight Stitches, working two flowers with baby pink as graphed, two with light blue and two with lavender. Work yellow French Knots in center of each flower.

4. Using photo as a guide, glue three flowers, one of each color, and three leaves to one side. Glue two flowers and two leaves to one corner of top; glue one flower and one leaf to opposite corner. ❖

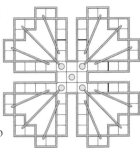

Raffia Bouquet Flower
13 holes x 13 holes
Cut 6
Stitch 2 with pink,
2 with light blue and
2 with lavender

Continue
pattern

Raffia Bouquet Side
31 holes x 41 holes
Cut 4

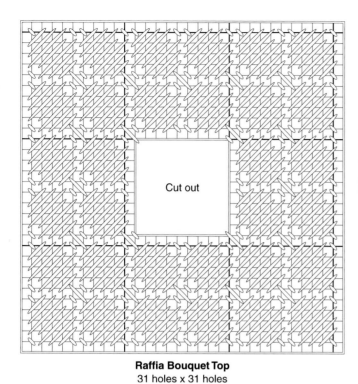

Raffia Bouquet Top
31 holes x 31 holes
Cut 1

COLOR KEY

Straw Satin Raffia Cord	Yards
□ White #3410-01	80
⁄ Baby pink #3410-02 Straight Stitch and Overcasting	6
Light blue #3410-13 Straight Stitch and Overcasting	6
⁄ Light green #3410-18 Straight Stitch and Overcasting	7
Lavender #3410-21 Straight Stitch and Overcasting	6
○ Yellow #3410-05 French Knot	2
Color numbers given are for Darice straw satin raffia cord.	

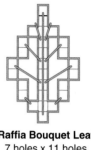

Raffia Bouquet Leaf
7 holes x 11 holes
Cut 5

Little Red Truck

Continued from page 99

7. Whipstitch bottom edge of tailgate to remaining edge of unstitched truck bottom. Overcast all remaining edges.

Painting & Drawing

1. Using flat paintbrush, paint 1-inch furniture button with flesh tone. Saw caps from axle pegs; paint caps with yellow. Allow to dry.

2. Paint wheels with black. Allow to dry. Spray all but backs of wheels with glossy acrylic spray. Allow to dry.

3. Following diagram given for dog's face, use black permanent marker to draw facial features on ½-inch furniture button.

4. Following diagram given for driver's face, use black permanent marker to draw eyes on painted 1-inch furniture button. Use detail brush to paint pink cheeks.

Assembly

1. Use photo as a guide throughout assembly. Lightly sand bottom of caps and wheels at center holes so glue will adhere; using wood glue, attach caps to center of wheels over holes.

2. Using hot glue through step 3, center and glue cab to front part of top, placing back of cab next to open-

ing. Stuff cab with fiberfill, and then center cab roof on cab, aligning back edges; glue in place.

3. Center and glue grill to truck front, making sure bottom edges are even. Glue front bumper to front corners near bottom, allowing bumper to arch. Center and glue back bumper flat against tailgate, just above bottom edge.

4. With tacky glue, attach driver to window of cab front on driver's side; glue dog in passenger's side window.

5. Cut doll hair into small pieces and carefully glue around side and top of face with hot glue. Tie ribbon in a tiny bow and glue to cab front under driver's head.

6. Using jewel glue, for headlights, glue one crystal faceted stone to front on each side of grill; glue red faceted stones to back bumper for taillights.

7. Using tacky glue through step 8, attach wheels to truck sides. Center and glue red bead for hood ornament to truck top behind grill.

8. Glue ears around top and sides of dog's head, placing straight edge next to cab side. Glue dog collar to window under dog's head.

9. Open tailgate and insert tissue box. ❖

Summertime Kitchen

Design by Michele Wilcox

Adorned with forget-me-nots, bumblebees, and a red and cream checkered pattern, this tissue box cover is just right for sprucing up your kitchen!

Skill Level: Beginner

Size: Fits regular-size tissue box

Materials

- 1½ sheets Uniek Quick-Count 7-count plastic canvas
- Uniek Needloft plastic canvas yarn as listed in color key
- DMC #5 pearl cotton as listed in color key
- #16 tapestry needle

Instructions

1. Cut plastic canvas according to graphs, cutting out gray area shown on front and back graph for front piece only, leaving back piece intact.

2. Stitch pieces following graphs, working uncoded areas with eggshell Continental Stitches. Fill in back continuing pattern given.

3. When background stitching is completed, Backstitch details on bees with black pearl cotton.

4. Using fern throughout, Whipstitch front and back to sides; Whipstitch front, back and sides to top, aligning edges on top and front pieces to create opening for tissues. Overcast all remaining edges. ❖

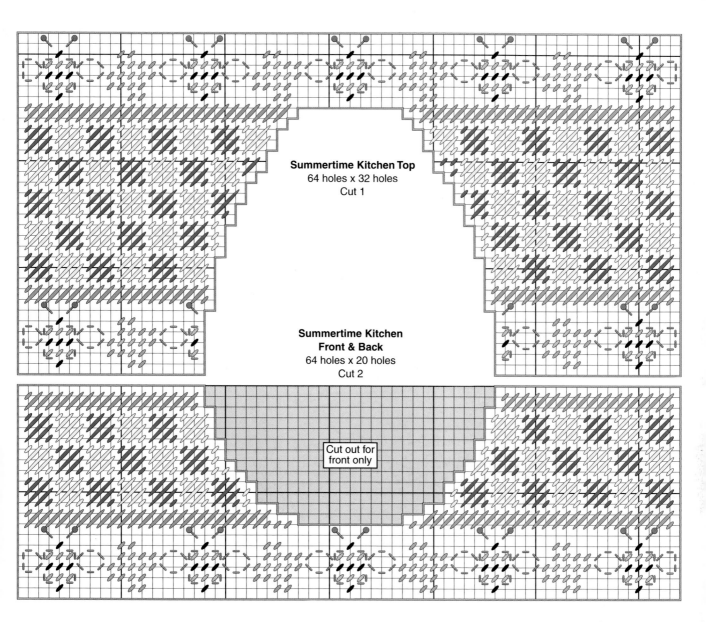

Summertime Kitchen Top
64 holes x 32 holes
Cut 1

**Summertime Kitchen
Front & Back**
64 holes x 20 holes
Cut 2

Cut out for
front only

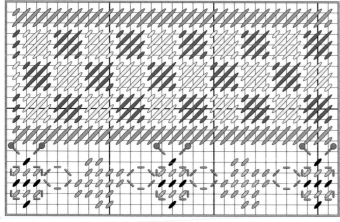

Summertime Kitchen Side
32 holes x 20 holes
Cut 2

COLOR KEY

Plastic Canvas Yarn	Yards
■ Black #00	10
■ Red #01	20
□ Tangerine #11	12
▨ Fern #23	25
□ Eggshell #39	55
▨ Turquoise #54	12

Uncoded areas are eggshell #39
Continental Stitches

#5 Pearl Cotton

╱ Black #310 Backstitch and Straight Stitch	10
● Black #310 French Knot	

Color numbers given are for Uniek Needloft plastic canvas
yarn and DMC #5 pearl cotton.

- DMC #3 pearl cotton embroidery floss as listed in color key
- DMC #8 pearl cotton embroidery floss as listed in color key
- DMC 6-strand embroidery floss as listed in color key
- #16 tapestry needle

Instructions

1. Cut plastic canvas according to graphs.

2. Following graphs, work borders with Two-Color Herringbone Stitch (Fig. 1), working mist green stitches first, then eggshell stitches. Work eggshell Slanting Gobelin Stitches on sides and top as indicated.

3. Work all remaining background stitches with Continental Stitches, working uncoded areas in corners, around angel and in center area of sides with eggshell.

Summer Angel

Design by Janelle Giese

This darling, ocean-loving angel is just what you need to add a sweet touch of heaven to your summertime decor!

Skill Level: Intermediate

Size: Fits boutique-style tissue box

Materials

- 1½ sheets 7-count plastic canvas
- Coats & Clark Red Heart Classic worsted weight yarn Art. E267 as listed in color key
- Kreinik Medium (#16) Braid as listed in color key

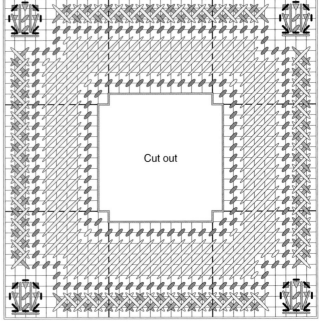

Summer Angel Top
30 holes x 30 holes
Cut 1

4. When background stitching is completed, work Cross Stitches for cheeks with 2-strands salmon floss. Embroider halo, lower portion of wings and scallop lines of skirt with Vatican gold medium (#16) braid.

5. Stitch lower portion of wings a second time with black #8 pearl cotton; work remaining black pearl cotton embroidery, passing over each eye six times.

6. Straight Stitch lines of seashells with light tawny #3 pearl cotton.

7. Overcast inside edges on top with mist green. Using eggshell, Whipstitch front and sides together; Whipstitch front and sides to top. Overcast bottom edges. ❖

Fig. 1
Two-Color Herringbone Stitch

Work a row of mist green stitches first, then work a row of eggshell stitches on top.

COLOR KEY	
Worsted Weight Yarn	**Yards**
◇ White #1	1
⬭ Eggshell #111	43
△ Cornmeal #220	1
◇ Sea coral #246	2
⬭ Silver #412	5
■ Light lavender #579	3
⬭ Honey gold #645	1
⬭ Mist green #681	13
⬭ Light seafoam #683	14
△ Lily pink #719	1
⬭ Light coral rose #749	1
★ Pale rose #755	3
▽ Pale blue #815	4
Uncoded areas are eggshell #111 Continental Stitches	
⁄ Light coral rose #749 Straight Stitch	
Medium (#16) Braid	
⁄ Vatican gold #102 Backstitch and Straight Stitch	1
#3 Pearl Cotton	
⁄ Light tawny #951 Straight Stitch	7
#8 Pearl Cotton	
⁄ Black #310 Backstitch and Straight Stitch	12
6-Strand Embroidery Floss	
✕ Salmon #760 Cross Stitch	1

Color numbers given are for Coats & Clark Red Heart Classic worsted weight yarn Art. E267, Kreinik Medium (#16) Braid and DMC pearl cotton and 6-strand embroidery floss.

Summer Angel Front
30 holes x 36 holes
Cut 1

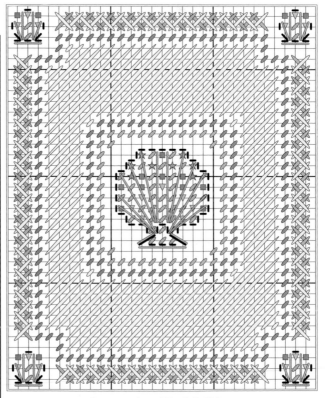

Summer Angel Back & Side
30 holes x 36 holes
Cut 3

Floral Hearts

Design by Ruby Thacker

Learn a pretty new stitch as you create this sweet project! Finished off with pearl beads, this tissue box will add beauty to your bedroom or bathroom!

Skill Level: Intermediate

Size: Fits regular-size tissue box

Materials

- 2 sheets 7-count plastic canvas
- Uniek Needloft plastic canvas yarn as listed in color key
- Nylon plastic canvas yarn as listed in color key
- #16 tapestry needle
- 1½ yards round white pearl beads on a string
- Sewing needle and white sewing thread

Instructions

1. Cut plastic canvas according to graphs.

2. Following graphs throughout, with lavender, stitch heart flowers using Heart Rhodes Stitch (Fig. 1). With moss, stitch leaves using Basic Leaf Stitch (Fig. 2) on top and Diagonal Leaf Stitch (Fig. 3) on sides. Work uncoded areas with baby pink Continental Stitches.

3. Using baby pink throughout, Overcast inside edges on top. Using Braided Cross Stitch (see stitch diagram on page 90), Whipstitch long sides to short sides; then Whipstitch sides to top. Overcast bottom edges. *Note: When working Braided Cross Stitch, work extra stitches at corners as necessary to cover.*

4. Using photo as a guide, with sewing needle and white sewing thread, attach pearl beads on a string around opening on top and around bottom edge. ❖

COLOR KEY

Plastic Canvas Yarn	Yards
■ Lavender #05	16
■ Moss #25	9
Uncoded areas are baby pink Continental Stitches	
⁄ Baby pink Overcasting and Whipstitching	90

Color numbers given are for Uniek Needloft plastic canvas yarn.

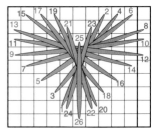

**Fig. 1
Heart Rhodes Stitch**

Working clockwise, bring needle up at 1, down at 2, up at 3, down at 4, etc.

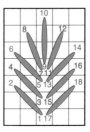

**Fig. 2
Basic Leaf Stitch**

Working clockwise, bring needle up at 1, down at 2, up at 3, down at 4, etc.

**Fig. 3
Diagonal Leaf Stitch**

Moving counterclockwise, work stitches in order given, working middle stitch last

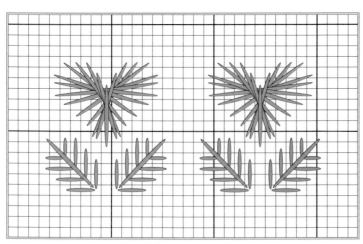

**Floral Hearts Short Side
34 holes x 21 holes
Cut 2**

Floral Hearts Long Side
66 holes x 21 holes
Cut 2

Floral Hearts Top
66 holes x 34 holes
Cut 1

Cut out

Bee My Honey

Design by Kathleen Hurley

Cheer up a shut-in or a sick friend with this dimensional tissue topper accented with pretty flowers and a buzzing bumble bee!

Skill Level: Beginner

Size: Fits boutique-style tissue box

Materials

- 1½ sheets 7-count plastic canvas
- Uniek Needloft plastic canvas yarn as listed in color key
- DMC #3 pearl cotton as listed in color key
- #16 tapestry needle
- 4 inches 24-gauge black craft wire
- Wire cutters
- Hot-glue gun

Instructions

1. Cut plastic canvas according to graphs.

2. Stitch cover pieces following graphs, working uncoded areas with white Continental Stitches. Work bee hives and borders, using two stitches per hole where indicated.

3. Work embroidery on front with pearl cotton when background stitching is completed.

4. Using white throughout, Overcast inside edges of top and bottom edges of front, back and sides. Whipstitch front and back to sides; Whipstitch front, back and sides to top.

5. Stitch and Overcast bees, flowers and leaves following graphs, working three flowers with pink and two each with lilac, purple and bright blue.

6. When background stitching is completed, work fern Straight Stitch on leaves, yellow French Knots in center of flowers and cinnamon French Knot on bees for eyes.

7. Using photo as a guide through step 8, cut wire in two 2-inch lengths. Fold each length in half. Bend and twist ends of wire as desire; glue one to back of each bee's head.

8. Glue leaves, flowers and bees to cover front as desired. ❖

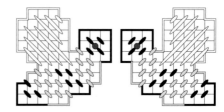

Bees
9 holes x 9 holes
Cut 1 each

Be My Honey Flower
6 holes x 6 holes
Cut 9
Stitch 3 with pink
and 2 each with lilac, purple
and bright blue

Be My Honey Leaf
5 holes x 9 holes
Cut 7

Bee My Honey Front
31 holes x 38 holes
Cut 1

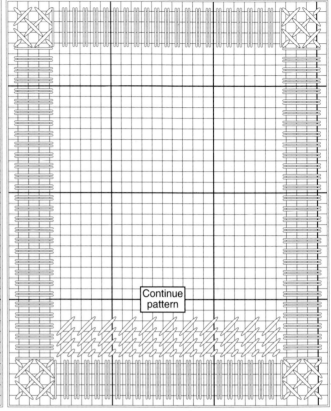

Continue pattern

Bee My Honey Back & Side
31 holes x 38 holes
Cut 3

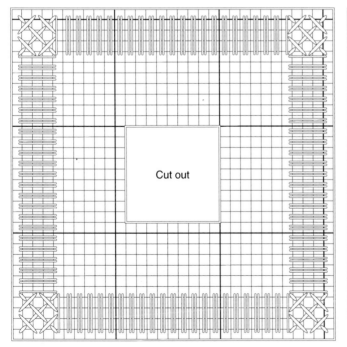

Cut out

Bee My Honey Top
31 holes x 31 holes
Cut 1

COLOR KEY

Plastic Canvas Yarn	Yards
■ Black #00	2
▢ Pink #07	3
■ Cinnamon #14	2
▨ Gold #17	6
▨ Fern #23	5
▢ White #41	70
Lilac #45	2
Purple #46	2
▢ Yellow #57	3
Bright blue #60	2
Uncoded areas are white #41	
Continental Stitches	
╱ Fern #23 Straight Stitch	
● Cinnamon #14 French Knot	
○ Yellow #57 French Knot	

#3 Pearl Cotton

╱ Black #310 Backstitch	2
╱ Ultra dark pistachio green #890 Backstitch and Straight Stitch	2

Color numbers given are for Uniek Needloft plastic canvas yarn and DMC #3 pearl cotton.

Sparkling Pastels

Design by Susan Leinberger

Add a beautiful sparkle to your bedroom or bathroom with this pretty tissue box cover. It is worked with pastel metallic cord in an interesting, textured pattern.

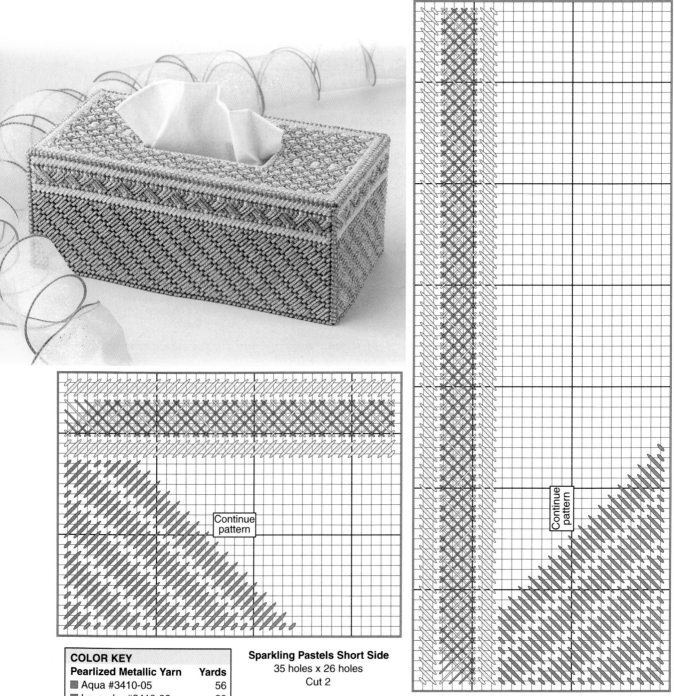

Continue pattern

Continue pattern

Sparkling Pastels Short Side
35 holes x 26 holes
Cut 2

Sparkling Pastels Long Side
68 holes x 26 holes
Cut 2

COLOR KEY	
Pearlized Metallic Yarn	**Yards**
■ Aqua #3410-05	56
■ Lavender #3410-06	30
□ Yellow #3410-07	24
Color numbers given are for Darice Bright Pearls pearlized metallic cord.	

Skill Level: Advanced

Size: Fits family-size tissue box

Materials

- 2 sheets Uniek Quick-Count 7-count plastic canvas
- Darice Bright Pearls pearlized metallic cord as listed in color key
- #16 tapestry needle

Instructions

1. Cut plastic canvas according to graphs..

2. Stitch sides following graphs, working band near top with a Six-Trip Herringbone Stitch (Fig. 1), beginning with yellow, then aqua, then lavender, then repeating the sequence.

3. Begin yellow and aqua trips as indicated. Continue stitching, starting lavender trip at hole A, second yellow trip at hole B, second aqua trip at hole C and second lavender trip at hole D.

4. Stitch top following graph, working Tied Double Cross Stitches (Fig. 2), beginning with large aqua Cross Stitches. Work yellow Upright Cross Stitches between large Cross Stitches, and lavender Upright Cross Stitches over large aqua Cross Stitch intersections.

5. Overcast inside edges of top with yellow; then work aqua Backstitches around opening.

6. Using lavender throughout, Overcast bottom edges of sides. Whipstitch long sides to short sides; then Whipstitch sides to top. ❖

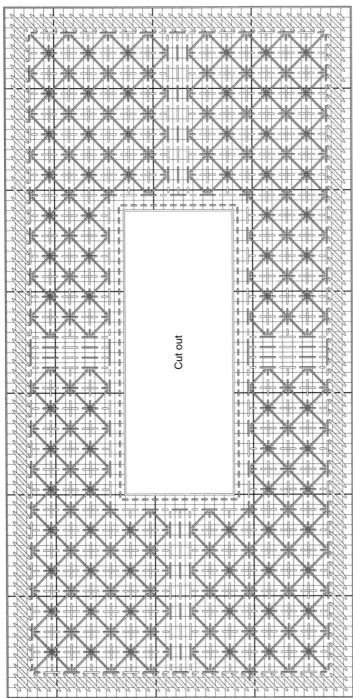

Cut out

Sparkling Pastels Top
68 holes x 35 holes
Cut 1

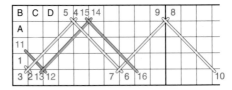

Fig. 1
Six-Trip Herringbone Stitch

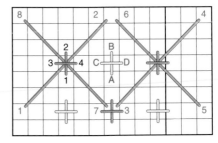

Fig. 2
Tied Double Cross Stitch

Autumn Glory!

Autumn brings with it crisp, cool days, breathtaking foliage, harvest time, Halloween and Thanksgiving! Stitch and celebrate the many wonders of autumn with this collection of creative, fall tissue box covers!

Country Apples

Design by Joan Green

*Here's a perfect appreciation gift for that wonderful teacher—
a charming tissue box decorated with appliqué-style apples!*

Skill Level: Beginner

Size: Fits boutique-style tissue box

Materials

- 2 sheets 7-count plastic canvas
- Coats & Clark Red Heart Classic worsted weight yarn Art. E267 as listed in color key
- Coats & Clark Red Heart Super Saver worsted weight yarn Art. E300 as listed in color key
- #16 tapestry needle

Instructions

1. Cut plastic canvas according to graphs.

2. Stitch pieces following graphs, leaving area indicated on each side unstitched.

3. When background stitching is completed, work burgundy Backstitches on apples and top.

4. Overcast apples with coffee, grass green and burgundy following graph. Overcast inside edges of top with paddy green.

5. Using tan throughout, Overcast bottom edges of sides. Whipstitch sides together, then Whipstitch sides to top.

6. Center one apple on each side, then tack in place every ½ inch to 1 inch around apple only; do not tack down leaves and stems. ❖

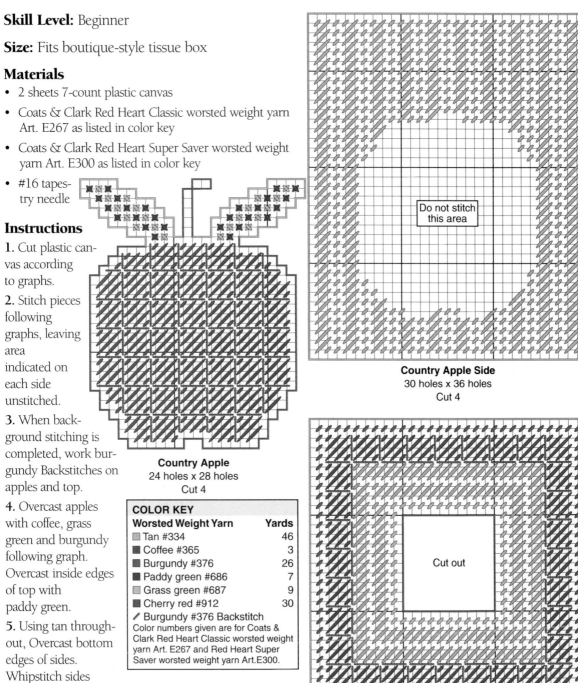

Country Apple Side
30 holes x 36 holes
Cut 4

Country Apple
24 holes x 28 holes
Cut 4

Do not stitch this area

Cut out

Country Apple Top
30 holes x 30 holes
Cut 1

COLOR KEY	
Worsted Weight Yarn	**Yards**
☐ Tan #334	46
■ Coffee #365	3
■ Burgundy #376	26
■ Paddy green #686	7
☐ Grass green #687	9
■ Cherry red #912	30
╱ Burgundy #376 Backstitch	
Color numbers given are for Coats & Clark Red Heart Classic worsted weight yarn Art. E267 and Red Heart Super Saver worsted weight yarn Art. E300.	

Log Cabin

Design by Angie Arickx

Capture the look of a pioneer's log cabin with this uniquely-shaped tissue box cover!
French Knot flowers and a basket-weave roof add extra dimension and texture!

Skill Level: Beginner

Size: Fits regular-size tissue box

Materials

- 2 sheets Uniek Quick-Count 7-count plastic canvas
- Uniek Needloft plastic canvas yarn as listed in color key
- #16 tapestry needle

Instructions

1. Cut plastic canvas according to graphs.

2. Stitch pieces following graphs, working uncoded window areas with black Continental Stitches.

3. When background stitching is completed, work French Knots in window boxes for flower blooms.

4. Overcast bottom edges of sides following graphs. Overcast indented roof edges (for chimney) with gold, leaving area between blue dots unworked at this time. Whipstitch long sides to short sides with brown.

5. Using eggshell, Overcast top edges of chimney pieces, then Whipstitch together along side edges.

6. Using gold throughout, Whipstitch long sides together along roof edges. Overcast bottom edges of chimney on opposite sides. Whipstitch remaining bottom edges of chimney to unstitched chimney edges on roof. ❖

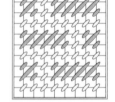

Log Cabin Chimney
9 holes x 10 holes
Cut 4

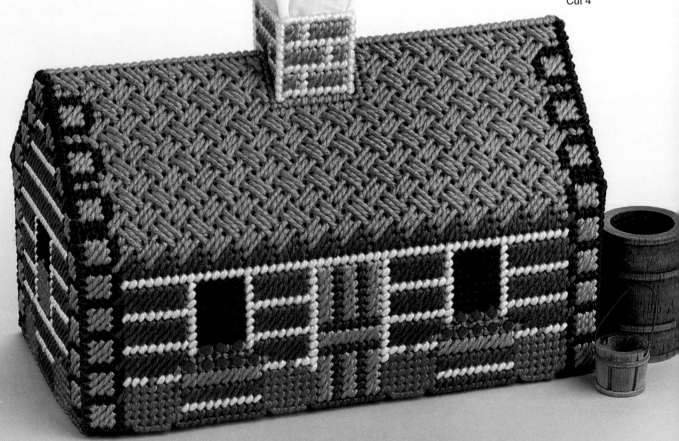

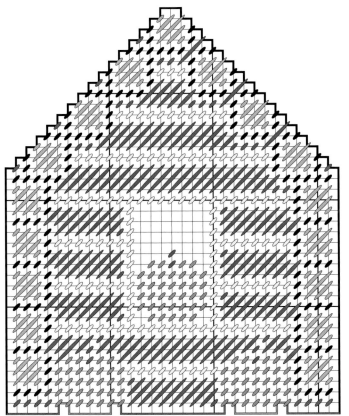

COLOR KEY

Plastic Canvas Yarn	Yards
■ Cinnamon #14	28
■ Brown #15	14
☐ Gold #17	42
■ Christmas green #28	3
☐ Eggshell #39	17
☐ Camel #43	19
■ Bittersweet #52	11
Uncoded window areas are black #00 Continental Stitches	5
● Red #01 French Knot	2

Color numbers given are for Uniek Needloft plastic canvas yarn.

Log Cabin Short Side
32 holes x 38 holes
Cut 2

Log Cabin Long Side
65 holes x 45 holes
Cut 2

Continue pattern

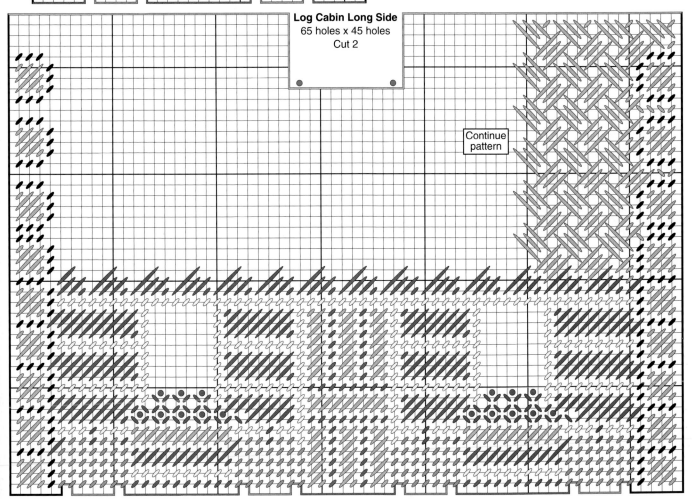

Autumn Angel

Design by Janelle Giese

Celebrate the bounty of autumn with this enchanting project! A darling angel carrying a basket of plump grapes will add thankfulness to your fall season.

Skill Level: Intermediate

Size: Fits boutique-style tissue box

Materials
- 1½ sheets 7-count plastic canvas
- Coats & Clark Red Heart Classic worsted weight yarn Art. E267 as listed in color key
- Kreinik Medium (#16) Braid as listed in color key
- DMC #3 pearl cotton floss as listed in color key
- DMC #8 pearl cotton as listed in color key
- DMC 6-strand as listed in color key
- #16 tapestry needle
- Thick white glue

Instructions

1. Cut plastic canvas according to graphs.

2. Following graphs, work borders with Two-Color Herringbone Stitch (Fig. 1), working maize stitches first, then eggshell stitches. Work eggshell Slanting Gobelin Stitches on sides and top as indicated.

3. Work all remaining background stitches with Continental Stitches, working uncoded areas in all corners, around angel and in center area of sides with eggshell.

4. When background stitching is completed, work Cross Stitches for cheeks with 2-strands salmon floss. Embroider halo and lower portion of wings with Vatican gold medium (#16) braid.

5. Stitch lower portion of wings a second time with black #8 pearl cotton, then work remaining black pearl cotton embroidery, passing over each eye six times.

6. Work French Knots for grapes with #3 pearl cotton, wrapping two times for each French Knot.

7. Backstitch basket handles with mid brown. Backstitch and Straight Stitch leaf accents with dark sage.

8. For hair bows, cut two lengths of light violet

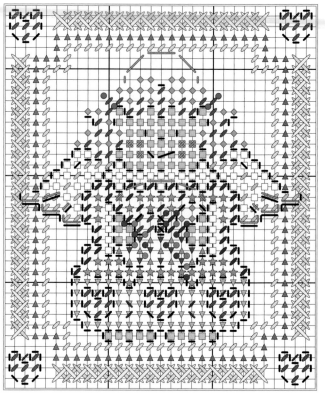

Autumn Angel Front
30 holes x 36 holes
Cut 1

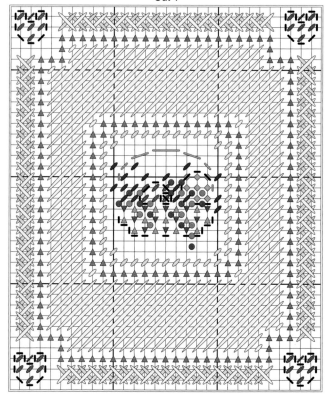

Autumn Angel Side
30 holes x 36 holes
Cut 3

pearl cotton. For each pigtail, thread ends of one length from back to front through holes indicated on graph. Tie each length in a tiny bow, trimming ends as desired. Secure with a dab of glue.

9. Overcast inside edges on top with maize. Using eggshell, Whipstitch sides together, then Whipstitch sides to top; Overcast bottom edges. ❖

Fig. 1
Two-Color Herringbone Stitch

1	C	B	5	4	G	F	9	8	K	J	12
A	3	2	E	D	7	6	I	H	11	10	L

Work a row of maize stitches first,
then work a row of eggshell
stitches on top.

COLOR KEY

Worsted Weight Yarn	Yards
☐ White #1	1
⊘ Eggshell #111	40
▲ Cornmeal #220	13
▣ Sea coral #246	2
⊘ Maize #261	12
◈ Medium clay #280	2
⬤ Bronze #286	4
▲ Mid brown #339	2
▼ Coffee #365	1
▽ Light sage #631	2
★ Medium sage #632	1
◢ Dark sage #633	3
⊘ Pale blue #815	1
Uncoded areas are eggshell #111 Continental Stitches	
⁄ Mid brown #339 Backstitch	
⁄ Dark sage #633 Backstitch and Straight Stitch	
Medium (#16) Braid	
⁄ Vatican gold #102 Backstitch and Straight Stitch	1
#3 Pearl Cotton	
● Very dark lavender #208 French Knot	2
● Light violet #554 French Knot	2
#8 Pearl Cotton	
⁄ Black #310 Backstitch and Straight Stitch	4
6-Strand Embroidery Floss	
✕ Salmon #760 Cross Stitch	1
● Attach Hair bow	

Color numbers given are for Coats & Clark Red Heart Classic worsted weight yarn Art. E267, Kreinik Medium (#16) Braid and DMC pearl cotton and 6-strand embroidery floss.

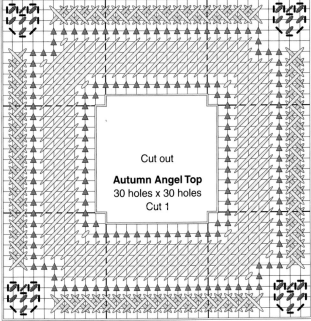

Cut out

Autumn Angel Top
30 holes x 30 holes
Cut 1

Learning the Ropes

Design by Judy Collishaw

This group of spiders is just too silly to be spooky!
Stitch this tissue topper to delight your Halloween visitors!

Skill Level: Beginner

Size: Fits family-size tissue box

Materials

- 2½ sheets 7-count plastic canvas
- Worsted weight yarn as listed in color key
- #16 tapestry needle
- 4 (9mm) round movable eyes
- 8 (7mm) round movable eyes
- 2 inches 24-gauge white stem wire
- Low-temperature glue gun

Instructions

1. Cut plastic canvas according to graphs (pages 119 and 120).

2. Stitch sides and top following graphs, working uncoded areas with yellow Continental Stitches.

3. When background stitching is completed, work gray Straight Stitches to complete spider webs.

4. Using yellow throughout, Overcast inside edges of top and bottom edges of sides. Whipstitch long sides to short sides, then Whipstitch sides to top.

5. Stitch spider pieces following graphs, reversing

Continued on page 120

Learning the Ropes Short Side
33 holes x 33 holes
Cut 2

COLOR KEY

Worsted Weight Yarn	Yards
■ Gray	30
■ Black	29
Uncoded areas are yellow Continental Stitches	98
⁄ Yellow Overcasting and Whipstitching	
⁄ Gray Straight Stitch	

Learning the Ropes Top
65 holes x 33 holes
Cut 2

Cut out

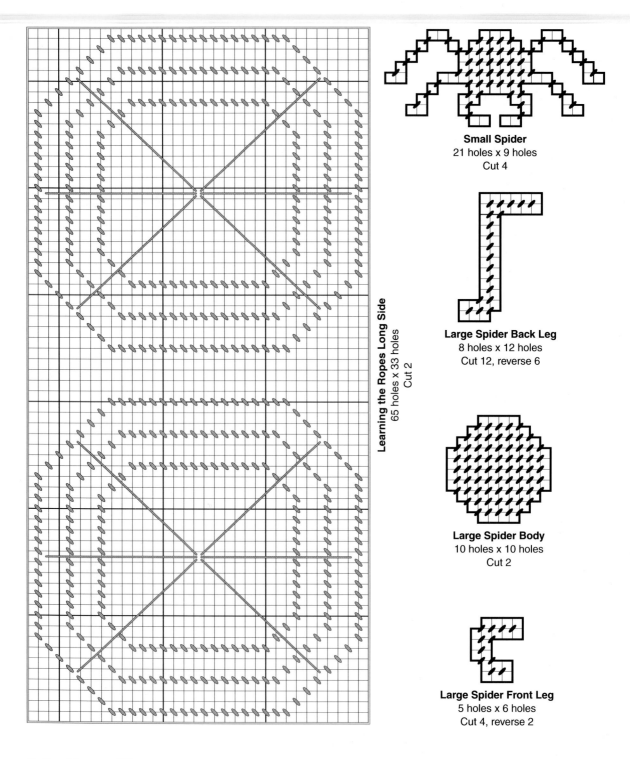

Small Spider
21 holes x 9 holes
Cut 4

Large Spider Back Leg
8 holes x 12 holes
Cut 12, reverse 6

Learning the Ropes Long Side
65 holes x 33 holes
Cut 2

Large Spider Body
10 holes x 10 holes
Cut 2

Large Spider Front Leg
5 holes x 6 holes
Cut 4, reverse 2

Continued from page 118

two large spider front legs and six large spider back legs before stitching. Overcast with black.

6. Using photo as a guide through step 8, glue 7mm eyes to small spiders and 9mm eyes to large spider bodies. Cut stem wire in half and bend each in a "U" shape to form mouths. Glue mouths below eyes on large spider bodies.

7. Glue two front legs to bottom backside of each large spider; glue six back legs (three on each side) to backs of each large spider around sides.

8. Glue one large and one small spider to webs on each long side and one small spider to web on each short side. ❖

Pumpkin Pocket

Design by Michele Wilcox

Tuck a package of tissues into this miniature tissue holder featuring a ripe, orange pumpkin on a royal blue background!

Skill Level: Beginner

Size: Fits pocket-size tissue package

Materials

- ½ sheet Uniek Quick-Count 7-count plastic canvas
- Uniek Needloft plastic canvas yarn as listed in color key
- DMC #5 pearl cotton as listed in color key
- #16 tapestry needle
- ½ yard ¼-inch-wide green satin ribbon

COLOR KEY	
Plastic Canvas Yarn	**Yards**
☐ Tangerine #11	5
☐ Pumpkin #12	8
■ Cinnamon #14	1
■ Royal #32	25
Uncoded areas are royal #32 Continental Stitches	
#5 Pearl Cotton	
╱ Dark golden brown #975 Backstitch	
Color numbers given are for Uniek Needloft plastic canvas yarn and DMC #5 pearl cotton.	

Instructions

1. Cut plastic canvas according to graphs.

2. Stitch pieces following graphs, working uncoded areas with royal Continental Stitches. Work dark golden brown Backstitches on pumpkin when background stitching is completed.

3. Using royal throughout, Overcast inside edges and top edges on front and back. Whipstitch wrong sides of front and back together along remaining edges.

4. For easier access, remove tissue from package before placing inside holder. Thread ribbon through holes on front and back; tie in a bow to close. ❖

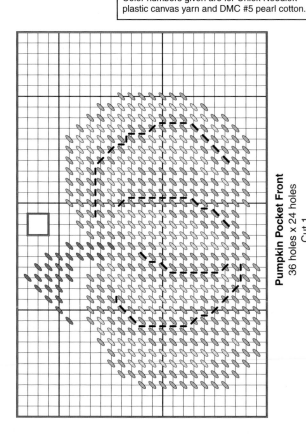

Pumpkin Pocket Front
36 holes x 24 holes
Cut 1

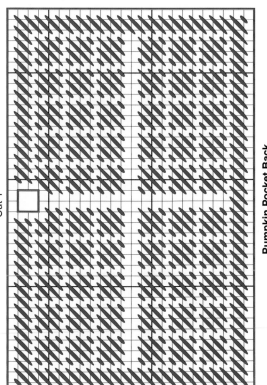

Pumpkin Pocket Back
36 holes x 24 holes
Cut 1

Country Barn

Design by Ronda Bryce

Celebrate a bumper crop with this down-on-the-farm fun tissue topper!
It's sure to remind retired farmers of those good-old-days on the farm!

Skill Level: Intermediate

Size: Fits boutique-style tissue box

Materials

- 2 sheets clear 7-count plastic canvas
- ½ sheet orange 7-count plastic canvas
- 3-inch plastic canvas round from Uniek
- Uniek Needloft plastic canvas yarn as listed in color key
- #16 tapestry needle

Cutting & Stitching

1. Following graphs (this page and pages 123 and 125) through step 4, cut barrel bottom from radial circle, cutting away gray area. Cut pumpkins from orange plastic canvas. Cut remaining pieces from clear plastic canvas. Barrel bottom will remain unstitched.

2. Stitch remaining pieces following graphs. When background stitching is completed, work brown Straight Stitches on barrel; work black Straight Stitches on barn back door.

3. Following graphs, Overcast shutters, barn doors and pumpkins; Overcast bottom edges of barn front, back and sides.

4. For hay, cut 40 (8-inch) lengths of tangerine yarn. Attach lengths where indicated on barn front graph with Lark's Head Knots, working from top down. When Lark's Head Knots are completed, trim hay to desired length.

Assembly

1. Use photo as a guide throughout assembly. Where indicated on graph with green lines, place one shutter on each side of window on barn front; tack in place with white yarn.

2. Where indicated on graph with blue lines, place one barn door on each side of barn front door; tack in place with

Barn Shutter
7 holes x 10 holes
Cut 2 from clear

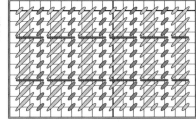

Barn Barrel
18 holes x 11 holes
Cut 1 from clear

COLOR KEY	
Plastic Canvas Yarn	**Yards**
■ Black #00	26
■ Christmas red #02	61
□ Tangerine #11	26
■ Maple #13	9
■ Brown #15	3
■ Christmas green #28	3
□ White #41	45
■ Bright orange #58	9
✦ Black #00 Straight Stitch	
✦ Brown #15 Straight Stitch	
◯ Tangerine #11 Lark's Head Knot	
╱ Attach door	
╱ Attach shutter	
╱ Attach barrel	
Color numbers given are for Uniek Needloft plastic canvas yarn.	

Christmas red. Tack pumpkins to open door area with bright orange.

3. Using maple throughout, Overcast around side and top edges of barrel, then Whipstitch bottom edge to rounded edge of barrel bottom. Tack side edges of barrel to one barn side where indicated on graph with lavender lines.

4. Using white, Whipstitch front and back to sides, then Whipstitch barn loft sides to top edges of barn sides.

5. Whipstitch cupola sides together with Christmas red and white following graph. Overcast top edges with white. Whipstitch bottom

edges to opening on roof top with Christmas red.

6. Using black, Whipstitch roof front and back to roof top. Whipstitch remaining edges of roof top to top edges of loft, then Whipstitch loft to roof front and back.

7. Using white, Whipstitch barn front and back to roof front and back. ❖

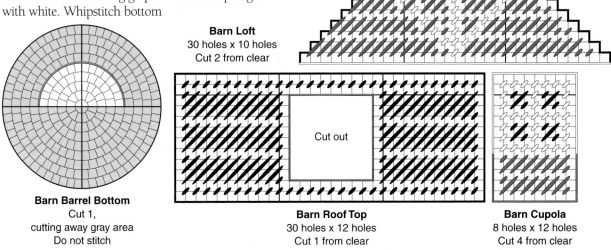

Barn Barrel Bottom
Cut 1,
cutting away gray area
Do not stitch

Barn Loft
30 holes x 10 holes
Cut 2 from clear

Barn Roof Top
30 holes x 12 holes
Cut 1 from clear

Cut out

Barn Cupola
8 holes x 12 holes
Cut 4 from clear

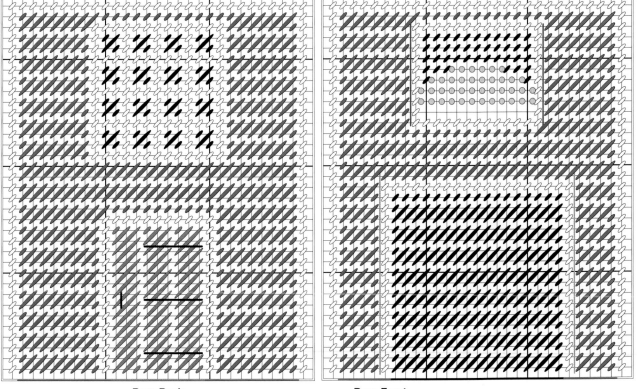

Barn Back
30 holes x 36 holes
Cut 1 from clear

Barn Front
30 holes x 36 holes
Cut 1 from clear

Graphs continued on page 125

Maple Leaves

Design by Lee Lindeman

Stitch this copper and gold-hued tissue topper to capture the yearly scene of maple leaves caught in a crisp, autumn breeze!

Skill Level: Beginner

Size: Fits boutique-style tissue box

Materials

- 2 sheets 7-count plastic canvas
- Worsted weight yarn as listed in color key
- #16 tapestry needle
- Hot-glue gun or tacky craft glue

Instructions

1. Cut plastic canvas according to graphs.

2. Stitch pieces following graphs, working uncoded areas with cream Continental Stitches. Work black Backstitches on side A when background stitching is completed.

3. Overcast inside edges of top and bottom edges of sides with cream.

4. Using cream and black and following graphs, Whipstitch sides together in alphabetical order (A–D), then Whipstitch sides A and D together; Whipstitch sides to top, making sure to match top edges with corresponding sides.

5. Stitch leaves following graphs, stitching one leaf with gold as graphed. Reverse three and stitch one with light copper, one with burgundy and one with deep yellow. Overcast with adjacent colors.

6. Glue one leaf to each side as desired. ❖

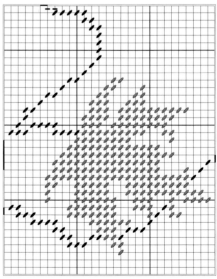

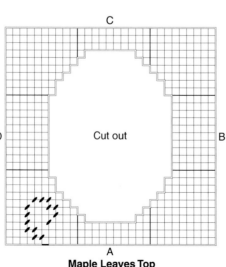

Maple Leaves Top
29 holes x 29 holes

Maple Leaves Side A
29 holes x 36 holes
Cut 1

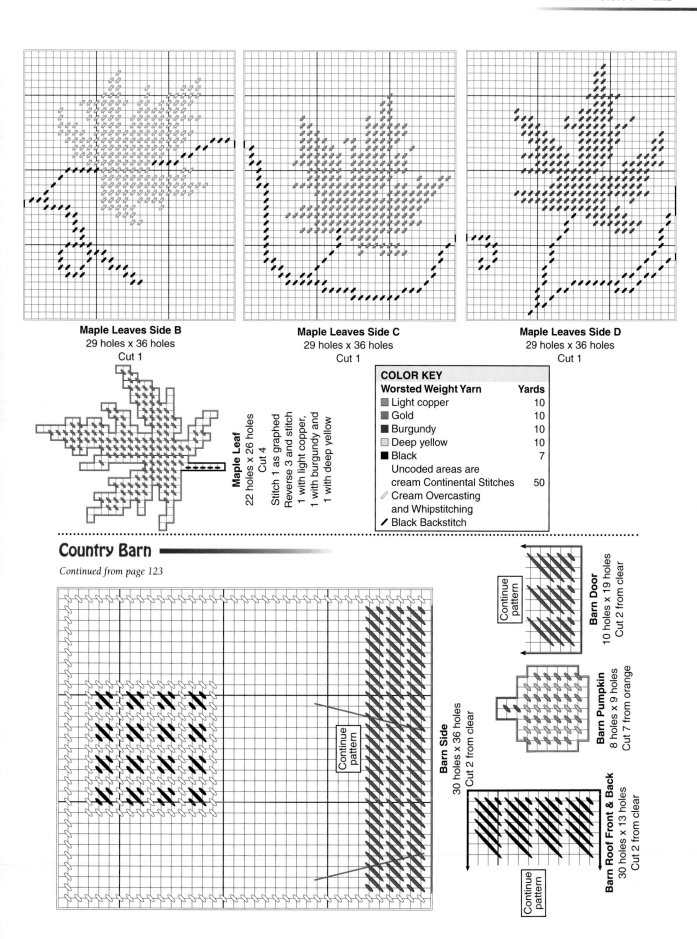

Maple Leaves Side B
29 holes x 36 holes
Cut 1

Maple Leaves Side C
29 holes x 36 holes
Cut 1

Maple Leaves Side D
29 holes x 36 holes
Cut 1

Maple Leaf
22 holes x 26 holes
Cut 4
Stitch 1 as graphed
Reverse 3 and stitch
1 with light copper,
1 with burgundy and
1 with deep yellow

COLOR KEY

Worsted Weight Yarn	Yards
Light copper	10
Gold	10
Burgundy	10
Deep yellow	10
Black	7
Uncoded areas are cream Continental Stitches	50
⁄ Cream Overcasting and Whipstitching	
✓ Black Backstitch	

Country Barn

Continued from page 123

Continue pattern

Barn Side
30 holes x 36 holes
Cut 2 from clear

Barn Door
10 holes x 19 holes
Cut 2 from clear
Continue pattern

Barn Pumpkin
8 holes x 9 holes
Cut 7 from orange

Barn Roof Front & Back
30 holes x 13 holes
Cut 2 from clear
Continue pattern

Autumn Silhouettes

Design by Ronda Bryce

Decorate your home with a different style of plastic canvas project with this unique tissue box cover. Black silhouettes standing out against a copper background make for an artistic design.

Skill Level: Intermediate

Size: Fits boutique-style tissue box

Materials

- 2 sheets Uniek Quick-Count black 7-count plastic canvas
- Coats & Clark Red Heart Super Saver worsted weight yarn Art. E301 as listed in color key
- #16 tapestry needle
- 3 (9-inch x 12-inch) sheets persimmon #3200 felt from Consumer Product Enterprises Inc. (CPE)
- Sewing needle and black sewing thread

Instructions

1. Cut plastic canvas according to graphs (this page and page 128), carefully cutting out openings on each piece.

COLOR KEY

Worsted Weight Yarn	Yards
■ Black #312	80

Color number given is for Coats & Clark Red Heart Super Saver worsted weight yarn Art. E301.

Continued on page 128

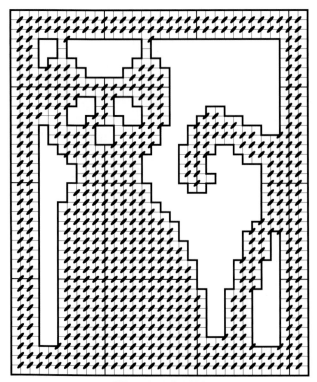

Silhouettes Cat Side
32 holes x 38 holes
Cut 1

Silhouettes Apple Side
32 holes x 38 holes
Cut 1

Thunderbird

Design by Joan Green

Create this artistically designed tissue topper to add a Southwest accent to your home. Silver beads and copper accents give this project an authentic Native American look and feel.

Skill Level: Beginner

Size: Fits boutique-style tissue box

Materials

- 1¼ sheets 7-count plastic canvas
- Coats & Clark Red Heart Classic worsted weight yarn Art. E267 as listed in color key
- ⅛-inch-wide Plastic Canvas 7 Metallic Needlepoint Yarn by Rainbow Gallery as listed in color key
- #16 tapestry needle
- 84 (4mm) round silver beads
- Sewing needle and black sewing thread

Instructions

1. Cut plastic canvas according to graphs (this page and page 128).

2. Stitch pieces following graphs, working uncoded areas with black Continental Stitches.

3. When background stitching is completed, work parakeet Backstitches and black French Knots for eyes with 4 plies yarn. Work black Backstitches and Straight Stitches on wings with 2 plies yarn.

4. Using sewing needle and black sewing thread, attach silver beads to top and sides where indicated on graphs.

5. Overcast opening on top with copper. Using black throughout, Overcast bottom edges of sides. Whipstitch sides together, then Whipstitch sides to top. ❖

Thunderbird Top
31 holes x 31 holes
Cut 1

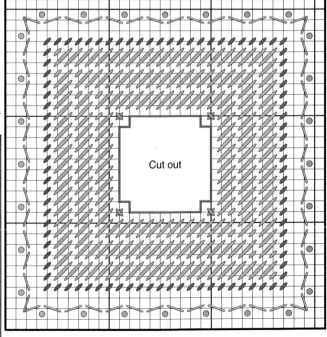

COLOR KEY	
Worsted Weight Yarn	**Yards**
▢ Medium clay #280	30
▨ Parakeet #513	32
Uncoded areas are black #12 Continental Stitches	28
⁄ Black #12 Backstitch, Overcasting and Whipstitching	
⁄ Parakeet #513 Backstitch	
● Black #12 French Knot	
⅛-Inch Metallic Needlepoint Yarn	
▪ Copper #PC3	14
⊙ Attach silver bead	
Color numbers given are for Coats & Clark Red Heart Classic worsted weight yarn Art. E267 and Rainbow Gallery Plastic Canvas 7 Metallic Needlepoint Yarn.	

Graphs continued on page 128

Thunderbird

Continued from page 127

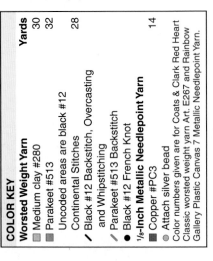

COLOR KEY

	Yards	
Worsted Weight Yarn		
▨ Medium clay #280	30	
▨ Parakeet #513	32	
Uncoded areas are black #12	28	
Continental Stitches		
╲ Black #12 Backstitch, Overcasting and Whipstitching		
╱ Parakeet #513 Backstitch		
● Black #12 French Knot		
1/8-Inch Metallic Needlepoint Yarn		
▨ Copper #PC3	14	
◯ Attach silver bead		

Color numbers given are for Coats & Clark Red Heart Classic worsted weight yarn Art. E267 and Rainbow Gallery Plastic Canvas 7 Metallic Needlepoint Yarn.

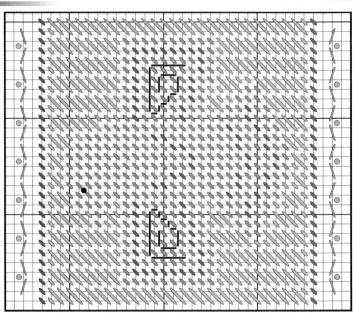

Thunderbird Side
31 holes x 37 holes
Cut 4

Autumn Silhouettes

Continued from page 126

2. From persimmon felt, cut four 4 ⅜-inch x 5 ½-inch pieces for sides and one 4 ½-inch x 4 ½-inch piece for top.

3. Using plastic canvas top piece as a template, cut out center opening on felt top piece, making opening on felt slightly larger than opening on plastic canvas piece.

4. Stitch pieces following graphs. With black, Overcast inside edges of top and inside and bottom edges of sides.

5. With sewing needle and black thread, stitch felt to sides and top, trimming as necessary to allow room for Whipstitching.

6. With black, Whipstitch sides together, then Whipstitch sides to top. ❖

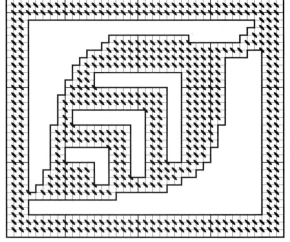

Silhouettes Leaf Side
32 holes x 38 holes
Cut 1

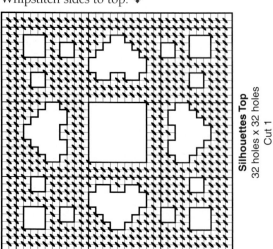

Silhouettes Top
32 holes x 32 holes
Cut 1

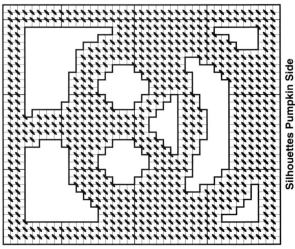

Silhouettes Pumpkin Side
32 holes x 38 holes
Cut 1

School Days Crayon Box

Design by Joan Green

Stitch this colorful tissue topper as a back-to-school surprise for your youngster! Bright yarn and cute buttons make it just right for kids of all ages!

Skill Level: Beginner

Size: Fits boutique-style tissue box

Materials

- 1¼ sheets 7-count plastic canvas
- Coats & Clark Red Heart Kids worsted weight yarn Art. E711 as listed in color key
- #16 tapestry needle
- Mill Hill Products ceramic buttons from Gay Bowles Sales:

  1 school bus #86116
  1 red crayon #86119
  1 yellow crayon #686120
  1 blue crayon #86121

- Sewing needle
- Red, yellow and blue sewing thread

Instructions

1. Cut plastic canvas according to graphs (this page and page 131).

2. Stitch pieces following graphs, working uncoded areas on crayons with black Continental Stitches.

3. When background stitching is completed, work Backstitches over black Continental Stitches on crayons.

4. Using sewing needle and matching color sewing thread, attach buttons to top where indicated on graph with blue dots.

5. Using white throughout, Overcast inside edges of top and bottom edges of sides. Whipstitch sides together, then Whipstitch sides to top. ❖

Graphs continued on page 131

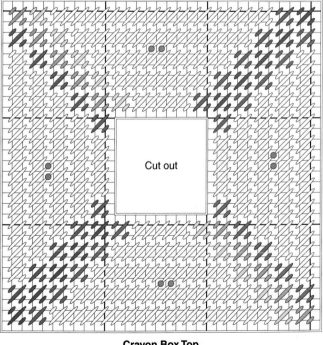

Crayon Box Top
31 holes x 31 holes
Cut 1

Mosaic Quilt

Design by Cynthia Roberts

Inspired by a favorite quilt style, this attractive tissue box cover makes a lovely gift for a needlecrafter, whether she loves sewing, quilting or plastic canvas stitching!

Skill Level: Beginner

Size: Fits boutique-style tissue box

Materials

- 1½ sheets 7-count plastic canvas
- Worsted weight yarn as listed in color key
- #16 tapestry needle

Instructions

1. Cut plastic canvas according to graphs.

2. Stitch pieces following graphs, working side A as graphed with a lavender Continental Stitch border, side B with a red Continental Stitch border, side C with a teal Continental Stitch border and side D with a yellow Continental Stitch border.

3. For inside edges on top, Overcast side A with lavender, side B with red, side C with teal and side D with yellow.

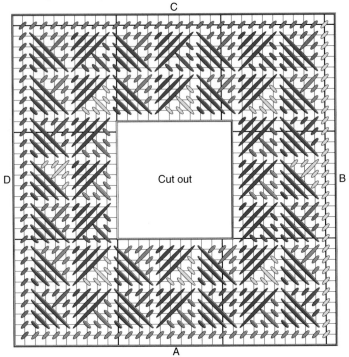

C

D — B

Cut out

A

Mosaic Quilt Top
31 holes x 31 holes
Cut 1

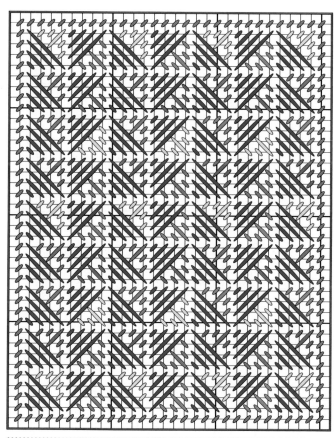

4. Using dark blue through step 5, Whipstitch sides together in alphabetical order, then Whipstitch sides A and D together; Overcast bottom edges.

5. Whipstitch sides to top, making sure to match top edges with corresponding sides. *Note: Border color on each side should match inside edge color on cover top.* ❖

COLOR KEY	
Worsted Weight Yarn	**Yards**
■ Dark blue	34
■ Lavender	10
■ Red	10
□ Yellow	10
■ Teal	10

Mosaic Quilt Side
31 holes x 39 holes
Cut 4
Stitch side A as graphed,
side B with a red Continental Stitch border,
side C with a teal Continental Stitch border,
side D with a yellow Continental Stitch border

Crayon Box

Continued from page 129

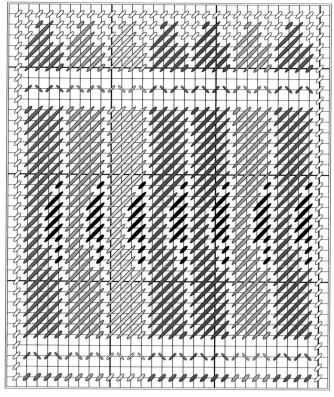

Crayon Box Side
31 holes x 36 holes
Cut 4

COLOR KEY	
Worsted Weight Yarn	**Yards**
□ White #2001	28
■ Black #2012	22
□ Yellow #2230	9
■ Orange #2252	9
■ Purple #2356	9
■ Red #2390	9
■ Green #2677	9
■ Blue #2845	9
■ Turquoise #2850	9

Uncoded areas are black
#2012 Continental Stitches
⟋ Yellow #2230 Backstitch
⟋ Orange #2252 Backstitch
⟋ Purple #2356 Backstitch
⟋ Red #2390 Backstitch
⟋ Green #2677 Backstitch
⟋ Blue #2845 Backstitch
⟋ Turquoise #2850 Backstitch
Color numbers given are for Coats & Clark
Red Heart Kids worsted weight yarn Art.
E711.

Fire Engine

Design by Christina Laws

Delight a youngster who dreams of being a firefighter with this fire-truck-shaped tissue box cover! It makes a practical decoration for any young child's room.

Skill Level: Beginner

Size: Fits regular-size tissue box

Materials

- 2 sheets 7-count plastic canvas
- Coats & Clark Red Heart Classic worsted weight yarn Art. E267 as listed in color key
- Coats & Clark Red Heart Super Saver worsted weight yarn Art. E301 as listed in color key
- #16 tapestry needle
- Hot-glue gun

Cutting & Stitching

1. Cut plastic canvas according to graphs (this page and pages 133 and 134). Cut one 36-hole x 6-hole piece for cab back, four 2-hole x 10-hole pieces for ladder holder front pieces and eight 2-hole x 2-hole pieces for ladder holder ends.

2. Continental Stitch ladder holder pieces with silver, Whipstitching one end piece to each short edge of front piece while Continental Stitching; Overcast remaining holder edges. Set aside.

3. Continental Stitch cab back with cherry red. Overcast ladders with white.

4. Stitch remaining pieces following graphs, reversing one truck side before stitching and working uncoded areas with cherry red Continental Stitches. Do not stitch bars indicated with blue lines on cab top at this time.

5. When background stitching is completed, work black Backstitches and grey heather Straight Stitches.

COLOR KEY	
Worsted Weight Yarn	**Yards**
☐ Eggshell #111	9
■ Black #312	25
■ Cherry red #319	60
☐ Bright yellow #324	1
■ Grey heather #400	4
☐ Silver #412	12
■ Olympic blue #849	4
Uncoded areas are cherry red #319 Continental Stitches	
⁄ White #311 Overcasting	5
⁄ Black #312 Backstitch	
⁄ Grey heather #400 Straight Stitch	
⁄ Attach ladder holder	
Color numbers given are for Coats & Clark Red Heart Classic worsted weight yarn Art. E267 and Red Heart Super Saver worsted weight yarn Art. E301.	

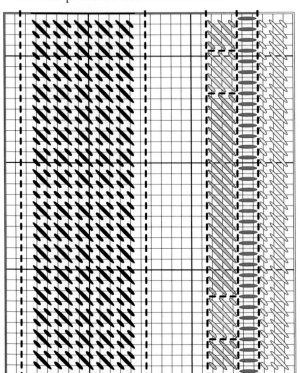

Fire Engine Front
34 holes x 28 holes
Cut 1

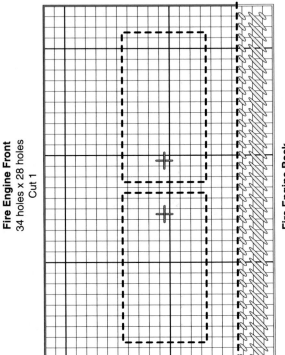

Fire Engine Back
34 holes x 22 holes
Cut 1

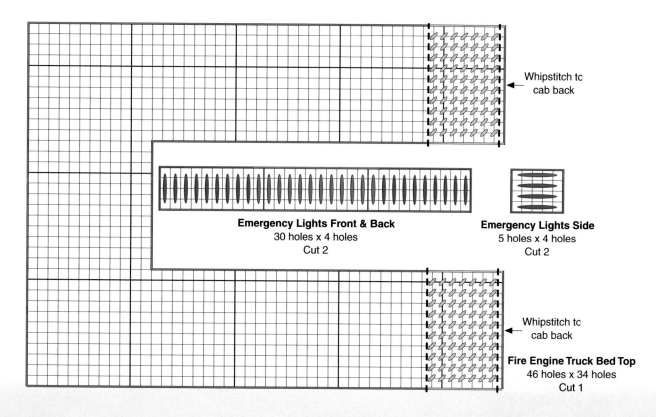

Whipstitch to cab back

Emergency Lights Front & Back
30 holes x 4 holes
Cut 2

Emergency Lights Side
5 holes x 4 holes
Cut 2

Whipstitch to cab back

Fire Engine Truck Bed Top
46 holes x 34 holes
Cut 1

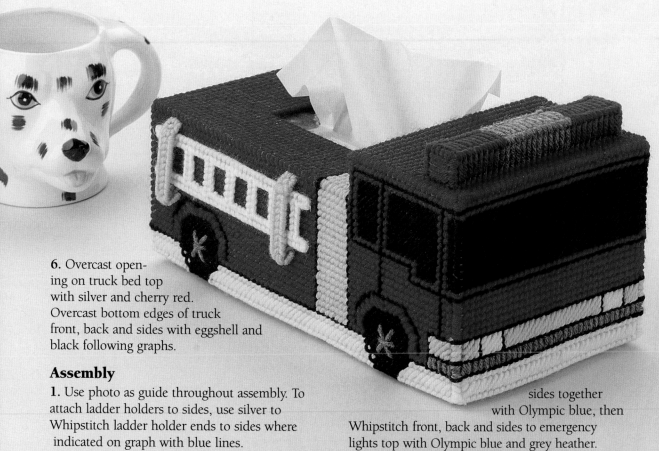

6. Overcast opening on truck bed top with silver and cherry red. Overcast bottom edges of truck front, back and sides with eggshell and black following graphs.

Assembly

1. Use photo as guide throughout assembly. To attach ladder holders to sides, use silver to Whipstitch ladder holder ends to sides where indicated on graph with blue lines.

2. For emergency lights, Whipstitch front, back and sides together with Olympic blue, then Whipstitch front, back and sides to emergency lights top with Olympic blue and grey heather. Using cherry red, Whipstitch bottom edges to cab top where indicated on graph with blue lines.

3. Following graphs, Whipstitch cab back to back edge of cab top. Whipstitch bottom edges of cab back to edges
indicated on truck bed top, Overcasting center portion on bottom edge while Whipstitching.

4. Whipstitch truck sides to truck front and back.

5. Whipstitch assembled top to front, back and sides, then work black embroidery stitches over edges where indicated on graphs.

6. Insert ladders into holders and glue to truck sides. ❖

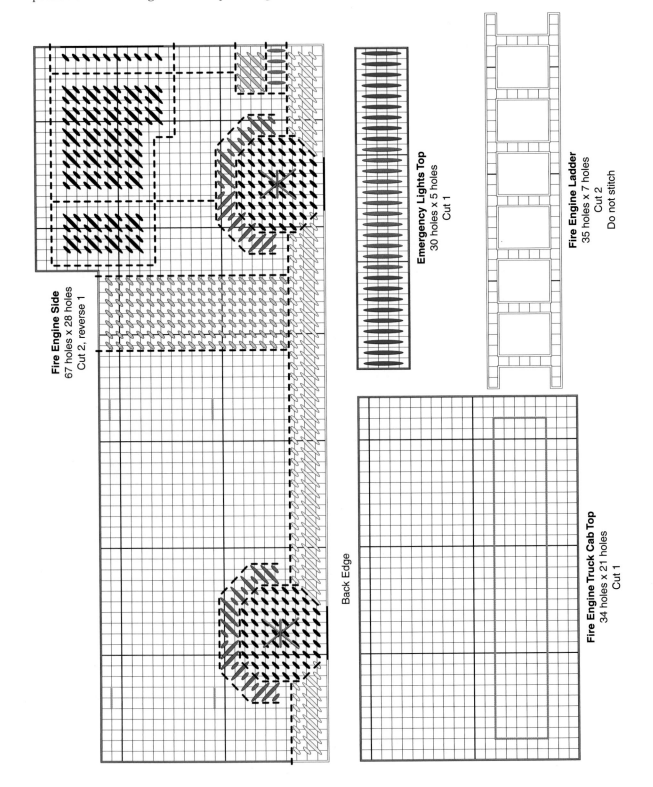

Fire Engine Side
67 holes x 28 holes
Cut 2, reverse 1

Back Edge

Emergency Lights Top
30 holes x 5 holes
Cut 1

Fire Engine Ladder
35 holes x 7 holes
Cut 2
Do not stitch

Fire Engine Truck Cab Top
34 holes x 21 holes
Cut 1

Mr. Bluebird

Design by Michele Wilcox

This charming bluebird pocket tissue holder is sure to add a cheery note to your day!

Skill Level: Beginner

Size: Fits pocket-size tissue package

Materials

- 1 sheet Uniek Quick-Count 7-count plastic canvas
- Uniek Needloft plastic canvas yarn as listed in color key
- DMC #5 pearl cotton as listed in color key
- #16 tapestry needle
- ½ yard ¼-inch-wide yellow satin ribbon
- Hot-glue gun

Instructions

1. Cut plastic canvas according to graphs.

2. Stitch pieces following graphs, working uncoded areas on front with baby blue Continental Stitches. Stitch back entirely with baby blue Continental Stitches.

3. Work black pearl cotton French Knot for bird's eye. Overcast bird pieces following graphs.

4. Using baby blue throughout, Overcast inside edges and top edges of front and back. Whipstitch wrong sides of front and back together

along remaining edges.

5. Using photo as a guide, glue bird to front.

6. For easier access, remove tissue from package before placing inside holder. Thread ribbon through holes on front and back; tie in a bow to close. ❖

COLOR KEY	
Plastic Canvas Yarn	**Yards**
■ Pumpkin #12	2
■ Royal #32	3
■ Sail blue #35	3
☐ White #41	5
☐ Yellow #57	1
Uncoded areas are baby blue #36 Continental Stitches	45
∕ Baby blue #36 Overcasting and Whipstitching	
#5 Pearl Cotton	
● Black #310 French Knot	
Color numbers given are for Uniek Needloft plastic canvas yarn and DMC #5 pearl cotton.	

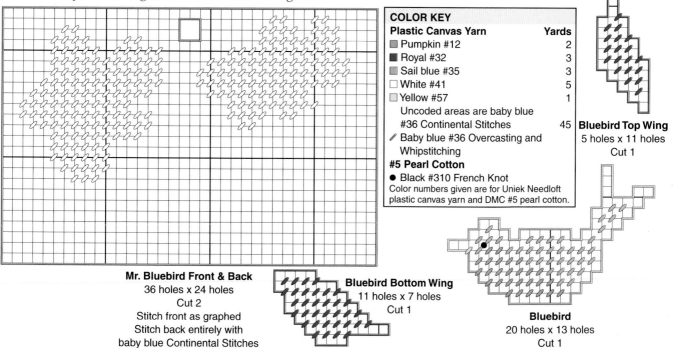

Mr. Bluebird Front & Back
36 holes x 24 holes
Cut 2
Stitch front as graphed
Stitch back entirely with
baby blue Continental Stitches

Bluebird Bottom Wing
11 holes x 7 holes
Cut 1

Bluebird Top Wing
5 holes x 11 holes
Cut 1

Bluebird
20 holes x 13 holes
Cut 1

King of the Coop

Design by Lee Lindeman

Chicken collectors will love stitching and displaying this dimensional tissue box cover featuring a very handsome rooster!

Skill Level: Beginner

Size: Fits boutique-style tissue box

Materials

- 2½ sheets 7-count plastic canvas
- Coats & Clark Red Heart Super Saver worsted weight yarn Art. E300 as listed in color key
- #16 tapestry needle
- Small amount black plastic foam
- 2 (9mm) round brown animal eyes
- Small amount fiberfill
- Hot-glue gun

Instructions

1. Cut plastic canvas according to graphs (pages 137 and 138). Cut two beaks from black craft foam using pattern given.

2. Stitch pieces following graphs, reversing one side, one head, one wing, one tail and one comb before stitching. Work uncoded areas with black Continental Stitches.

3. Overcast inside edges of top with black. Following graphs, Whipstitch front and back to sides, then Whipstitch front, back and sides to top; Overcast bottom edges.

4. Using adjacent colors throughout, Overcast wattles and wings. Overcast tail edges along straight edge from dot to dot and neck edges on head pieces along straight edge from dot to dot.

5. Use photo as a guide through step 9. Whipstitch remaining edges of head pieces together. Stuff head and neck with fiberfill, then center and glue neck to upper portion of front.

6. Whipstitch remaining edges of tail pieces together. Stuff with fiberfill; center and glue to upper portion of back.

7. Place beak pieces together, then glue to front edge of head, placing edge in indent. Glue eyes to head where indicated on graph.

8. Glue top portion of one wattle to each side of head below beak. Whipstitch wrong sides of comb

pieces together with cherry red, then glue to top of head.

9. Glue wing edges from dot to dot to sides. Stuff a small amount of fiberfill up under wings, making sure it stays hidden under wings. ❖

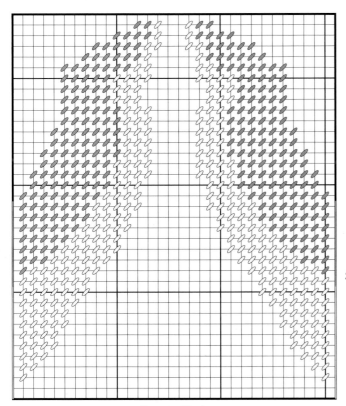

Rooster Back
31 holes x 36 holes
Cut 1

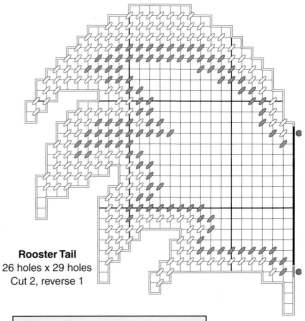

Rooster Tail
26 holes x 29 holes
Cut 2, reverse 1

COLOR KEY	
Worsted Weight Yarn	**Yards**
■ Medium clay #280	30
□ Aran #313	33
■ Cherry red #319	6
Uncoded areas are black #312	
Continental Stitches	55
╱ Black #312 Overcasting and Whipstitching	
● Attach eye	

Color numbers given are for Coats & Clark Red Heart Super Saver worsted weight yarn Art. E300.

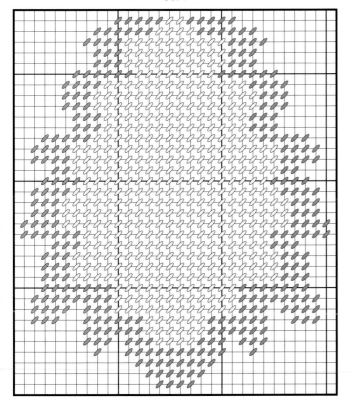

Rooster Front
31 holes x 36 holes
Cut 1

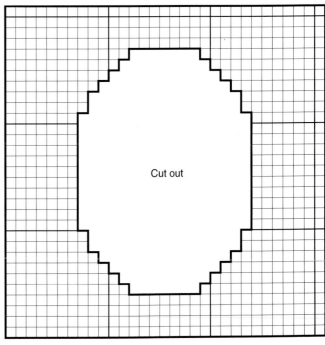

Cut out

Rooster Top
31 holes x 31 holes
Cut 1

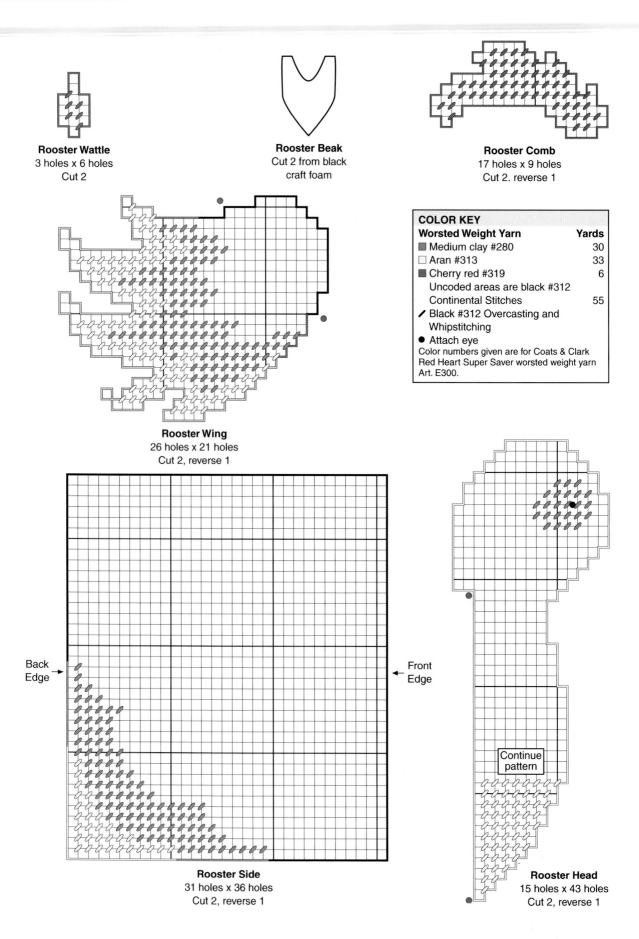

Rooster Wattle
3 holes x 6 holes
Cut 2

Rooster Beak
Cut 2 from black
craft foam

Rooster Comb
17 holes x 9 holes
Cut 2. reverse 1

Rooster Wing
26 holes x 21 holes
Cut 2, reverse 1

COLOR KEY	
Worsted Weight Yarn	**Yards**
■ Medium clay #280	30
☐ Aran #313	33
■ Cherry red #319	6
Uncoded areas are black #312	
Continental Stitches	55
✒ Black #312 Overcasting and Whipstitching	
● Attach eye	

Color numbers given are for Coats & Clark
Red Heart Super Saver worsted weight yarn
Art. E300.

Back
Edge →

← Front
Edge

Continue
pattern

Rooster Side
31 holes x 36 holes
Cut 2, reverse 1

Rooster Head
15 holes x 43 holes
Cut 2, reverse 1

African Animals

Design by Nancy Marshall

You'll almost hear the call of the wild as you stitch this unique topper depicting four African animal skins.

Skill Level: Beginner

Size: Fits boutique-style tissue box

Materials

- 1½ sheets Uniek Quick-Count 7-count plastic canvas
- Uniek Needloft plastic canvas yarn as listed in color key
- #16 tapestry needle

Instructions

1. Cut plastic canvas according to graphs (this page and page 141).

2. Stitch pieces following graphs, working uncoded areas with Black Continental Stitches.

3. Using black throughout, Overcast inside edges of top and bottom edges of sides. Whipstitch sides together, then Whipstitch sides to top. ❖

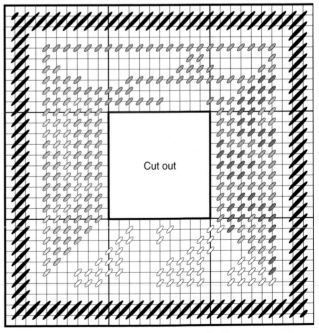

African Animals Top
30 holes x 30 holes
Cut 1

COLOR KEY	
Plastic Canvas Yarn	**Yards**
■ Black #00	44
□ Tangerine #11	6
▨ Pumpkin #12	5
▨ Maple #13	11
■ Cinnamon #14	6
▨ Sandstone #16	5
□ Flesh tone #56	6
Uncoded areas are black #00 Continental Stitches	
Color numbers given are for Uniek Needloft plastic canvas yarn.	

Graphs continued on page 141

Desert Designs

Design by Angie Arickx

Capture the distinctive look of Native American design with this Southwest tissue topper.

Skill Level: Beginner

Size: Fits boutique-style tissue box

Materials

- 1½ sheets Uniek Quick-Count 7-count plastic canvas
- Uniek Needloft plastic canvas yarn as listed in color key
- #16 tapestry needle

Instructions

1. Cut and stitch plastic canvas according to graphs.

2. Overcast inside edges of top with eggshell and bottom edges of sides with cinnamon.

3. Using cinnamon throughout, Whipstitch sides together, then Whipstitch sides to top. ❖

Desert Designs Side
31 holes x 37 holes
Cut 4

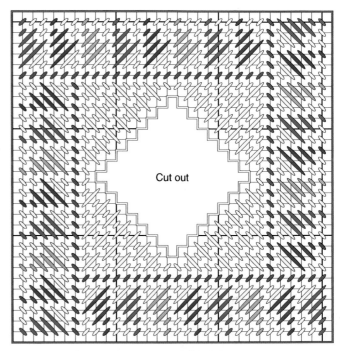

Desert Designs Top
31 holes x 31 holes
Cut 1

COLOR KEY	
Plastic Canvas Yarn	**Yards**
■ Burgundy #03	12
▨ Rust #09	12
■ Cinnamon #14	12
□ Eggshell #39	40
▨ Turquoise #54	18
Color numbers given are for Uniek Needloft plastic canvas yarn.	

African Animals

Continued from page 139

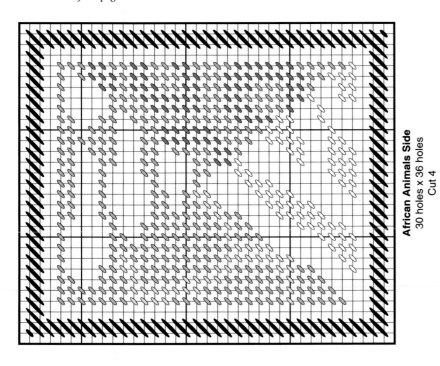

African Animals Side
30 holes x 36 holes
Cut 4

COLOR KEY	
Plastic Canvas Yarn	**Yards**
■ Black #00	44
□ Tangerine #11	6
▨ Pumpkin #12	5
▨ Maple #13	11
▨ Cinnamon #14	6
▨ Sandstone #16	5
□ Flesh tone #56	6
Uncoded areas are black #00 Continental Stitches	
Color numbers given are for Uniek Needloft plastic canvas yarn.	

Nighty-Night Bear

Design by Vicki Blizzard

*Keep this charming tissue topper close at hand in your
child's room for those occasional late night sniffles!*

Skill Level: Beginner

Size: Fits boutique-style tissue box

Materials

- 2 sheets Uniek Quick-Count 7-count plastic canvas

- Uniek Needloft plastic canvas yarn as listed in color key

- ⅛-inch-wide Plastic Canvas 7 Metallic Needlepoint Yarn by Rainbow Gallery as listed in color key

- DMC #3 pearl cotton as listed in color key

- #16 tapestry needle

- 5mm round black cabochon from The Beadery

- 84 star-shaped metal heat-set trims from Creative Crystals

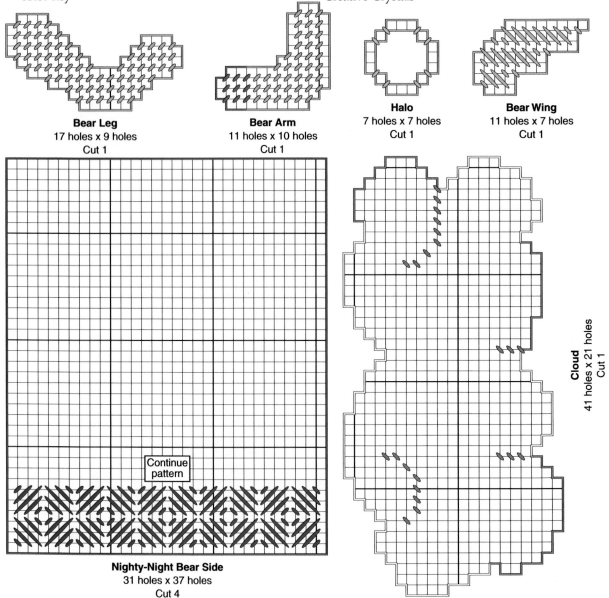

Bear Leg
17 holes x 9 holes
Cut 1

Bear Arm
11 holes x 10 holes
Cut 1

Halo
7 holes x 7 holes
Cut 1

Bear Wing
11 holes x 7 holes
Cut 1

Continue
pattern

Nighty-Night Bear Side
31 holes x 37 holes
Cut 4

Cloud
41 holes x 21 holes
Cut 1

- BeJeweler heat-set tool from Creative Crystals Co.
- Hot-glue gun

Instructions

1. Cut plastic canvas according to graphs.

2. Following graphs through step 4, stitch and Overcast halo. Stitch remaining pieces, working uncoded area with white plastic canvas yarn Continental Stitches. Fill in around opening on top with a partial dark royal pattern.

3. Using dark royal for topper pieces, Overcast inside edges of top and bottom edges of sides. Whipstitch sides together, then Whipstitch sides to top.

4. Overcast remaining pieces, then work pearl cotton embroidery.

5. Use photo as a guide through step 7. Using hot-

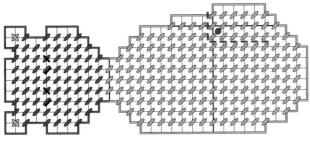

Bear
29 holes x 12 holes
Cut 1

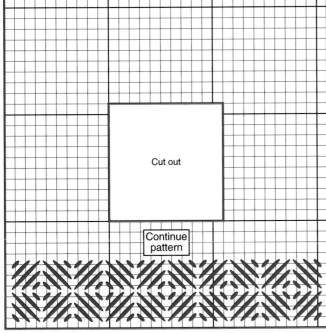

Nighty-Night Bear Top
31 holes x 31 holes
Cut 1

glue gun, glue cloud to one side near bottom edge. Glue bear body to cloud.

6. Glue muzzle to face. Glue arm to body with hand at face. Glue leg and wing to body. Glue black cabochon to muzzle for nose where indicated on graph. Glue halo to head.

7. Using heat-set tool, attach 11 stars to side above cloud, then glue 18 stars to each remaining side and 18 stars to top. Attach remaining star to halo. ❖

COLOR KEY	
Plastic Canvas Yarn	**Yards**
■ Maple #13	2
■ Moss #25	7
■ Beige #40	1
■ Lilac #45	2
■ Dark royal #48	85
Uncoded areas are white #41 Continenal Stitches	11
⁄ White #41 Overcasting	
⅛-Inch Metallic Needlepoint Yarn	
■ Gold #PC1	1
■ White pearl #PC10	1
#3 Pearl Cotton	
⁄ Black #310 Backstitch	1
⁄ Green #699 Backstitch	1
● Green #699 French Knot	
○ Attach cabochon	

Color numbers given are for Uniek Needloft plastic canvas yarn, Rainbow Gallery Plastic Canvas 7 Metallic Needlepoint Yarn and DMC #3 pearl cotton.

Bear Muzzle
5 holes x 4 holes
Cut 1

Instructions

1. Cut plastic canvas according to graphs (this page and page 146).

2. Stitch pieces following graphs, working uncoded areas on top piece and above pumpkins on sides with light blue Continental Stitches; work uncoded areas below pumpkins with rust Continental Stitches.

3. When background stitching is completed, using 4 plies yarn, work black mouth and eyes on scarecrow and tangerine beak and feet on crows. Work yellow Straight Stitches for straw hands and hair on scarecrow, going through each hole three times.

4. Using 2 plies yarn, work medium blue Straight Stitches for eyes on crows, rust Backstitches on pumpkins, red Backstitches on shirt and remainder of black Backstitches on and around scarecrow and pumpkin.

5. Overcast inside opening on top with light blue and bottom edges of sides with rust. Whipstitch sides together with light blue and rust; Whipstitch sides to top with light blue. ❖

Graphs continued on page 146

Pumpkin Patch Scarecrow

Design by Kimberly A. Suber

This friendly scarecrow is decked out in his autumn best—a green and red plaid shirt and patched pants! Stitch him to add a touch of country charm to your home.

Skill Level: Beginner

Size: Fits boutique-style tissue box

Materials

- 1½ sheets 7-count plastic canvas
- Worsted weight yarn as listed in color key
- #16 tapestry needle

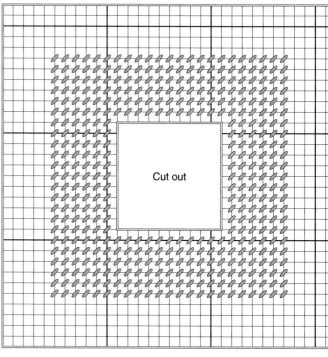

Pumpkin Patch Scarecrow Top
32 holes x 32 holes
Cut 1

Autumn Sampler

Design by Terry Ricioli

Stitched on colored plastic canvas, this tissue box cover
pictures all the bounty of the autumn harvest.

Skill Level: Beginner

Size: Fits boutique-style tissue box

Materials

- 1½ sheets beige 7-count plastic canvas
- Uniek Needloft plastic canvas yarn as listed in color key
- #16 tapestry needle

Instructions

1. Cut plastic canvas according to graphs.

2. Stitch pieces following graphs, working each leaf, pumpkin, acorn and apple separately so yarn cannot be seen behind unstitched areas.

3. Using cinnamon throughout, Overcast inside edges of top and bottom edges of sides. Whipstitch sides together, then Whipstitch sides to top. ❖

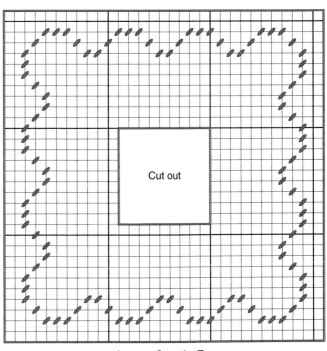

Autumn Sampler Top
31 holes x 31 holes
Cut 1

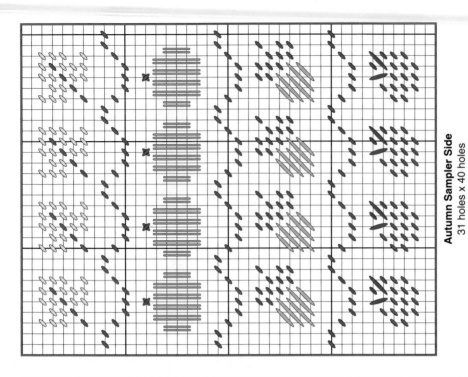

Autumn Sampler Side
31 holes x 40 holes
Cut 4

COLOR KEY	
Plastic Canvas Yarn	**Yards**
Red #01	10
Rust #09	8
Pumpkin #12	8
Maple #13	8
Cinnamon #14	35
Christmas green #28	4
Color numbers given are for Uniek	
Needloft plastic canvas yarn.	

Pumpkin Patch Scarecrow

Continued from page 144

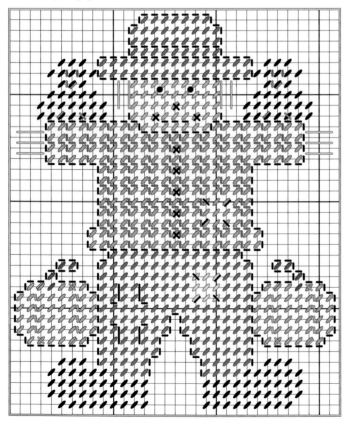

Pumpkin Patch Scarecrow Side
32 holes x 38 holes
Cut 4

COLOR KEY	
Worsted Weight Yarn	**Yards**
Bright green	12
Black	9
Medium blue	8
Bright orange	5
Yellow	5
Brown	3
Light tan	3
Red	2
Dark green	1
Uncoded areas above pumpkins and on top are light blue Continental Stitches	22
Uncoded areas below pumpkins are rust Continental Stitches	8
⁄ Light blue Overcasting and Whipstitching	
⁄ Rust Backstitch, Overcasting and Whipstitching	
⁄ Red Backstitch	
⁄ Black Backstitch and Straight Stitch	
⁄ Tangerine Straight Stitch	1
⁄ Medium blue Straight Stitch	
⁄ Yellow Straight Stitch	
● Black French Knot	

Falling Leaves

Design by Joan Green

Cool, crisp days and colorful, falling leaves are just two of the highlights of autumn! Create this seasonal project to bring autumn's glory indoors!

Skill Level: Beginner

Size: Fits boutique-style tissue box

Materials

- 1¼ sheets 7-count plastic canvas
- Coats & Clark Red Heart Classic worsted weight yarn Art. E267 as listed in color key
- ⅛-inch-wide Plastic Canvas 7 Metallic Needlepoint Yarn by Rainbow Gallery as listed in color key
- ¹⁄₁₆-inch-wide Plastic Canvas 10 Metallic Needlepoint Yarn by Rainbow Gallery as listed in color key
- #16 tapestry needle

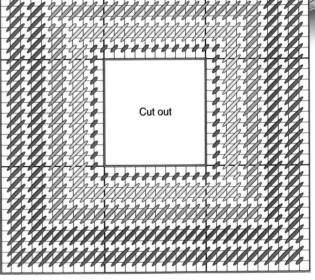

Falling Leaves Top
30 holes x 30 holes
Cut 1

Instructions

1. Cut plastic canvas according to graphs (this page and page 149).

2. Stitch pieces following graphs. Work Backstitches, Straight Stitches and French Knots when background stitching is completed.

3. Using coffee throughout, Overcast opening on top and bottom edges of sides. Whipstitch sides together, then Whipstitch sides to top. ❖

Continued on page 149

Give Thanks

Design by Michele Wilcox

This colorful tissue box cover remembers the very first Thanksgiving when the Native Americans introduced corn to the pilgrims!

Skill Level: Beginner

Size: Fits boutique-style tissue box

Materials

- 1¼ sheets Uniek Quick-Count 7-count plastic canvas
- Uniek Needloft plastic canvas yarn as listed in color key
- DMC #5 pearl cotton as listed in color key
- #16 tapestry needle
- 68 multi-colored seed beads
- 56–64 multi-colored "E" 6/0 beads
- Beading needle and white sewing thread

Instructions

1. Cut plastic canvas according to graphs.

2. Stitch pieces following graphs, working uncoded areas with eggshell Continental Stitches.

3. When background stitching is completed, work embroidery with pearl cotton.

4. Using beading needle and white sewing thread, attach seed beads to head bands and moccasins where indicated on graph.

5. Using black pearl cotton, attach "E" beads to top where indicated on graph.

6. For each necklace, thread a length of pearl cotton from back to front through one hole indicated on graph, securing on backside. String on eight to 10 beads, then thread pearl cotton through remaining hole indicated. Pull pearl cotton to desired length and secure on backside.

7. For each braid, cut three 10-inch lengths of black yarn. Place lengths together and tie at midpoint with another length of yarn. Thread ends of this length from front to back where indicated on graph and tie ends in a knot.

8. Divide the six strands into three sections; braid yarn until braid measures 1½ inches. Wrap a length of pearl cotton around bottom of braid to secure, then tack down. Cut ends ½ inch from pearl cotton.

9. Overcast inside edges on top with red. Using eggshell, Whipstitch sides together, then Whipstitch sides to top; Overcast bottom edges. ❖

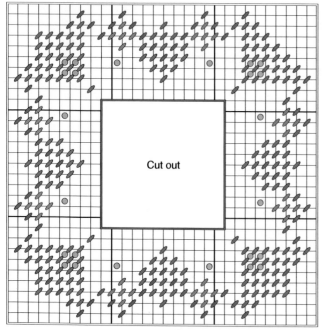

Cut 2

Give Thanks Top
30 holes x 30 holes
Cut 1

Cut out

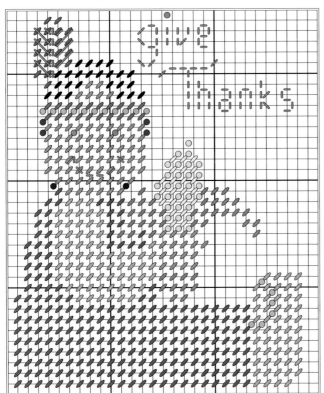

COLOR KEY

Plastic Canvas Yarn	Yards
■ Black #00	8
■ Red #01	4
■ Rust #09	6
■ Cinnamon #14	15
■ Fern #23	3
□ Yellow #57	2
■ Royal #32	4
■ Camel #43	8
Uncoded areas are eggshell #39	
Continental Stitches	45
⁄ Eggshell Overcasting and Whipstitching	

#5 Pearl Cotton

⁄ Black #310 Backstitch and Straight Stitch	
○ Variegated yellow-orange #108 French Knot	
● Black #310 French Knot	
○ Attach seed bead	
○ Attach "E" bead	
● Attach necklace	
● Attach braid	

Color numbers given are for Uniek Needloft plastic canvas yarn and DMC #5 pearl cotton.

Give Thanks Side
30 holes x 36 holes
Cut 4

Falling Leaves

Continued from page 147

COLOR KEY

Worsted Weight Yarn	Yards
■ Medium coral #252	8
■ Coffee #365	50
□ Honey gold #645	8
■ Country red #914	8
1/8-Inch Metallic Needlepoint Yarn	
■ Copper #PC3	7
■ Red #PC5	7
□ Yellow gold #PC7	7
⁄ Copper #PC3 Backstich and Straight Stitch	
⁄ Red #PC5 Backstitch and Straight Stitch	
⁄ Yellow gold #PC7 Backstitch and Straight Stitch	
1/16-Inch Metallic Needlepoint Yarn	
○ Yellow gold #PM57 French Knot	6

Color numbers given are for Coats & Clark Red Heart Classic worsted weight yarn Art. E267 and Rainbow Gallery Plastic Canvas 7 Metallic Needlepoint Yarn and Plastic Canvas 10 Metallic Needlepoint Yarn.

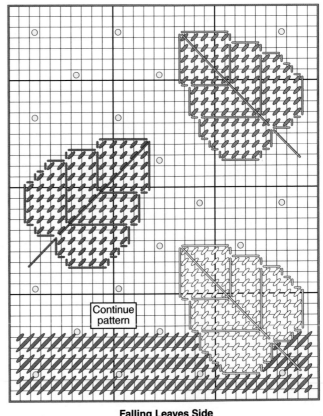

Continue pattern

Falling Leaves Side
30 holes x 37 holes
Cut 4

Winter Sparkles!

Add to your winter festivities with this collection of delightful tissue toppers! Jingle bells and Christmas lights, and snowflakes and snowmen alike will bring warmth and charm into your winter home!

Snappy Snowman

Design by Janelle Giese

Donned with his best top hat and bright red scarf,
this handsome snowman is ready for a night of holiday festivities!

Skill Level: Beginner

Size: Fits boutique-style tissue box

Materials

- 1½ sheets Uniek Quick-Count 7-count plastic canvas
- Uniek Needloft yarn as listed in color key
- DMC #3 pearl cotton as listed in color key
- #16 tapestry needle

Instructions

1. Cut plastic canvas according to graphs.

2. Stitch pieces following graphs, working uncoded areas on front with white Continental Stitches. Do not work Whipstitch lines highlighted with blue at this time.

3. When background stitching is completed, work white yarn Straight Stitches for eye highlights. Use black pearl cotton for Backstitches and Straight Stitches on face and scarf. Do not work Backstitch on scarf over blue highlighted line at this time.

4. Overcast inside edges of top with white. On front, Overcast extended edges and bottom edge following graph.

5. With right sides facing and using colors indicated, Whipstitch one side to front along one vertical Whipstitch line, using Continental Stitches where indicated. Repeat, stitching second side to front along remaining vertical Whipstitch line.

6. Work remaining black pearl cotton stitch on scarf over Whipstitch line.

7. Following instructions in step 5, Whipstitch top to front along horizontal Whipstitch line.

8. Using baby blue, Whipstitch sides together, then Whipstitch sides to top; Overcast remaining bottom edges. ❖

COLOR KEY	
Plastic Canvas Yarn	**Yards**
■ Black #00	11
■ Red #01	3
■ Christmas red #02	2
■ Royal #32	3
■ Baby blue #36	25
□ White #41	42
■ Lilac #45	1
■ Watermelon #55	1
■ Bright blue #60	2
Uncoded areas are white #41 Continental Stitches	
╱ White #41 Straight Stitch	
#3 Pearl Cotton	
╱ Black #310 Backstitch and Straight Stitch	3
Color numbers given are for Uniek Needloft plastic canvas yarn and DMC #3 pearl cotton.	

Snappy Snowman Front
43 holes x 48 holes
Cut 1

Snappy Snowman Top
30 holes x 30 holes
Cut 1

Cut out

Continue pattern

Front Edge

Continue pattern

Snappy Snowman Side
30 holes x 36 holes
Cut 3

Snowflake Quilt

Design by Angie Arickx

*Square by square, this attractive tissue box cover will remind you of all those
quiet winter nights when the snowflakes fall softly to the ground!*

Skill Level: Beginner

Size: Fits regular-size tissue box

Materials

- 2 sheets Uniek Quick-Count 7-count plastic canvas
- Uniek Needloft plastic canvas yarn as listed in color key
- #16 tapestry needle

Instructions

1. Cut and stitch plastic canvas according to graphs.

2. Using sail blue throughout, Overcast inside edges on top and bottom edges of sides. Whipstitch long sides to short sides, then Whipstitch sides to top. ❖

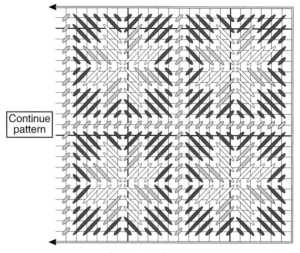

Snowflake Quilt Long Slide
66 holes x 22 holes
Cut 2

Snowflake Quilt Short Slide
33 holes x 22 holes
Cut 2

COLOR KEY	
Plastic Canvas Yarn	**Yards**
▨ Sail blue #35	34
☐ White #41	22
■ Dark royal #48	44
Color numbers given are for Uniek Needloft plastic canvas yarn.	

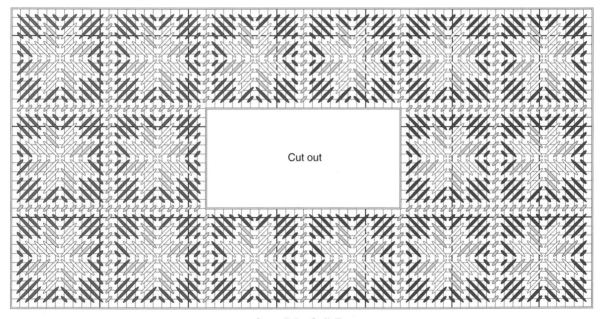

Snowflake Quilt Top
66 holes x 33 holes
Cut 1

Country Snowman

Design by Michele Wilcox

Warm up your winter home with this friendly, country snowman!
He's just right for adding a sweet, country touch!

Skill Level: Beginner

Size: Fits boutique-style tissue box

Materials

- 1¼ sheets 7-count plastic canvas
- Uniek Needloft plastic canvas yarn as listed in color key
- #5 pearl cotton as listed in color key
- #16 tapestry needle

Instructions

1. Cut plastic canvas according to graphs (this page and page 161).

2. Stitch pieces following graphs, working uncoded areas with baby blue Continental Stitches.

3. When background stitching is completed, work pearl cotton embroidery on snowmen and brooms.

4. Overcast bottom edges of sides with eggshell. Using baby blue, Overcast inside edges of top; Whipstitch sides together, then Whipstitch sides to top. ❖

Graphs continued on page 161

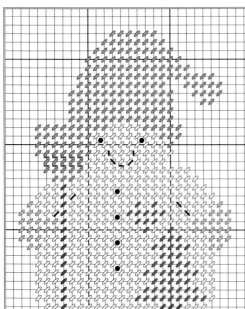

Country Snowman Side
30 holes x 36 holes
Cut 4

COLOR KEY

Plastic Canvas Yarn	Yards
■ Red #01	2
■ Tangerine #11	2
■ Cinnamon #14	2
■ Sandstone #16	5
■ Fern #23	4
■ Christmas green #28	8
□ Eggshell #39	20
■ Camel #43	4
Uncoded areas are baby blue #36 Continental Stitches	31
✎ Baby blue #35 Overcasting and Whipstitching	
#5 Pearl Cotton	
✎ Black Backstitch and Straight Stitch	3
✎ Red Backstitch	1
● Black French Knot	
Color numbers given are for Uniek Needloft plastic canvas yarn.	

Snowman With Heart

Design by Michele Wilcox

This friendly snowman will be ever-so-pleased to keep your purse tissues tidy and clean!

Skill Level: Beginner

Size: Fits purse-size tissue package

Materials

- ½ sheet 7-count plastic canvas
- Uniek Needloft plastic canvas yarn as listed in color key
- DMC #5 pearl cotton as listed in color key
- #16 tapestry needle
- ½ yard ¼-inch-wide blue satin ribbon

Instructions

1. Cut plastic canvas according to graphs.

2. Stitch pieces following graphs, working uncoded areas with sail blue Continental Stitches.

3. Work black pearl cotton French Knots on snowman when background stitching is completed.

4. Using sail blue throughout, Overcast inside edges and top edges on front and back. Whipstitch wrong sides of front and back together.

5. For easier access, remove tissue from package before placing inside holder. Thread ribbon through holes on front and back; tie in a bow to close. ❖

COLOR KEY	
Plastic Canvas Yarn	**Yards**
■ Red #01	1
▨ Pumpkin #12	1
■ Cinnamon #14	1
■ Sail blue #35	18
☐ White #41	8
Uncoded areas are sail blue #35 Continental Stitches	
#5 Pearl Cotton	
● Black #310 French knot	1
Color numbers given are for Uniek Needloft plastic canvas yarn and DMC #5 pearl cotton.	

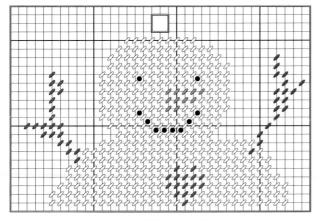

Snowman With Heart Front
36 holes x 24 holes
Cut 1

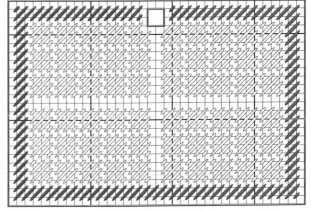

Snowman With Heart Back
36 holes x 24 holes
Cut 1

Peppermint & Poinsettias

Design by Kimberly A. Suber

At a glance, your holiday guests will think this is a specially-wrapped gift from Santa!
With its bright Christmas colors and touch of gold, it is sure to be a family favorite!

Skill Level: Beginner

Size: Fits boutique-style tissue box

Materials

- 1¼ sheets 7-count plastic canvas
- Worsted weight yarn as listed in color key
- Metallic craft cord as listed in color key
- #16 tapestry needle

Instructions

1. Cut plastic canvas according to graphs (this page and page 158.

2. Stitch pieces following graphs, working uncoded areas with green Continental Stitches.

3. Alternating red and white throughout for a striped look, Overcast bottom edges of sides and inside edges of top. Whipstitch sides together, then Whipstitch sides to top. ❖

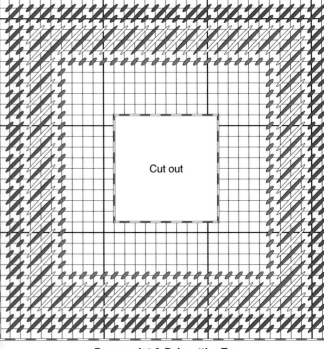

Peppermint & Poinsettias Top
32 holes x 32 holes
Cut 1

COLOR KEY	
Worsted Weight Yarn	**Yards**
■ Green	36
■ Red	21
□ White	17
▨ Medium yellow	2
Uncoded areas are green	
Continental Stitches	
Metallic Craft Cord	
■ Gold	6

Graphs continued on page 158

Christmas Gift

Design by Angie Arickx

Cover that small box of tissues with this fun and festive gift-wrap topper!

Skill Level: Beginner

Size: Fits travel-size tissue box

Materials

- 1 sheet Uniek Quick-Count 7-count plastic canvas
- Uniek Needloft plastic canvas yarn as listed in color key
- #16 tapestry needle

Instructions

1. Cut plastic canvas according to graphs (this page and page158).

2. Stitch pieces following graphs. Do not work Christmas red Backstitches at this time.

3. Using Christmas red throughout, Overcast inside edges on top. Overcast long sides on one bow piece, then Whipstitch short sides together, forming a loop. Repeat with remaining bow pieces.

4. Backstitch loops to top where indicated on graphs, working through all three layers.

5. Following graphs, Whipstitch long sides to short sides, then Whipstitch sides to top. Overcast bottom edges. ❖

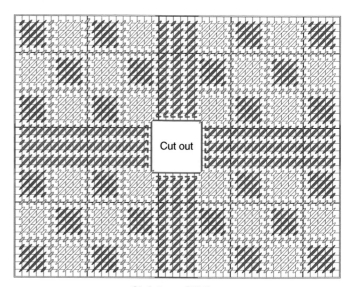

Christmas Gift Top
45 holes x 35 holes
Cut 1

COLOR KEY	
Plastic Canvas Yarn	**Yards**
■ Christmas red #02	24
☐ Fern #23	16
■ Holly #27	14
☐ White #41	14
╱ Christmas red #02 Backstitch	
Color numbers given are for Uniek Needloft plastic canvas yarn.	

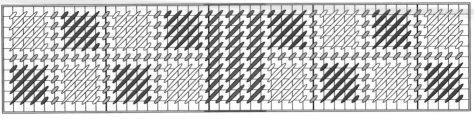

Christmas Gift Long Side
45 holes x 10 holes
Cut 2

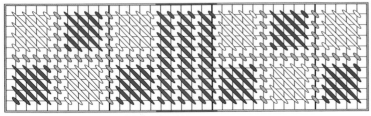

Christmas Gift Short Side
35 holes x 10 holes
Cut 2

COLOR KEY	
Plastic Canvas Yarn	**Yards**
■ Christmas red #02	24
▨ Fern #23	16
■ Holly #27	14
☐ White #41	14
✎ Christmas red #02 Backstitch	

Color numbers given are for Uniek Needloft plastic canvas yarn.

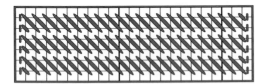

Christmas Gift Bow
23 holes x 7 holes
Cut 4

Peppermint & Poinsettias

Continued from page 156

COLOR KEY	
Worsted Weight Yarn	**Yards**
■ Green	36
■ Red	21
☐ White	17
☐ Medium yellow	2
Uncoded areas are green	
Continental Stitches	
Metallic Craft Cord	
■ Gold	6

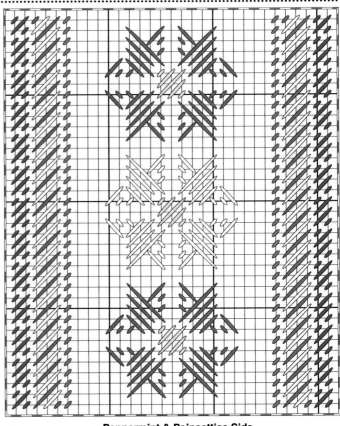

Peppermint & Poinsettias Side
32 holes x 38 holes
Cut 4

Four Seasons Window Boxes

Design by Celia Lange Designs

Celebrate the changing seasons with this charming project! With scraps of fabric and silk flowers, you can make each side a different season!

Skill Level: Beginner

Size: Fits boutique-style tissue box

Materials
- 2 sheets Darice Ultra-Stiff 7-count plastic canvas
- Coats & Clark Red Heart Classic worsted weight yarn Art. E 267 as listed in color key
- #16 tapestry needle
- 4 (9-inch x 2-inch) strips mini print fabric in color desired for each season
- Pinking shears
- Sewing needle and sewing thread
- Assorted miniature silk flowers, leaves, greenery, berries and pinecones for each season
- Sheet natural or white tissue paper
- Hot-glue gun

Instructions

1. Cut plastic canvas according to graphs (this page and pages 160 and 161).

**Four Seasons Window Box
Bottom**
27 holes x 3 holes
Cut 4

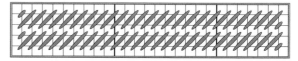

**Four Seasons Window Box
Front & Back**
27 holes x 5 holes
Cut 8

Four Seasons Window Box Side
3 holes x 5 holes
Cut 8

2. Using warm brown through step 4, stitch window frames, window box pieces and top following graphs.

3. Overcast inside edges of window frames and top. Overcast bottom edges of window frames and top edges of window box fronts, backs and sides.

4. For each window box, Whipstitch front and back to sides, then Whipstitch front, back and sides to bottom.

5. Stitch sky panels following graph, working winter panel as graphed. For spring and autumn panels, work sky with blue jewel and clouds with white only. Work summer panel entirely in light periwinkle, eliminating clouds. Do not Overcast panels.

Assembly

1. Using photo as guide throughout assembly, trim one long edge (bottom edge) of each fabric strip with pinking shears. Baste along top edge of each strip with sewing needle and sewing thread, then gather evenly.

2. Glue top edges of fabric strips to back of window frames for valances; trimming if necessary to allow room for Whipstitching.

3. Center and glue sky panels behind corresponding window frames, holding fabric in place.

4. With warm brown, Whipstitch window frames together, then Whipstitch frames to top.

5. Crumple then glue a piece of tissue paper in each window box to partially fill and provide surface to glue flowers.

6. Arrange and glue each season's flowers, greenery, etc., in a box, then glue boxes to lower part of corresponding frames. ❖

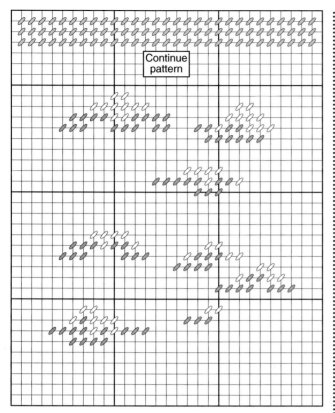

Four Seasons Sky Panel
30 holes x 37 holes
Cut 1
Stitch 1 as graphed for winter
Stitch 2 with white clouds and blue
jewel sky for spring and autumn
Stitch 1 entirely with light
periwinkle for summer

Country Snowman

Continued from page 154

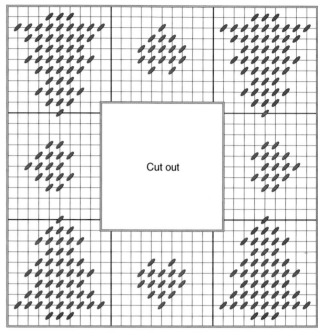

Country Snowman Top
30 holes x 30 holes
Cut 1

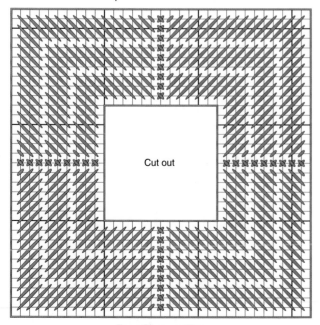

Four Seasons Top
32 holes x 32 holes
Cut 1

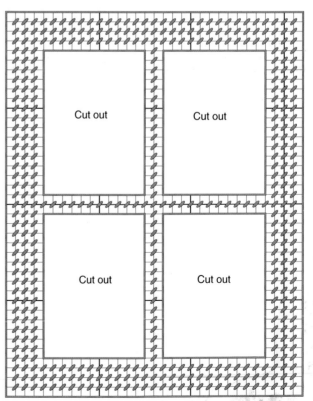

Four Seasons Window Frame
32 holes x 40 holes
Cut 4

Winter Angel

Design by Janelle Giese

You'll enjoy a spirit of peace and tranquility as you stitch this keepsake tissue box cover!

Skill Level: Intermediate

Size: Fits boutique-style tissue box

Materials

- 1½ sheets 7-count plastic canvas
- Coats & Clark Red Heart Classic worsted weight yarn Art. E267 as listed in color key
- Kreinik Medium (#16) Braid as listed in color key
- DMC #3 pearl cotton embroidery floss as listed in color key
- DMC #8 pearl cotton embroidery floss as listed in color key
- DMC 6-strand embroidery floss as listed in color key
- #16 tapestry needle

Instructions

1. Cut plastic canvas according to graphs.

2. Following graphs, stitch borders with Two-Color Herringbone Stitch (Fig. 1), working pale blue stitches first, then eggshell stitches. Work eggshell Slanting Gobelin Stitches on sides and top as indicated.

Fig. 1
Two-Color Herringbone Stitch

Work a row of pale blue stitches first,
then work a row of eggshell
stitches on top.

3. Work all remaining background stitches with Continental Stitches, working uncoded areas in corners, around angel and in center area of sides with eggshell.

4. When background stitching is completed, work Cross Stitches for cheeks with 2-strands salmon

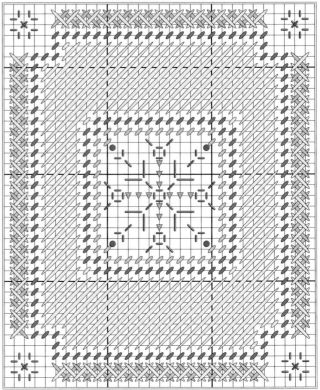

Winter Angel Side
30 holes x 36 holes
Cut 3

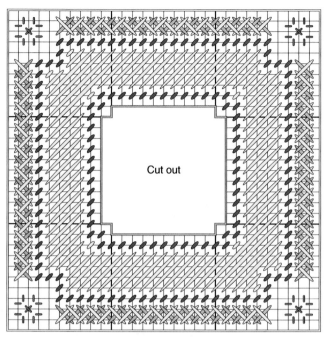

Winter Angel Top
30 holes x 30 holes
Cut 1

floss. Embroider halo and lower portion of wings with Vatican gold medium (#16) braid.

5. Stitch lower portion of wings a second time with black #8 pearl cotton, then work remaining black pearl cotton embroidery, passing over each eye six times.

6. Work white #3 pearl cotton embroidery on angel, wrapping one time for French Knots on dress and hair.

7. Work embroidery in corners and in center area of sides with very dark lavender #3 pearl cotton, wrapping one time for French Knots.

8. Overcast inside edges on top with pale blue. Using eggshell, Whipstitch front and sides together, then Whipstitch front and sides to top. Overcast bottom edges. ❖

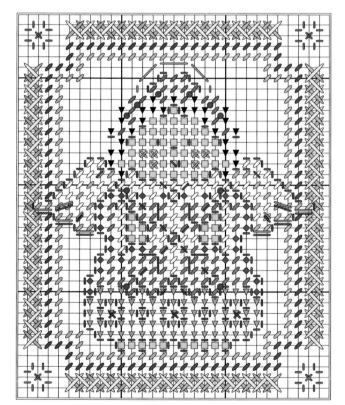

Winter Angel Front
30 holes x 36 holes
Cut 1

COLOR KEY	
Worsted Weight Yarn	**Yards**
⊘ White #1	2
▼ Black #12	1
⊘ Eggshell #111	43
▢ Sea coral #246	2
⊘ Coffee #365	1
⊘ Light plum #531	2
◆ Dark plum #533	1
▽ Light lavender #579	2
⊘ Pale blue #815	12
⊘ Country blue #882	13
Uncoded areas are eggshell #111 Continental Stitches	
Medium (#16) Braid	
⊘ Vatican gold #102 Backstitch and Straight Stitch	1
#3 Pearl Cotton	
⊘ White Backstitch and Straight Stitch	2
⊘ Very dark lavender #208 Backstitch and Straight Stitch	7
● White French Knot	
● Very dark lavender #208 French Knot	
#8 Pearl Cotton	
⊘ Black #310 Backstitch and Straight Stitch	12
6-Strand Embroidery Floss	
✕ Salmon #760 Cross Stitch	1
Color numbers given are for Coats & Clark Red Heart Classic worsted weight yarn Art. E267, Kreinik Medium (#16) Braid and DMC pearl cotton and 6-strand embroidery floss.	

Winter Maiden

Design by Janelle Giese

Beautiful, detailed stitching makes this tissue box cover simply breathtaking. Exquisitely detailed snowflakes on three sides accent the portrait of a winter maiden on the front.

Skill Level: Intermediate

Size: Fits boutique-style tissue box

Materials

- 1½ sheets 7-count plastic canvas
- Coats & Clark Red Heart Classic worsted weight yarn Art. E267 as listed in color key
- DMC #5 pearl cotton as listed in color key
- #16 tapestry needle

Instructions

1. Cut plastic canvas according to graphs.

2. Stitch pieces following graphs, working uncoded areas with pale blue Continental Stitches.

3. When background stitching is completed, use sea coral to Straight Stitch eyelids. With ultra dark coffee brown, work a Straight Stitch under each eyelid, then work mouth and hair accents. Work cameo rose pin stitch at bottom of mouth.

4. Work eye and ear of rabbit with 2 plies pale rose. Work remaining embroidery on maiden with dark steel grey, wrapping pearl cotton once around needle for French Knots.

5. Using white yarn throughout, work Straight Stitches and French Knots in center area of sides, wrapping yarn around needle once for French Knots. Work one Straight Stitch in each corner of each piece.

6. Work remaining embroidery in corners with white pearl cotton, wrapping pearl cotton twice around needle for French Knots.

7. Overcast inside edges of top with white yarn. Using light periwinkle, Whipstitch sides and front together, then Whipstitch sides and front to top; Overcast bottom edges. ❖

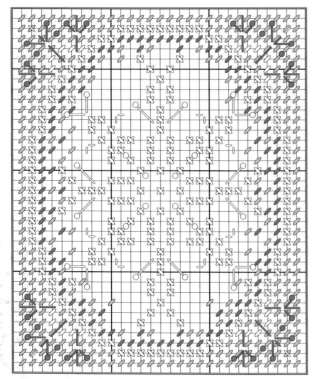

Winter Maiden Side
30 holes x 36 holes
Cut 3

Winter Maiden Front
30 holes x 36 holes
Cut 1

COLOR KEY

Worsted Weight Yarn	Yards
⬭ White #1	33
⬭ Eggshell #111	2
⬭ Sea coral #246	1
◆ Tan #334	1
▲ Warm brown #336	1
⬭ Light sage #631	1
◻ Lily pink #719	1
⬭ Pale rose #755	1
⬭ Cameo rose #759	1
⬭ Blue jewel #818	27
⬭ Light periwinkle #827	17
Uncoded areas are pale blue #815 Continental Stitches	22
⬭ White #1 Straight Stitch	
⬭ Sea coral #246 Straight Stitch	
⬭ Pale rose #755 Straight Stitch	
⬭ Cameo rose #759 Pin Stitch	
○ White #1 French Knot	

#5 Pearl Cotton

⬭ White Backstitch and Straight Stitch	13
⬭ Dark steel grey #414 Backstitch	4
⬭ Ultra dark coffee brown #938 Backstitch and Straight Stitch	
⬤ White French Knot	1
⬤ Dark steel grey #414 French Knot	

Color numbers given are for Coats & Clark Red Heart Classic worsted weight yarn Art. E267 and DMC #5 pearl cotton.

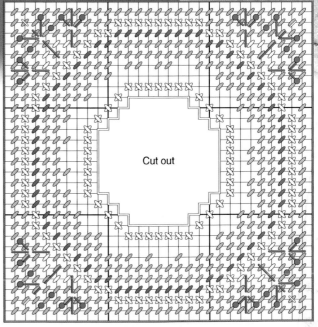

Winter Maiden Top
30 holes x 30 holes
Cut 1

Santa Bear

Design by Michele Wilcox

Stitch this sweet Santa bear tissue holder as a quick-to-stitch gift for a friend or co-worker.

Skill Level: Beginner

Size: Fits purse-size tissue package

Materials

- ½ sheet 7-count plastic canvas
- Uniek Needloft plastic canvas yarn as listed in color key
- DMC #5 pearl cotton as listed in color key
- #16 tapestry needle
- ½ yard ¼-inch-wide red plaid ribbon

Instructions

1. Cut plastic canvas according to graphs.

2. Stitch pieces following graphs, working uncoded areas with lemon Continental Stitches.

3. Work black pearl cotton Backstitches and French Knots when background stitching is completed.

4. Using holly throughout, Overcast inside edges and top edges on front and back. Whipstitch wrong sides of front and back together.

5. For easier access, remove tissue from package before placing inside holder. Thread ribbon through holes on front and back; tie in a bow to close. ❖

COLOR KEY	
Plastic Canvas Yarn	**Yards**
■ Red #01	2
■ Holly #27	30
▨ Beige #40	2
□ White 41	2
■ Camel #43	4
Uncoded areas are lemon #20 Continental Stitches	3
#5 Pearl Cotton	
╱ Black #310 Backstitch	1
● Black #310 French Knot	
Color numbers given are for Uniek Needloft plastic canvas yarn and DMC #5 pearl cotton.	

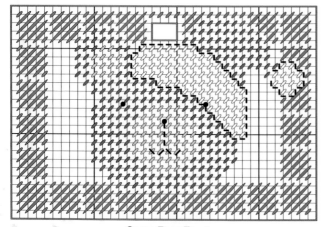

Santa Bear Front
37 holes x 25 holes
Cut 1

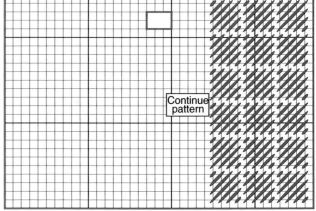

Continue pattern

Santa Bear Back
37 holes x 25 holes
Cut 1

Santa's Li'l Helpers

Design by Angie Arickx

Show off your favorite little "elves" in this picture frame tissue topper! Each side has an opening for displaying favorite photos!

Skill Level: Beginner

Size: Fits boutique-style tissue box

Materials

- 2 sheets Uniek Quick-Count 7-count plastic canvas
- Uniek Needloft plastic canvas yarn as listed in color key
- #16 tapestry needle

Instructions

1. Cut plastic canvas according to graphs..

2. Stitch pieces following graphs, working uncoded areas with Christmas green Continental Stitches.

3. Using Christmas green and white and following graphs, Overcast inside edges on sides. Using Christmas green throughout, Overcast inside edges

on top and bottom edges on sides. Whipstitch sides together, then Whipstitch sides to top.

4. Attach photos as desired. ❖

COLOR KEY	
Plastic Canvas Yarn	**Yards**
■ Christmas red #02	4
☐ White #41	4
☐ Yellow #57	12
Uncoded areas are Christmas green #28 Continental Stitches	60
╱ Christmas green #28 Overcasting and Whipstitching	
Color numbers given are for Uniek Needloft plastic canvas yarn.	

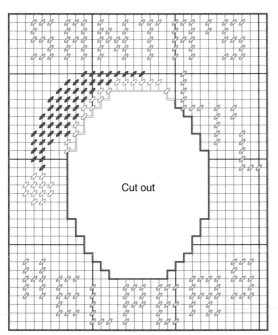

Santa's Li'l Helpers Side
31 holes x 37 holes
Cut 4

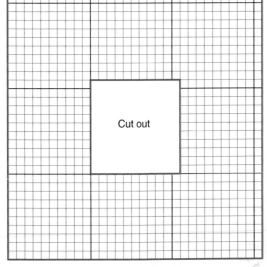

Santa's Li'l Helpers Top
31 holes x 31 holes
Cut 1

Cuddly Snowbear

Design by Nancy Dorman

Everyone loves snowmen and teddy bears! Stitch this charming project featuring a cute-as-a-button snowbear!

Skill Level: Intermediate

Size: Fits boutique-style tissue box

Materials

- 2 sheets 7-count plastic canvas
- Worsted weight yarn: 5 yards mauve and as listed in color key
- Fine metallic braid as listed in color key
- 6-strand embroidery floss as listed in color key
- #16 tapestry needle
- 28 tiny white pearl beads
- Sewing needle and white sewing thread
- Hot-glue gun

Instructions

1. Cut plastic canvas according to graphs.

2. Stitch sides and top following graphs, working Smyrna Cross borders first. Fill in center areas with blue Reversed Mosaic Stitches.

3. When background stitching is completed, work metallic silver braid Backstitches between white and blue stitching. Attach pearl beads to sides with sewing needle and white sewing thread where indicated on graph.

4. Stitch and Overcast snowbears following graph, working uncoded areas with white Continental Stitches.

5. When background stitching is completed, work black yarn French Knots for eyes and buttons. Using 6 strands black embroidery floss, work noses and mouths.

6. Stitch and Overcast brooms following graph. Work blue Straight Stitch around edges of each broom where indicated.

7. Using white and a Braided Cross Stitch throughout, Overcast inside edges on top and bottom edges of sides. Whipstitch sides together, then Whipstitch sides to top.

8. For scarves, cut 12 (15-inch) lengths of mauve yarn. Knot three lengths together about ½ inch from end and braid strands until braid measures 7 inches. Knot end and trim as desired. Repeat with remaining mauve strands to make a total of four scarves.

9. Using photo as a guide throughout, tie one scarf around each snowbear's neck and secure ends with a dab of glue. Glue broom to each snowbear. Stitch or glue one snowbear to each side. ❖

Braided Cross Stitch

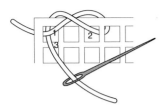

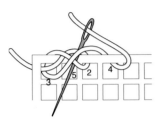

COLOR KEY	
Worsted Weight Yarn	**Yards**
■ Blue	60
□ White	60
■ Light gray	5
■ Gold	4
Uncoded areas are white	
Continental Stitches	
╱ Blue Straight Stitch	
● Black French Knot	3
Fine Metallic Braid	
╱ Silver Backstitch	10
6-Strand Embroidery Floss	
╱ Black Backstitch	1
● Black French Knot	
● Attach pearl bead	

Pulling yarn tight with each stitch,
continue by bringing needle over edge
and from back to front at 4,
over edge and from back to front at 5, etc.

Reversed Mosaic Stitch

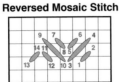

Cuddly Snowbear Broom
18 holes x 18 holes
Cut 4

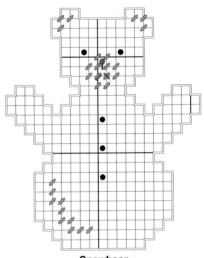

Snowbear
21 holes x 25 holes
Cut 4

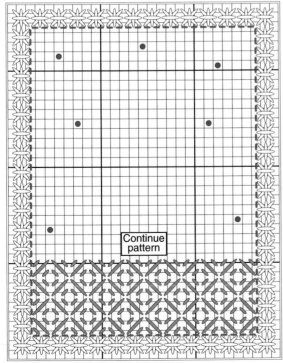

Cuddly Snowbear Side
29 holes x 37 holes
Cut 4

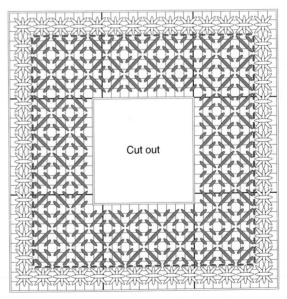

Cuddly Snowbear Top
29 holes x 29 holes
Cut 1

Christmas Wishes

Design by Roseanna Beck

What do you wish for at Christmas? A goodie-filled stocking, candy canes, candle-glow and a bell decorate this festive topper!

Skill Level: Beginner

Size: Fits boutique-style tissue box

Materials

- 2 sheets 7-count plastic canvas
- Worsted weight yarn as listed in color key
- Metallic plastic canvas yarn as listed in color key
- #16 tapestry needle
- 20 (2½-mm) round metallic gold beads
- 11 (⅞-inch) metallic green snowflake sequins
- Sewing needle and white and gold sewing thread

Cutting & Stitching

1. Cut plastic canvas according to graphs (this page and pages 171 and 173).

2. Stitch sides and top following graphs, working uncoded areas with white Continental Stitches.

3. When background stitching is completed, work

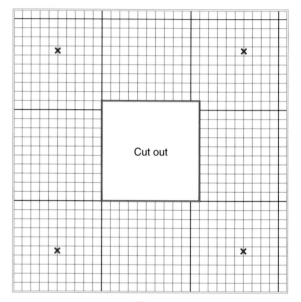

Top
31 holes x 31 holes
Cut 1

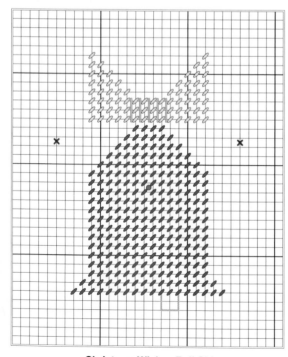

Christmas Wishes Bell Side
31 holes x 37 holes
Cut 1

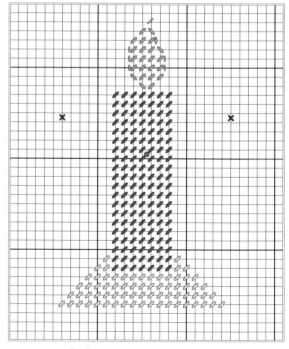

Christmas Wishes Candle Side
31 holes x 37 holes
Cut 1

Backstitches with red, white and orange worsted weight yarn and Straight Stitches with gold metallic plastic canvas yarn.

4. Stitch one candy cane following graph. Reverse remaining candy cane and stitch, reversing direction of stitches.

5. Overcast inside opening of top with red. Overcast candy canes and bottom edges of sides with white.

Continued on page 173

COLOR KEY	
Worsted Weight Yarn	**Yards**
☐ White	75
■ Red	16
■ Emerald green	16
☐ Orange	2
Uncoded areas are white Continental Stitches	
⁄ White Backstitch	
⁄ Red Backstitch	
⁄ Orange Backstitch	
Metallic Plastic Canvas Yarn	
☐ Gold	5
⁄ Gold Straight Stitch	
⊔ Attach gold beads for bell clapper	
✘ Attach snowflake and gold bead	
● Attach yarn bow	

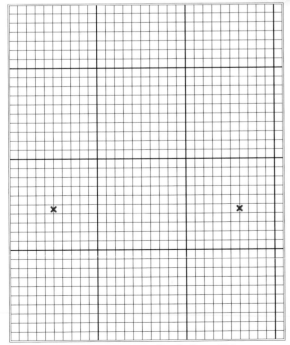

Christmas Wishes Candy Cane Side
31 holes x 37 holes
Cut 1

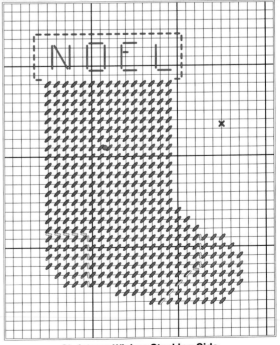

Christmas Wishes Stocking Side
31 holes x 37 holes
Cut 1

Bargello Hearts

Design by Joan Green

Stitch and share this pretty tissue topper with someone you love!
It makes a wonderful gift for anniversaries or Valentine's Day!

Skill Level: Beginner

Size: Fits boutique-style tissue box

Materials

- 1¼ sheets 7-count plastic canvas
- Coats & Clark Red Heart Super Saver worsted weight yarn Art. E300 as listed in color key
- ⅛-inch-wide Plastic Canvas 7 Metallic Needlepoint Yarn by Rainbow Gallery as listed in color key
- #16 tapestry needle

Instructions

1. Cut plastic canvas according to graphs.

2. Stitch pieces following graphs, working top with Slanting Gobelin Stitches. Work bottom two rows

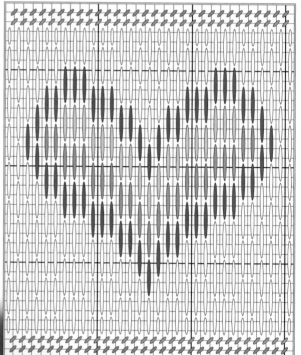

Bargello Hearts Side
31 holes x 37 holes
Cut 4

and top two rows on sides with Continental Stitches.

3. Work remainder of sides with Bargello Stitches, working soft white, raspberry and light raspberry worsted weight yarn stitches with 6 plies yarn in 1 yard lengths. When working with metallic needlepoint yarn, keep yarn smooth and flat for best coverage.

4. Overcast inside edges on top with fuchsia. Using petal pink, Whipstitch sides together, then Whipstitch sides to top; Overcast bottom edges. ❖

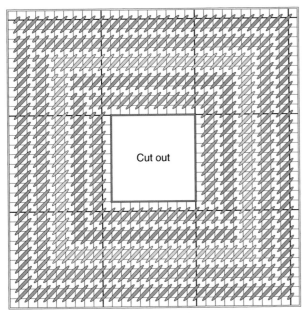

Bargello Hearts Top
31 holes x 31 holes
Cut 1

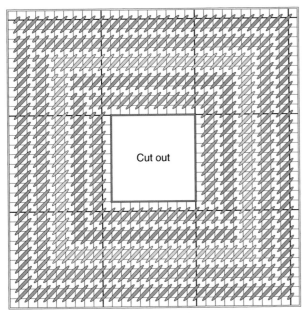

Cut out

COLOR KEY	
Worsted Weight Yarn	**Yards**
☐ Soft white #316	42
☐ Petal pink #373	10
☐ Raspberry #375	18
☐ Light raspberry #774	18
⅛-Inch Metallic Needlepoint Yarn	
☐ Fuchsia #PC13	12
Color numbers given are for Coats & Clark Red Heart Super Saver worsted weight yarn Art. E300 and Rainbow Gallery Plastic Canvas 7 Metallic Needlepoint Yarn.	

Christmas Wishes

Continued from page 171

Assembly

1. Use photos as guides throughout assembly. Using sewing needle and gold sewing thread through step 2, for bell clapper, sew a cluster of nine gold beads inside area indicated on graph.

2. Attach snowflakes and beads to top and sides where indicated on graphs by coming up from wrong side, through center of snowflake, through gold bead and back down through snowflake; knot off thread on wrong side.

3. Cut four 10-inch lengths each of emerald green and red yarn. Place two lengths of each color together and tie in a bow so there are two emerald green bows and two red bows.

4. Where indicated on graph, attach one emerald green bow to one candy cane with two or three Straight Stitches of gold metallic plastic canvas yarn. Repeat with remaining bows, attaching remaining green bow to candle and red bows to stocking and bell.

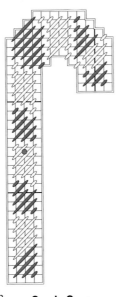

Candy Cane
12 holes x 30 holes
Cut 2, reverse 1,
reversing direction of stitches

5. Crisscross candy canes and tack together with needle and white sewing thread; center and tack candy canes to candy cane side.

6. Using white, Whipstitch sides together, so that candy canes and candle are opposite each other and stocking and bell are opposite each other. Whipstitch sides to top. ❖

Fun in the Snow

Design by Janelle Giese

The young and young-at-heart will adore this delightful tissue box cover designed with two cuddly bears building a snowbear!

Skill Level: Beginner

Size: Fits boutique-style tissue box

Materials

- 1½ sheets 7-count plastic canvas
- Coats & Clark Red Heart Classic worsted weight yarn Art. E267 as listed in color key
- DMC #5 pearl cotton as listed in color key
- DMC #8 pearl cotton as listed in color key
- DMC #12 pearl cotton as listed in color key
- #16 tapestry needle

Instructions

1. Cut plastic canvas according to graphs (this page and page 179).

2. Stitch pieces following graphs, working uncoded areas with blue jewel Continental Stitches.

3. When background stitching is completed, work medium delft blue # 8 pearl cotton Backstitches in corners. Work light periwinkle yarn Straight Stitches for each bird's scarf.

Continued on page 179

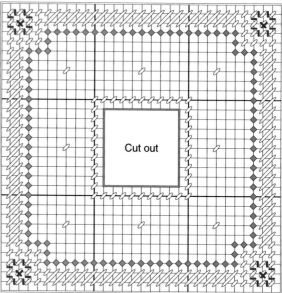

Fun in the Snow Top
30 holes x 30 holes
Cut 1

COLOR KEY	
Worsted Weight Yarn	**Yards**
⊘ White #1	35
⬦ Teal #48	1
⊘ Yellow #230	1
⊘ Tan #334	1
◆ Warm brown #336	1
⬦ Nickel #401	1
▽ Peacock green #508	1
△ Honey gold #645	1
⊘ Pale blue #815	2
◆ Light periwinkle #827	10
△ Country red #914	2
⬦ Cardinal #917	1
Uncoded areas are blue jewel #37 Continental Stitches	37
╱ Light periwinkle #827 Straight Stitch	
#5 Pearl Cotton	
╱ Black #310 Backstitch and Straight Stitch	7
● Black #310 French Knot	
#8 Pearl Cotton	
╱ Medium delft blue #799 Backstitch	5
#12 Pearl Cotton	
╱ Black #310 Backstitch and Straight Stitch	1
Color numbers given are for Coats & Clark Red Heart Classic worsted weight yarn Art. E267 and DMC pearl cotton.	

Winter Rabbit

Design by Janelle Giese

Can you see the rabbit with his pure white fur? Creative stitchers will enjoy creating and displaying this artistic tissue box cover.

Skill Level: Beginner

Size: Fits boutique-style tissue box

Materials

- 1½ sheets Uniek Quick-Count 7-count plastic canvas
- Uniek Needloft plastic canvas yarn as listed in color key
- Kreinik Heavy (#32) Braid as listed in color key
- DMC 6-strand embroidery floss as listed in color key
- DMC #3 pearl cotton as listed in color key
- DMC #5 pearl cotton as listed in color key
- #16 tapestry needle
- Sharp needle

COLOR KEY	
Plastic Canvas Yarn	**Yards**
☐ Sandstone #16	1
☐ Baby blue #36	23
■ Silver #37	19
☐ Gray #38	1
☐ White #41	45
☐ Orchid #44	1
Uncoded areas are white #41 Continental Stitches	
Heavy (#32) Braid	
☐ Vatican gold #102	22
⟋ Vatican gold #102 Backstitch and Straight Stitch	
○ Vatican gold #102 French Knot	
#3 Pearl Cotton	
⟋ Medium pistachio green #320 Straight Stitch	1
⟋ Medium beige brown #840 Backstitch	1
● Light shell pink #223 French Knot	1
#5 Pearl Cotton	
⟋ Dark steel grey #414 Backstitch and Straight Stitch	3
6-Strand Embroidery Floss	
⟋ White Straight Stitch	1
Color numbers given are for Uniek Needloft plastic canvas yarn, Kreinik Heavy (#32) Braid and DMC pearl cotton and 6-strand embroidery floss.	

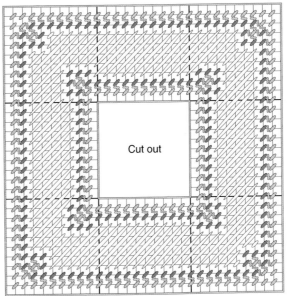

Cut out

Winter Rabbit Top
30 holes x 30 holes
Cut 1

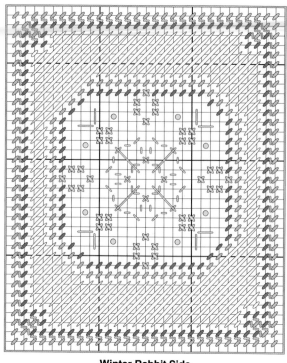

Winter Rabbit Side
30 holes x 36 holes
Cut 3

Winter Rabbit Front
30 holes x 36 holes
Cut 1

Instructions

1. Cut plastic canvas according to graphs (this page and page 175).

2. Stitch pieces following graphs, working uncoded areas on front and in center of sides with white Continental Stitches.

3. When background stitching is completed, work French Knot for eye on rabbit using light shell pink, wrapping pearl cotton two times around needle. For eye highlight, using sharp needle and four strands white floss, bring needle up outside eye and pierce into center of French Knot.

4. Use a double strand of medium pistachio green pearl cotton to Straight Stitch leaves; use one strand for remaining pearl cotton embroidery.

5. For heavy (#32) braid embroidery, work Backstitches first, then Straight Stitches over Backstitches on sides. Wrap braid one time around needle for French Knots.

6. Using baby blue throughout, Overcast inside edges of top and bottom edges of front and sides. Whipstitch front and sides together, then Whipstitch front and sides to top. ❖

COLOR KEY	
Plastic Canvas Yarn	**Yards**
☐ Sandstone #16	1
☐ Baby blue #36	23
■ Silver #37	19
■ Gray #38	1
☐ White #41	45
☐ Orchid #44	1
Uncoded areas are white	
#41 Continental Stitches	
Heavy (#32) Braid	
☐ Vatican gold #102	22
╱ Vatican gold #102 Backstitch	
and Straight Stitch	
○ Vatican gold #102 French Knot	
#3 Pearl Cotton	
╱ Medium pistachio green	
#320 Straight Stitch	1
╱ Medium beige brown	
#840 Backstitch	1
● Light shell pink #223 French Knot	1
#5 Pearl Cotton	
╱ Dark steel grey #414	
Backstitch and Straight Stitch	3
6-Strand Embroidery Floss	
╱ White Straight Stitch	1
Color numbers given are for Uniek Needloft plastic canvas yarn, Kreinik Heavy (#32) Braid and DMC pearl cotton and 6-strand embroidery floss.	

Silent Night Nativity

Design by Alida Macor

Remember that most special night in Bethlehem with this nativity-scene tissue box cover featuring Joseph, Mary and Baby Jesus.

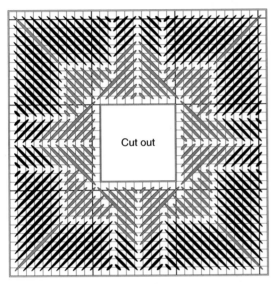

Nativity Top
31 holes x 31 holes
Cut 1

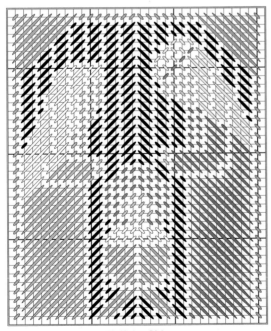

Nativity Side
31 holes x 37 holes
Cut 4

Skill Level: Beginner

Size: Fits boutique-style tissue box

Materials

- 1½ sheets 7-count plastic canvas
- Darice Nylon Plus plastic canvas yarn as listed in color key
- Worsted weight yarn as listed in color key
- Darice metallic cord as listed in color key
- #16 tapestry needle

Instructions

1. Cut plastic canvas according to graphs.

2. Stitch pieces following graphs, working black background last.

3. Overcast inside edges on top with white/gold.

Using flesh tone throughout, Whipstitch sides together, then Whipstitch sides to top. Overcast bottom edges. ❖

COLOR KEY	
Plastic Canvas Yarn	**Yards**
☐ White #01	7
▨ Dusty rose #12	10
▨ Flesh tone #14	20
☐ Lemon #25	4
▨ Baby green #28	8
▨ Avocado #30	1
Worsted Weight Yarn	
■ Black	27
☐ Peach	4
Metallic Cord	
■ White/gold #34021-149	10
Color numbers given are for Darice Nylon Plus plastic canvas yarn and metallic cord.	

Victorian Valentine

Design by Susan Leinberger

Whether stitched for a loved one, or simply for yourself, this pretty project is sure to add a touch of Victorian charm to the home!

Skill Level: Intermediate

Size: Fits boutique-style tissue box

Materials

- 1½ sheets Uniek Needloft 7-count plastic canvas
- Uniek Needloft plastic canvas yarn as listed in color key
- ¼-inch-wide satin ribbon as listed in color key
- #16 tapestry needle

Instructions

1. Cut and stitch plastic canvas according to graphs.

2. When background stitching is completed, work Lazy Daisy Stitches with green satin ribbon, then work each rose with 1 yard burgundy ribbon following Fig. 1.

**Fig. 1
Rose Stitch**

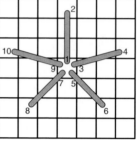
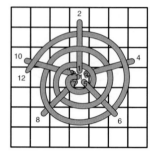

First, work five spokes from the same center hole. Next, bring needle up through center hole and begin weaving over and under spokes, keeping tension slightly loose. Continue weaving from center out until all spokes are covered. Draw ribbon slightly, so ribbon will resemble petals. Bring needle to backside and fasten off.

COLOR KEY	
Plastic Canvas Yarn	**Yards**
■ Burgundy #03	38
□ White #41	20
▨ Orchid #44	16
¼-Inch-Wide Satin Ribbon	
✎ Burgundy Rose Stitch	4
ᴑ Green Lazy Daisy Stitch	2
Color numbers given are for Uniek Needloft plastic canvas yarn.	

3. Using burgundy yarn throughout, Overcast inside edges of top and bottom edges of sides. Whipstitch sides together, then Whipstitch sides to top. ❖

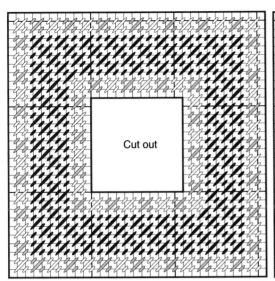

Cut out

Victorian Valentine Top
31 holes x 31 holes
Cut 1

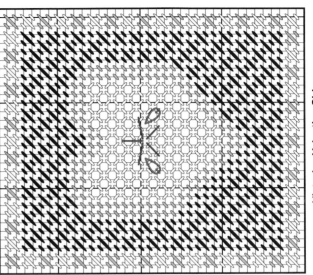

Victorian Valentine Side
31 holes x 37 holes
Cut 4

Fun in the Snow

Continued from page 174

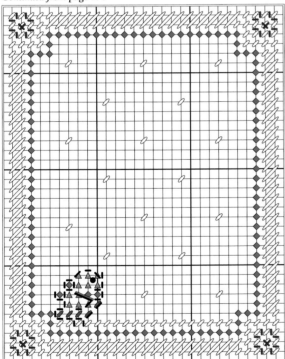

Fun in the Snow Side
30 holes x 37 holes
Cut 3

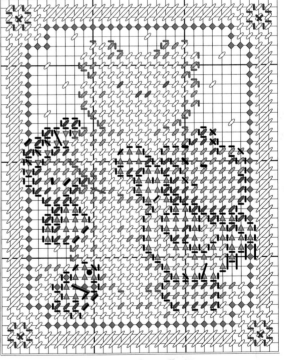

Fun in the Snow Front
30 holes x 37 holes
Cut 1

4. Work black #12 pearl cotton Backstitches to outline and accent snowman.

5. Work remaining embroidery with black #5 pearl cotton passing over eyes and noses on bears four times. ***Note:*** *Eyes and noses are the thicker black embroidery lines on bears' faces.*

Work French Knots for birds' eyes wrapping pearl cotton one time.

6. Overcast inside edge of top with light periwinkle. Using white, Whipstitch sides and front together, then Whipstitch front and sides to top; Overcast bottom edges. ❖

Holiday Bells

Design by Susan Leinberger

A row of gold jingle bells adds an extra festive touch to this merry tissue box cover!

Skill Level: Beginner

Size: Fits regular-size tissue box

Materials

- 2 sheets Uniek Needloft 7-count plastic canvas
- Uniek Needloft plastic canvas yarn as listed in color key
- Uniek Needloft solid metallic craft cord as listed in color key
- #16 tapestry needle
- #18 tapestry needle
- 2 yards ¼-inch-wide gold metallic ribbon
- 20 (½-inch) gold jingle bells
- Hot-glue gun

Instructions

1. Cut plastic canvas according to graphs.

2. Using #16 tapestry needle, stitch pieces following graphs, working uncoded areas with holly Continental Stitches.

3. For holly border on top piece, work three Straight Stitches, then draw them together in the center with a horizontal tie-down stitch. Repeat until border is completed.

4. Overcast edges of small openings around top with red, then work Backstitches around these openings.

5. Using holly and #18 tapestry needle, attach jingle bells to sides by working first stitch of Cross Stitch, then threading on jingle bell when working second stitch.

6. Cut a 25-inch length of gold metallic ribbon. Glue one end to wrong side of top beside opening A. Keeping ribbon smooth and flat, thread ribbon

COLOR KEY	
Plastic Canvas Yarn	**Yards**
■ Red #01	47
Uncoded areas are holly #27 Continental Stitches	
╱ Red #01 Backstitch	
╱ Holly #27 Straight Stitch and Overcasting	47
Solid Metallic Craft Cord	
□ Solid gold #55020	20
✖ Attach jingle bell	
Color numbers given are for Uniek Needloft plastic canvas yarn and solid metallic craft cord.	

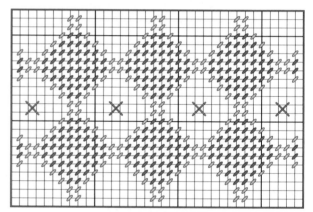

Holiday Bells Short Side
35 holes x 23 holes
Cut 2

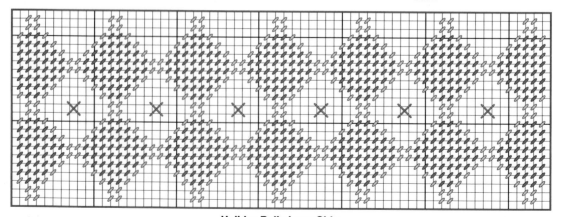

Holiday Bells Long Side
65 holes x 23 holes
Cut 2

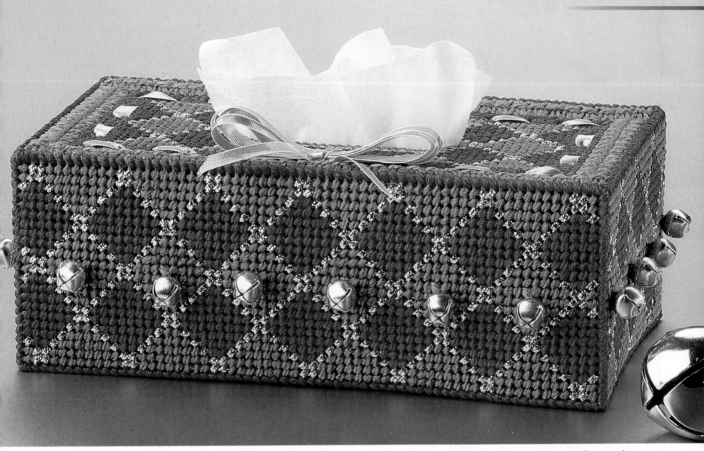

up through opening A to front and down through opening B to back.

7. Continue weaving ribbon through all openings until starting point is reached. Trim end if necessary and glue to backside.

8. Overcast tissue opening on top with holly. Using red throughout, Whipstitch long sides to short sides, then Whipstitch sides to top. Overcast bottom edges.

9. Make a multi-looped bow with remaining ribbon, trimming ends as desired. Glue to top, referring to photo for placement. ❖

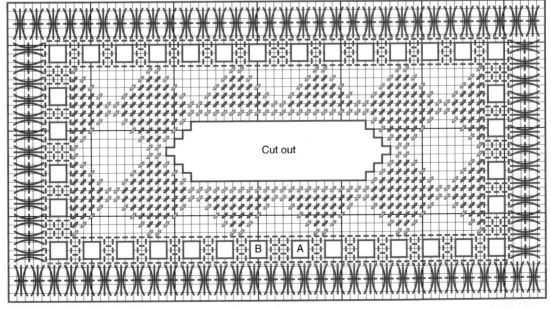

Holiday Bells Top
65 holes x 35 holes
Cut 1

Christmas Lights

Design by Ruby Thacker

*Stitched with metallic yarn, this strand of Christmas lights
will always add sparkle and light to your home!*

Skill Level: Beginner

Size: Fits boutique-style tissue box

Materials

- 1¼ sheets 7-count plastic canvas
- Uniek Needloft plastic canvas yarn as listed in color key
- Metallic craft cord as listed in color key
- #16 tapestry needle

Instructions

1. Cut plastic canvas according to graphs (this page and page 184).

2. Stitch pieces following graphs. For light bulbs, stitch four with red as graphed, three each with magenta, royal blue, gold and silver, two each with teal and purple and one each with green and yellow.

3. Using white throughout, Overcast inside edges of top and bottom edges of sides. Whipstitch sides together.

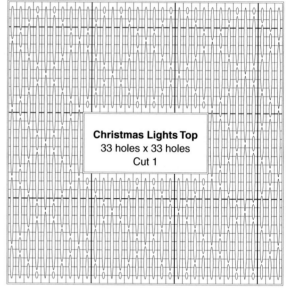

Christmas Lights Top
33 holes x 33 holes
Cut 1

COLOR KEY

Plastic Canvas Yarn	Yards
■ Forest #29	14
□ White #41	56
⌀ Forest #29 Chain Stitch	
Metallic Craft Cord	
■ Red	4
Royal blue	3
Magenta	3
Gold	3
Silver	3
Teal	2
Purple	2
Green	1
Yellow	1

Color numbers given are for Uniek Needloft plastic canvas yarn.

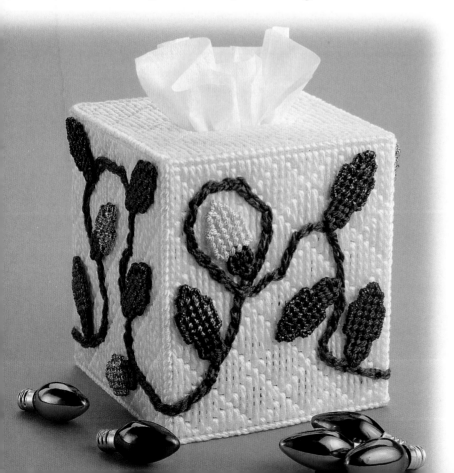

4. For Christmas lights wire, work forest Chain Stitches on sides in the following order: side A, side B, side A and side B, working stitches over edges and connecting the last stitch on side B to the beginning stitch on side A.

5. Whipstitch top to sides with white.

6. Glue bulbs as desired to sides, placing bottom edge of each bulb on wire. ❖

Graphs continued on page 184

Sparkling Ornaments

Design by Joan Green

Rich with texture and color, this gorgeous project has a dimensional ornament on each side accented with touches of gold!

Skill Level: Beginner

Size: Fits boutique-style tissue box

Materials

- 1½ sheets 7-count plastic canvas
- Coats & Clark Red Heart Super Saver worsted weight yarn Art. E301 as listed in color key
- ⅛-inch-wide Plastic Canvas 7 Metallic Needlepoint Yarn by Rainbow Gallery as listed in color key
- ¹⁄₁₆-inch-wide Plastic Canvas 10 Metallic Needlepoint Yarn by Rainbow Gallery as listed in color key
- #16 tapestry needle
- 152 (3mm) gold round beads
- Sewing needle and gold sewing thread
- 4 (3-inch x 3-inch) squares lightweight batting

Instructions

1. Cut plastic canvas according to graphs (this page and page 184).

2. Stitch pieces following graphs, working uncoded areas with royal Continental Stitches. Do not stitch area indicated on each side.

3. When background stitching is completed, work embroidery with ¹⁄₁₆-inch-wide gold metallic yarn and ⅛-inch-wide fuchsia metallic yarn.

4. Using sewing needle and gold thread, attach gold beads to ornaments where indicated on graph.

5. Overcast ornaments and inside

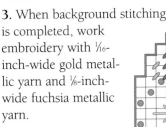

Sparkling Ornament
19 holes x 24 holes
Cut 4

COLOR KEY	
Worsted Weight Yarn	**Yards**
■ Burgundy #376	46
Uncoded areas are royal #385	
Continental Stitches	28
⅛-Inch Metallic Needlepoint Yarn	
■ Gold #PC1	12
■ Navy #PC6	10
■ Fuchsia #PC13	11
○ Fuchsia #PC13 French Knot	
¹⁄₁₆-Inch Metallic Needlepoint Yarn	
✎ Gold #PM51 Backstitch and Straight Stitch	22
○ Gold #PM51 French Knot	
● Attach gold bead	
Color numbers given are for Coats & Clark Red Heart Super Saver worsted weight yarn Art. E301 and Rainbow Gallery Plastic Canvas 7 Metallic Needlepoint Yarn and Plastic Canvas 10 Metallic Needlepoint Yarn.	

edges of top with ⅛-inch-wide gold metallic yarn

6. To attach one ornament to each side, fold a square of batting in half twice. Sandwich folded batting between ornament and unstitched portion of side. Using ⅛-inch-wide gold metallic yarn, tack ornament to side, taking a stitch every ½ inch around entire ornament.

7. Using burgundy throughout and being careful not to poke French Knots through to wrong side, Whipstitch sides together, then Whipstitch sides to top. Overcast bottom edges. ❖

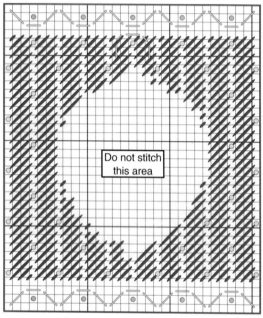

Sparkling Ornaments Side
31 holes x 36 holes
Cut 4

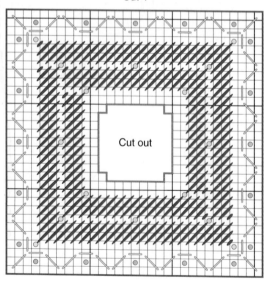

Sparkling Ornaments Top
31 holes x 31 holes
Cut 1

Christmas Lights

Continued from page 182

Christmas Lights Bulb
5 holes x 11 holes
Cut 22
Stitch 4 as graphed;
3 each with magenta,
royal blue, gold, and silver;
2 each with teal and purple;
1 each with green and yellow

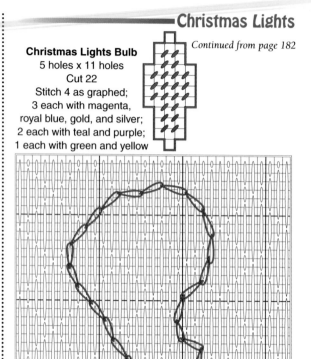

Christmas Lights Side A
33 holes x 37 holes
Cut 2

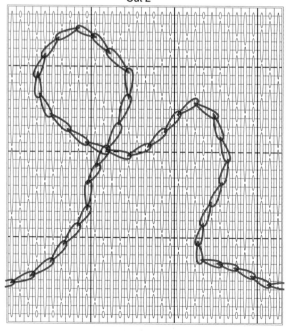

Christmas Lights Side B
33 holes x 37 holes
Cut 2

Rudolph

Design by Christina Laws

*Your children will be especially delighted with this lovable tissue
box cover! With his sparkling eyes and bright red nose,
Rudolph will make your holiday wishes come true!*

Skill Level: Intermediate

Size: Fits boutique-style tissue box

Materials

- 2 sheets 7-count plastic canvas
- Worsted weight yarn as listed in color key
- Metallic craft cord as listed in color key
- #16 tapestry needle
- Hot-glue gun

Instructions

1. Cut plastic canvas according to graphs.

2. Following graphs through step 5, stitch cover front from bottom to blue Whipstitch line, leaving blue line unworked at this time. Turn front piece over and stitch back of head and antlers above blue line.

3. Stitch cover back, leaving blue Whipstitch line unworked at this time.

4. Stitch cover sides, cover top, nose, head front and tail front working uncoded area on head front with brown Continental Stitches.

5. When background stitching is completed, work white Straight Stitches on Rudolph's eyes and gold Straight Stitches on cover sides.

6. Overcast nose with red, inside edges of top with burgundy and bottom edges of cover front, back

COLOR KEY	
Worsted Weight Yarn	**Yards**
■ Brown	47
■ Burgundy	18
■ Black	9
■ Tan	8
■ Green	5
□ White	2
■ Red	1
Uncoded areas are brown Continental Stitches	
⁄ White Straight Stitch	
Metallic Craft Cord	
⁄ Gold Straight Stitch	2

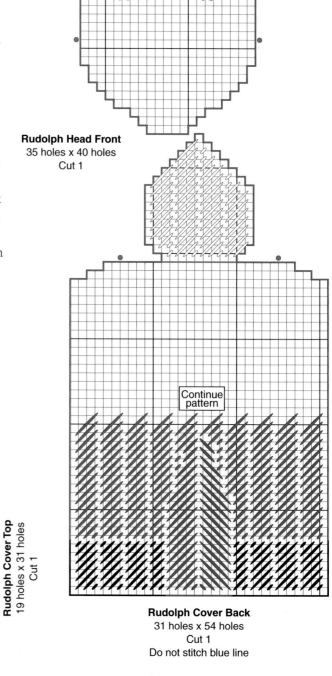

Rudolph Head Front
35 holes x 40 holes
Cut 1

Continue pattern

Rudolph Cover Back
31 holes x 54 holes
Cut 1
Do not stitch blue line

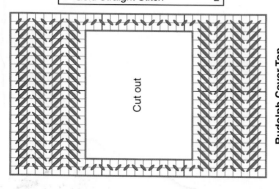

Rudolph Cover Top
19 holes x 31 holes
Cut 1

Cut out

and sides with black and green. Overcast around side and bottom edges of head front from dot to dot with brown.

Assembly

1. Use photo as guide throughout assembly. Using brown through step 3, Whipstitch wrong sides of tail front and tail back together around sides and top.

2. Whipstitch one short edge of top to cover back along top edge/Whipstitch line between blue dots, catching bottom edge of tail front along blue line while stitching.

3. Whipstitch remaining short edge of top to cover front along Whipstitch line.

4. Using brown and burgundy and following graphs, Whipstitch top

edges of cover sides to long edges of cover top with brown and burgundy.

5. Following graphs, Whipstitch front and back to sides with brown and black, easing edges around top curves

6. Matching edges and using brown and tan, Whipstitch wrong sides of head front and back together along remaining unstitched edges.

7. Glue lower portion of head front to cover front. Glue nose to center bottom of head. ❖

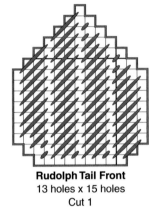

Rudolph Tail Front
13 holes x 15 holes
Cut 1

Rudolph Nose
7 holes x 7 holes
Cut 1

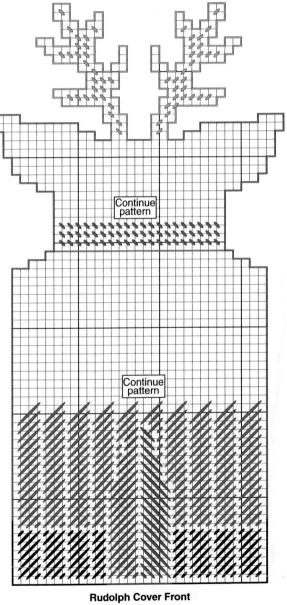

Rudolph Cover Front
35 holes x 68 holes
Cut 1
Stitch up to blue line
turn over and stitch above blue line
Do not stitch blue line

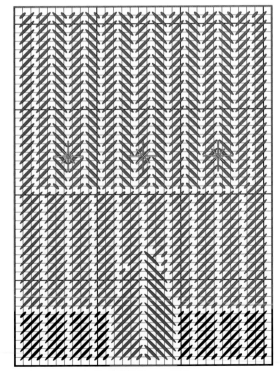

Rudolph Cover Side
31 holes x 42 holes
Cut 2

Star of David

Design by Mary K. Perry

Share this golden star of David inspirational tissue topper with a friend of Jewish heritage.

Skill Level: Beginner

Size: Fits boutique-style tissue box

Materials

- 1½ sheets 7-count plastic canvas
- Worsted weight yarn as listed in color key
- 2mm GlissenGloss Braid Ribbon 2 by Source Marketing as listed in color key
- #16 tapestry needle

Instructions

1. Cut and stitch plastic canvas according to graphs.

2. When background stitching is completed, work each Star of David with dark gold Straight Stitches.

3. Using dark blue throughout, Overcast inside edges on top and bottom edges of sides. Whipstitch sides together, then Whipstitch sides to top. ❖

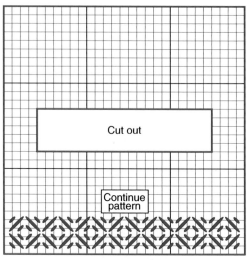

Star of David Top
29 holes x 29 holes
Cut 1

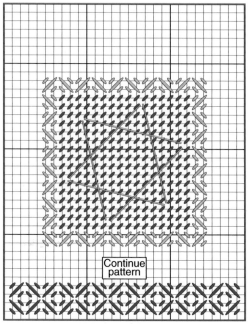

Star of David Side
29 holes x 37 holes
Cut 4

COLOR KEY	
Worsted Weight Yarn	**Yards**
■ Dark blue	64
2mm Braid Ribbon	
▨ Dark gold #9201	9
⁄ Dark gold #9201 Straight Stitch	
Color numbers given are for 2mm GlissenGloss Braid Ribbon 2 by Source Marketing.	

Lion & Lamb

Design by Mary K. Perry

This tissue box anticipates the promised time when the earth is filled with peace—from the lion and lamb event to we humans.

Skill Level: Beginner

Size: Fits boutique-style tissue box

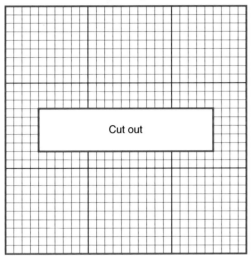

Lion & Lamb Top
29 holes x 29 holes
Cut 1

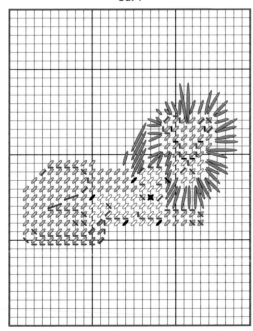

Lion & Lamb Side
29 holes x 37 holes
Cut 4

Materials

- 1½ sheets 7-count plastic canvas
- Worsted weight yarn as listed in color key
- DMC #5 pearl cotton as listed in color key
- #16 tapestry needle

Instructions

1. Cut plastic canvas according to graphs.

2. Stitch pieces following graphs, working uncoded areas with dark blue Continental Stitches.

3. When background stitching is completed, work Backstitches and Straight Stitches with black yarn and pearl cotton.

4. Using dark blue throughout, Overcast inside edges on top and bottom edges of sides. Whipstitch sides together, then Whipstitch sides to top. ❖

COLOR KEY	
Worsted Weight Yarn	**Yards**
▨ Light golden brown	9
▨ Golden brown	7
☐ White	3
■ Black	2
☐ Off-white	2
Uncoded areas are dark blue Continental Stitches	62
╱ Dark blue Overcasting and Whipstitching	
╱ Black Backstitch and Straight Stitch	
#5 Pearl Cotton	
╱ Black #310 Backstitch and Straight Stitch	5
Color number given is for DMC #5 pearl cotton.	

Stitch Guide

Use the following diagrams to expand your plastic canvas stitching skills. For each diagram, bring needle up through canvas at the red number one and go back down through the canvas at the red number two. The second stitch is numbered in green. Always bring needle up through the canvas at odd numbers and take it back down through the canvas at the even numbers.

Background Stitches

The following stitches are used for filling in large areas of canvas. The Continental Stitch is the most commonly used stitch. Other stitches, such as the Condensed Mosaic and Scotch Stitch, fill in large areas of canvas more quickly than the Continental Stitch because their stitches cover a larger area of canvas.

Continental Stitch

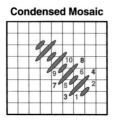

Condensed Mosaic

Alternating Continental

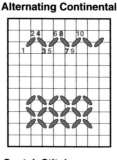

Cross Stitch

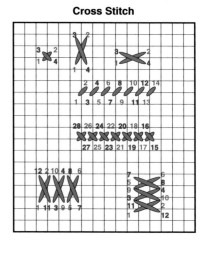

Long Stitch

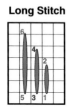

Slanting Gobelin

Scotch Stitch

Embroidery Stitches

These stitches are worked on top of a stitched area to add detail to the project. Embroidery stitches are usually worked with one strand of yarn, several strands of pearl cotton or several strands of embroidery floss.

Lattice Stitch

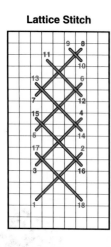

Chain Stitch

Straight Stitch

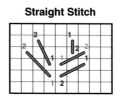

Fly Stitch

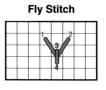

Running Stitch

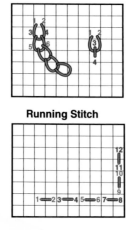

Couching

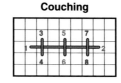

Backstitch

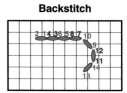

Embroidery Stitches

French Knot

Bring needle up through canvas.

Wrap yarn around needle 1 to 3 times, depending on desired size of knot; take needle back through canvas through same hole.

Lazy Daisy

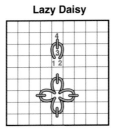

Bring yarn needle up through canvas, then back down in same hole, leaving a small loop.

Then, bring needle up inside loop; take needle back down through canvas on other side of loop.

Loop Stitch/Turkey Loop Stitch

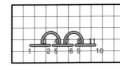

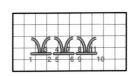

The top diagram shows this stitch left intact. This is an effective stitch for giving a project dimensional hair. The bottom diagram demonstrates the cut loop stitch. Because each stitch is anchored, cutting it will not cause the stitches to come out. A group of cut loop stitches gives a fluffy, soft look and feel to your project.

Specialty Stitches

The following stitches can be worked either on top of a previously stitched area or directly onto the canvas. Like the embroidery stitches, these too add wonderful detail and give your stitching additional interest and texture.

Diamond Eyelet

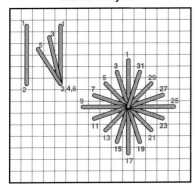

For each stitch, bring needle up at odd numbers and down through canvas at center hole.

Smyrna Cross

Satin Stitches

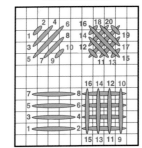

This stitch gives a "padded" look to your work.

Finishing Stitches

Overcast/Whipstitch

Overcasting and Whipstitching are used to finish the outer edges of the canvas. Overcasting is done to finish one edge at a time. Whipstitching is used to stitch two or more pieces of canvas together along an edge. For both Overcasting and Whipstitching, work one stitch in each hole along straight edges and inside corners, and two or three stitches in outside corners.

Lark's Head Knot

The Lark's Head Knot is used for a fringe edge or for attaching a hanging loop.

SPECIAL THANKS

We would like to acknowledge and thank the following designers whose original work has been published in this collection. We appreciate and value their creativity and dedication to designing quality plastic canvas projects!

Angie Arickx
Christmas Gift, Cottage Garden, Desert Designs, Log Cabin, Patchwork Tulips, Quilted Stars & Stripes, Santa's Li'l Helpers, Snowflake Quilt, Sunflower Fantasy, Watermelon Delight

Roseanna Beck
Christmas Wishes

Vicki Blizzard
Cheery Cherries, Count Your Bless-You's!, Garden Fence Buzz, Hog Wash, Nighty-Night Bear, Seeds of the Spirit, Strawberry Patch

Janna Britton
Puppy Love, Summer Jewels

Ronda Bryce
Autumn Silhouettes, Country Barn, Country Basket

Celia Lange Designs
Daisy Delight,

Four Seasons Window Boxes, Ikebana, Springtime Plaid

Judy Collishaw
Friendly Froggy, Hearts & Daisies, Learning the Ropes, Liberty Stars

Nancy Dorman
Cuddly Snowbear, Floral Bouquet, Panda Bear

Janelle Giese
Autumn Angel, Fun in the Snow, Snappy Snowman, Spring Angel, Summer Angel, Winter Angel, Winter Maiden, Winter Rabbit

Joan Green
Bargello Hearts, Country Apples, Falling Leaves, Folk Art Chickens, Maritime Flags, School Days Crayon Box, Sparkling Ornaments, Thunderbird, You're the Star!

Robin Howard-Will
April Showers

Kathleen Hurley
Bee My Honey

Christina Laws
County Fair Carousel, Fire Engine, Mini Critters Tissue Pockets, Pampered Pets, Rudolph, Unicorn's Rainbow

Susan Leinberger
Checks & Cherries, Forget-Me-Not, Holiday Bells, Sparkling Pastels, Victorian Valentine

Lee Lindeman
Bunny Bouquet, King of the Coop, Little Red Truck, Maple Leaves

Alida Macor
Silent Night Nativity

Nancy Marshall
African Animals, Rose Lattice

Mary K. Perry
Lion & Lamb, Star of David

Robin Petrina
Baby Love, Bait Shop, Raffia Bouquet

Terry Ricioli
Autumn Sampler, Painted Daisies

Cynthia Roberts
Bless You!, Mosaic Quilt

Kimberly A. Suber
Just for Dad, Peppermint & Poinsettias, Pumpkin Patch Scarecrow

Ruby Thacker
Christmas Lights, Floral Hearts, Wishing Well

Michele Wilcox
Bees & Blooms, Country Cottage, Country Snowman, Give Thanks, Happy Easter, Little Mouse, Mr. Bluebird, Pumpkin Pocket, Santa Bear, Snowman With Heart, Spring Garden, Summertime Kitchen, Thyme Began

BUYER'S GUIDE

When looking for a specific material, first check your local craft and retail stores. If you are unable to locate a product locally, contact the manufacturers listed below for the closest retail source in your area or a mail-order source.

The Beadery
P.O. Box 178 • Hope Valley, RI 02832 • (401) 539-2432

Coats & Clark
Consumer Service • P.O. Box 12229 • Greenville, SC 29612-0229 • (800) 648-1479 • www.coatsandclark.com

CPE Inc.
P.O. Box 649 • Union, SC 29379 • (800) 327-0059

Creative Crystals Co.
P.O. Box 1476 • Middletown, CT 06457 • (800) 578-0716
www.creativecrystals.com

Darice
Mail-order source: **Schrock's International**
P.O. Box 538 • Bolivar, OH 44612 • (330) 874-3700

DMC Corp.
Hackensack Ave. Bldg. 10A • South Kearny, NJ 07032-4688
(800) 275-4117 • www.dmc-usa.com

Gay Bowles Sales Inc.
P.O. Box 1060 • Janesville, WI 53545 • (800) 447-1332
www.millhill.com

Jesse James Button & Co.
615 N. New St. • Allentown, PA 18102 • (610) 435-7899

Kreinik Mfg. Co. Inc.
3106 Timanus Ln., #101 • Baltimore, MD 21244-2871
(800) 537-2166

Natural Science Industries Ltd. (NSI)
910 Orlando Ave. • West Hempstead, NY 11552
(888) 425-9113

C.M. Offray & Son Inc./Lion Ribbon Co. Inc.
Rte. 24, Box 601 • Chester, NJ 07930 • (800) 551-LION
www.offray.com

Rainbow Gallery
Mail-order source:
Designs by Joan Green
3897 Indian Ridge Woods • Oxford, OH 45056
(513) 523-0437 (Mon.–Fri., 9 a.m.–5 p.m.)

Source Marketing
600 E. Ninth St. • Michigan City, IN 46360-3655
(219) 873-1000

Uniek
Mail-order source: **Annie's Attic Catalog**
1 Annie Ln. • Big Sandy, TX 75755 • (800) 582-6643
www.anniesattic.com